T0281646

Character Rigging and Advanced Animation

Bring Your Character to Life Using Autodesk 3ds Max

Purushothaman Raju

Apress®

Character Rigging and Advanced Animation

Purushothaman Raju
Bangalore, Karnataka, India

ISBN-13 (pbk): 978-1-4842-5036-5 ISBN-13 (electronic): 978-1-4842-5037-2
https://doi.org/10.1007/978-1-4842-5037-2

Managing Director, Apress Media LLC: Welmoed Spahr
Acquisitions Editor: Spandana Chatterjee
Development Editor: Siddhi Chavan
Coordinating Editor: Divya Modi

Cover designed by eStudioCalamar

Cover image designed by Freepik (www.freepik.com)

Distributed to the book trade worldwide by Springer Science+Business Media New York, 233 Spring Street, 6th Floor, New York, NY 10013. Phone 1-800-SPRINGER, fax (201) 348-4505, e-mail orders-ny@springer-sbm.com, or visit www.springeronline.com. Apress Media, LLC is a California LLC and the sole member (owner) is Springer Science + Business Media Finance Inc (SSBM Finance Inc). SSBM Finance Inc is a **Delaware** corporation.

For information on translations, please e-mail rights@apress.com, or visit http://www.apress.com/rights-permissions.

Apress titles may be purchased in bulk for academic, corporate, or promotional use. eBook versions and licenses are also available for most titles. For more information, reference our Print and eBook Bulk Sales web page at http://www.apress.com/bulk-sales.

Any source code or other supplementary material referenced by the author in this book is available to readers on GitHub via the book's product page, located at www.apress.com/978-1-4842-5036-5. For more detailed information, please visit http://www.apress.com/source-code.

Printed on acid-free paper

This book is dedicated to the most special women in my life, Rajeshwari (mom) and Rashmi (Wifey), without their support this book would not have been possible.

Table of Contents

About the Author

Purushothaman Raju has over 17 years of experience in multiple domains comprising online gaming and academic coaching. During his tenure in academics, he has trained and mentored more than 800 students on diverse projects in the field of multimedia. He holds an advanced professional diploma in multimedia. Currently, he works as an associate senior professor teaching 3D, multimedia, and post-production at NICC International College of Design, Bangalore.

About the Technical Reviewer

Olivier Henley holds a BFA from Concordia University and a BEE from Polytechnique Montreal. He regularly works as a software contractor for Autodesk Inc. and has previously evolved within Ubisoft Entertainment SA as a generalist game programmer on titles such as *Rainbox Six: Siege, For Honor* and *Your Shape: Fitness Evolved.* He also invented some original work on temporal filtering (patent US8884949B1) for the Microsoft Kinect camera. In his spare time, he likes to do carpentry, welding, and multimedia art installation, as well as build web servers and maintain an Awesome list about the Ada programming language.

Acknowledgments

I would like to thank Spandana Chatterjee for putting my name forth for such a wonderful opportunity, Divya Modi for pushing me to complete the book, as the deadlines were missed time and again, all the while being patient, Siddhi Chavan for proofreading the chapters and providing valuable feedback that made the book better in terms of readability and Olivier Henley for tech reviewing and providing me with valuable feedback to improve the book.

I would also like to thank Mel Naoke, from EndlessReference.com, for providing me with the content video and for permission to use their content in Chapter 8.

Thanks to all my friends and family members who supported me while I wrote this book. Special thanks to everyone else who was a part of this book.

Thanks to you all.

Introduction

Character Rigging and Advanced Animation is a book for people who are familiar with 3ds Max at a basic level and want to learn character rigging and animation. The book is split into three major modules, which are further split into chapters.

The first module is the foundational module. In this module, the book begins by baselining the importance of the 12 principles of animation with reference to classical real-world examples. It uses famous movies/animation shots to help you understand keyframe and graph editors, which will help you obtain fluid motion in animations. Practical examples are used to explain which feature suits a particular scenario.

The second module is the backbone module. In this module, you are introduced to deformation tools and their use in character animation. Further chapters introduce you to driven animations, constraints bones, bipeds, and the CAT tools available in 3ds Max 2019.

The final module, the lifeline module, is where you bring your character to life by applying the principles you learned in the previous modules. You will be guided in how to use advanced concepts to retarget animation from one character to other characters or rigs. Once you have completed the exercises and followed along with the book, you should be able to create characters rigs for bipeds or quadrupeds with ease and animate them for lifelike motion.

CHAPTER 1

Beginning Animation

Many people are inspired by animation from favorite cartoon shows, movies, and games, but only a few have ventured into character animation as a career path. Character animation is not rocket science when you know the fundamentals and the operational principles of how it works. This book will help allay any fears of complexity you have about animation techniques and help you begin the journey of bringing your 3D characters to life.

Animation is a form of art and is mastered by practice. In other words, you'll get better at it by repeatedly handling the tools and trying the techniques. For example, everyone has arms and legs, but not everyone can dance. What makes someone a great dancer is that they master the art of moving their body in a rhythmic pace, which is acquired by practicing over time.

In the early days of animation, when the animators at Disney were trying to create lifelike animations, they came up with *The 12 Principles of Animation.* These principles were developed by Ollie Johnston and Frank Thomas, in their book, *The Illusion of Life: Disney Animation.* The book won several awards and serves as a base for anyone willing to learn animation.

This first chapter focuses on the core principles of animation, with examples. It explains why and how a principle makes a difference in an animation. Note that the principles are not mentioned in any particular order.

Let's begin!

The Principles of Animation

This section looks at the principles of animation, with images, and explains how each principle can be applied in the further sections of this chapter.

P. Raju, *Character Rigging and Advanced Animation*, https://doi.org/10.1007/978-1-4842-5037-2_1

Squash and Stretch

The first principle we discuss is the *squash and stretch* principle. A classic example is a ball-bouncing animation. Take the time to analyze Figures 1-1 through 1-3. The images are also available in your contents folder for each chapter that can be downloaded from the github location provided in the Introduction part of the book.

If you notice in Figure 1-1 the first ball does not deform/squash when it hits the floor, while the ball in Figure 1-2 does deform/squash. Using this principle, we can show mass/rigidity of an object without the texture or color. The first ball might be made of concrete while the second one is a tennis ball or a rubber ball.

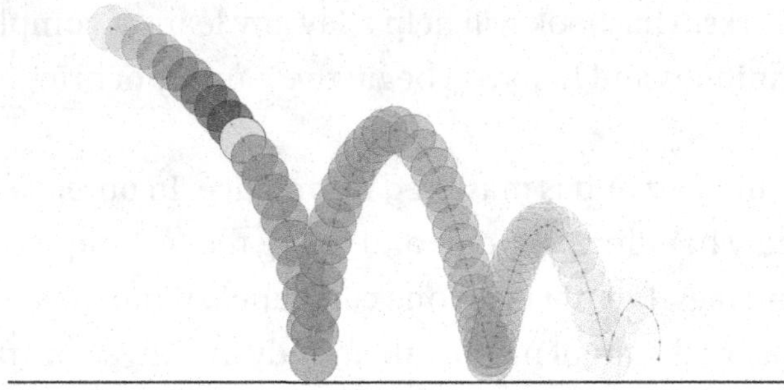

Figure 1-1. *No squash and stretch applied to the animation of a ball*

Figure 1-2 shows how a ball deforms/squashes as it hits the floor.

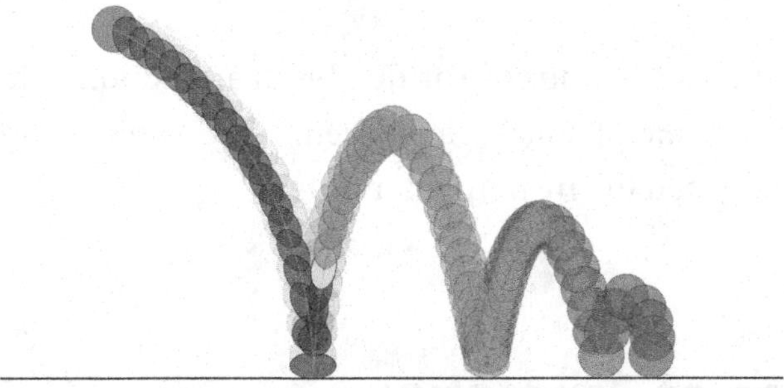

Figure 1-2. *Squash and stretch applied to the animation of a ball*

Now let's look at the same principle with another example in relation to character animation. Here I explain this principle using a character that is jumping, as shown in Figure 1-3.

***Figure 1-3.** Squash and stretch applied to a cartoon character*

In the sprite sheet in Figure 1-3, you can see a silhouette of a character jumping. Let's break down the phases as labeled to understand this process better.

- (a): The character is standing idle before the jump. This is the idle phase, before any form of squash is applied to prepare for a jump. By the same token, (i) shows the idle phase after recovering from the jump.
- (b): This is the phase when the character goes into a sit-up pose and squashes itself to gain momentum for the leap. This is the first squash for the jump cycle, while (h) shows the phase where the character squashes itself to soften the landing.
- (c): During this phase, the character begins to release itself from the squash pose and gain momentum for the jump. At phase (g), the character prepares itself for the squash landing.
- (d): During this phase, the character stretches itself to gain maximum momentum to attain the desired height. Phase (f) is where the character begins stretching itself to align its legs and body to the landing spot.
- (e): During this phase, the character has reached the peak zone, also known as the *transition zone,* which is from the jump to land phase. The character has reached the desired/anticipated jump height.

Other examples of squashing are when a character shows surprise, disappointment, or a freaking out moment. This technique is often seen in cartoons, such as in the *Tom and Jerry* cartoon, when you see Jerry surprised by Tom. He freaks out and elongates before he makes a run for his life. The same technique can be seen with the Roadrunner cartoon, where the coyote squashes after falling down the cliff.

Key principles to keep in mind when using squash and stretch for animation is to maintain the volume of the animated object and keep the duration of the squash/stretch short, often within a span of a few frames.

Squash and stretch can be used in conjunction with other animation principles, such as *anticipation* and *follow-through,* which are explained in the upcoming sections.

Note The amount of squash and stretch should be used wisely, depending on the animation type. For example, the squash and stretch can be more evidently seen or overdone in cartoon animations but should be very subtle in lifelike animations.

Anticipation

Anticipation is a must-follow principle for character animation. It helps create the illusion of lifelike motion and prepares the audience/viewers for an action. Anticipation is often used as a preparation to motion. It can make the shot more interesting or intense, as needed. See Figure 1-4.

Figure 1-4. *Anticipation and action*

Anticipation is often used to direct the viewer's attention toward an imminent animation and convey the intensity of the shot before the action happens.

Let's take a look at a couple of examples:

- A boxer punching: A character punching someone is a typical example, with the punch being the action and the arms pulling back/ winding up to show how intense the punch is going to be. In this case, it allows the viewer to anticipate of the force of the punch.
- Wood chopping: In this case, the animation is chopping wood, but when the woodcutter swings his axe, he draws the axe back above his head and slams it down on the piece of wood. How much he pulls the axe back determines the attack speed, which is our anticipated motion here.
- Throwing a ball: We have all done this at some point while playing with a kid or a friend. The intensity of the throw is based on how much you pull your arm back. The pull-back here is the anticipated motion.

Note To preserve realism, try to follow human movements based on joint rotations and limitations when animating a character. In real life, people cannot twist their bodies like rope to unwind and punch someone, as is often seen in cartoons. Anticipation, when it's overdone, is called exaggeration. Refer to the exaggeration examples to get a better idea of that technique.

Exaggeration

Since we mentioned exaggeration in the previous section, let's discuss it before proceeding further. In its simplest form, *exaggeration* is when an action is overdone to make the overall animation look more intense or even humorous. Exaggeration is seen often in cartoon animations, but it can be used in any setting. Let's take a look at the examples we used for anticipation and see how they can be exaggerated.

- A boxer punching: Exaggeration can be shown by having the character wind up more than once around his body, which is unnatural for the human body.

- Wood chopping: In order to exaggerate this action, we can have our woodcutter bend too much backward as he pulls back the axe and jump in the air as the axe chops the wood.
- Throwing a ball: Exaggeration can be shown by elongating arms and legs to gain momentum and force. This is often seen in cartoon animations. Another typical example seen in cartoons is a character running in place for a second and two and then moving off at incredible speeds (often a puff of smoke is shown).

Figure 1-5. *Exaggeration of action*

Exaggeration can also be done by adding more assets/props and giving the character more appeal to suit the need. For example, if you want to show your character as a sad/depressed person, you could just show this by the way he dresses and his facial expression, but it can be exaggerated by adding elements/props that showcase his current state. We will explore this further when we introduce the principle of staging and appeal.

Note In real life, a person cannot twist his body like a rope to unwind and punch someone, as is often seen in cartoons. Anticipation, when overdone, is called exaggeration.

Follow-Through Animation and Overlapping Action

Follow-through and *overlapping actions* are based on real-world physics and emulate real-world motion. Let's consider an example of moving in a bus. Our bodies move along within the bus, but when the bus makes a sudden stop, our bodies continue to move forward or are dragged forward due to what is called *inertia*. They take a moment to stop. This is an example of follow-through.

Let's use the example of our character throwing a ball, which we used for anticipation, but this time, we focus on the ball thrower (see Figure 1-6).

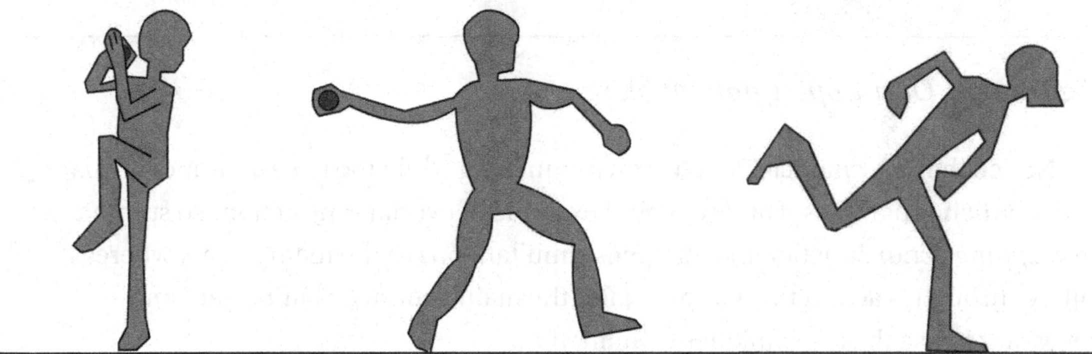

Figure 1-6. *Follow-through animation principle*

Note that the character doesn't stop once he releases the ball. The momentum developed while throwing has to decelerate before the character can stop his movement. This follow-up animation is depicted in the third image. This kind of dynamic movement happens all the time in real life. Try to throw a ball or an object and observe how your motion does not stop immediately once the object leaves your hand.

Now let's look at an overlapping action. Let's examine the example of our boxer punching once again, this time in Figure 1-7.

Figure 1-7. *Overlapping animation principle*

Notice that the character's right arm is punching while the left arm is moving back as the punch progresses. This is a typical example of overlapping action. To summarize, *overlapping action* is action that happens simultaneous to the main action, whereas follow-through is action that happens after the main action. It is important and necessary to use these techniques in animation.

Secondary Action

Secondary action is often related to follow-through and overlapping action; the only difference being that secondary action carries more dynamic realism. It is a logical follow-up to some previous action that set the mood or added complexity to the situation. Let's look at an example.

Imagine a scenario in which a person is waiting at a bus stop. The main action here is waiting for the bus. By adding a few animation changes, *a secondary action,* we can alter the mood of the scene.

- Option 1: We can have the character check his watch repeatedly to show a sense of urgency. Just by adding this simple gesture of looking at his watch over and over, we achieve a sense of impatience and maybe lateness.

- Option 2: We can have the character take out a newspaper and read it by flipping pages repeatedly until the bus arrives. This changes the mood of the shot completely. Now our character seems to enjoy waiting for the bus.

We were able to change the mood by adding an animation to follow-through or by overlapping our existing animation of waiting for the bus. See Figure 1-8.

Figure 1-8. *Secondary action used to alter the mood*

Arc

Every living being moves its body parts in arcs. Let's look at a few examples:

- Waving goodbye: Your arm waves around your elbow joint in an arc fashion.
- Slamming your fist on a table: Your arms arc to hit the table with your fist.
- Nodding yes or no: Your head arcs left to right to say no and up and down to say yes from your neck.
- Walking animation:
    - Your arms swing in the form of an arch back and forth.
    - Your body sways left and right to compensate and balance as you walk.

Let's look at this movement with our character who is chopping wood, as seen previously when talking about anticipation. Consider the arcs marked by arrows drawn in Figure 1-9. This gives you a good idea of their predominance.

Figure 1-9. *Arcs*

Appeal

Appeal is used to emphasize a character's characteristics, personality, or mood. Let's try to depict a sad/depressed person. This can be achieved in many ways.

- Facial expression and body language
- Clothes they are wearing
- The space they live in

Take a look at the illustration in Figure 1-10 and compare the left and right scenes. With the addition of a few props, we can sense a mood.

Figure 1-10. *Appeal*

Timing and Spacing

Timing and spacing are critical for achieving the expected animation effect. If these are off, you will not get the result you desire. We will be going over the tools to use in Chapter 2, but for now let's look at the basics.

Animation is derived from the interpolation of keyframes. Keyframes are containers/holders that stores an object's position/rotation and scale in the timeline. Note that they are not limited to these properties only, many more can be stored. Interpolation is the process where the software calculates the current position/rotation/scale of an object based on the immediate before and after keyframe. In order to create an animation, you need at least two keyframes. Let's consider a scenario of a ball animation.

There are two points, A and B, which are 100 meters apart and a ball that is going to travel from A to B. The animation is 25 frames per second. See Figure 1-11.

- Case 1: Ball A starts at frame 0 and reaches destination B at frame 100. If you play it back, you will notice that the ball takes four seconds to reach the destination.
- Case 2: Let's alter the ball's position so that it reaches destination B at frame 50. Now the ball will reach its destination in two seconds.
- A quick formula to calculate:
    - Time = Total frames/frames per sec

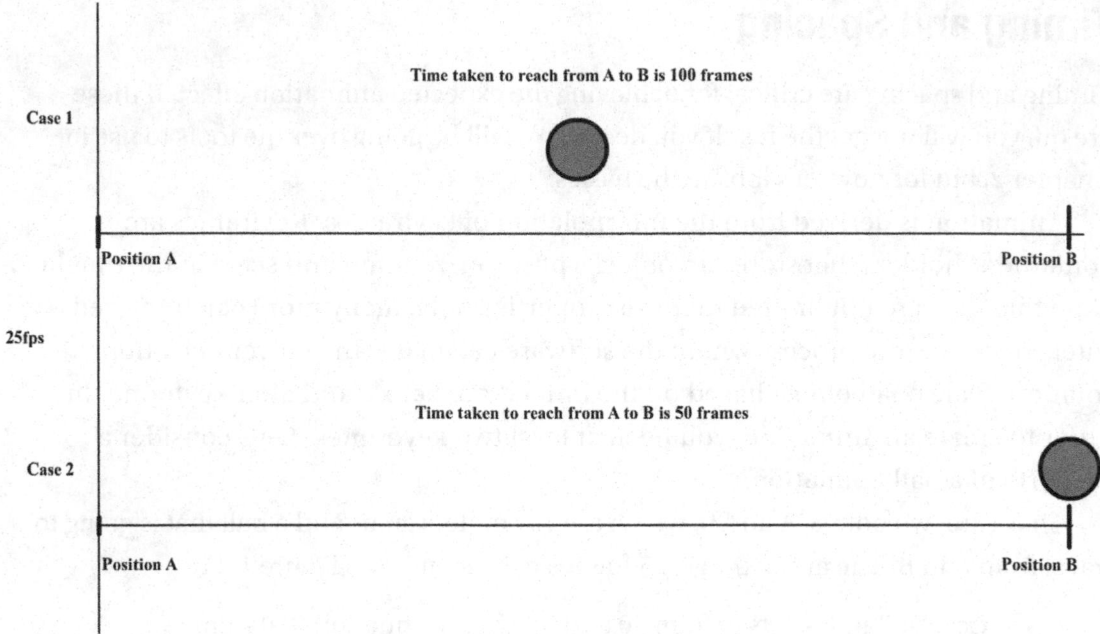

Figure 1-11. *Timing*

We adjusted the timing of the animation by repositioning the ball to reach the destination earlier. The ball in case 2 will reach destination at twice the speed of case 1.

We will look at this with a practical exercise about the Track Editor in Chapter 2.

Let's look at spacing now. For this case, we have three points (A, B, and C), which determine the position of our ball at various times.

- Case 1: Ball A starts at 0 and reaches B (which is midway) at frame 50 and its destination C at frame 100. The result is the same as in case 1 of the timing example.
- Case 2: Ball A starts at 0 and reaches B at frame 20 and its destination C at frame 100. In this result, the ball accelerates to B quickly and slows down on its way to C.
- Case 3: Ball A starts at 0 and reaches B at frame 80 and its destination C at frame 100.

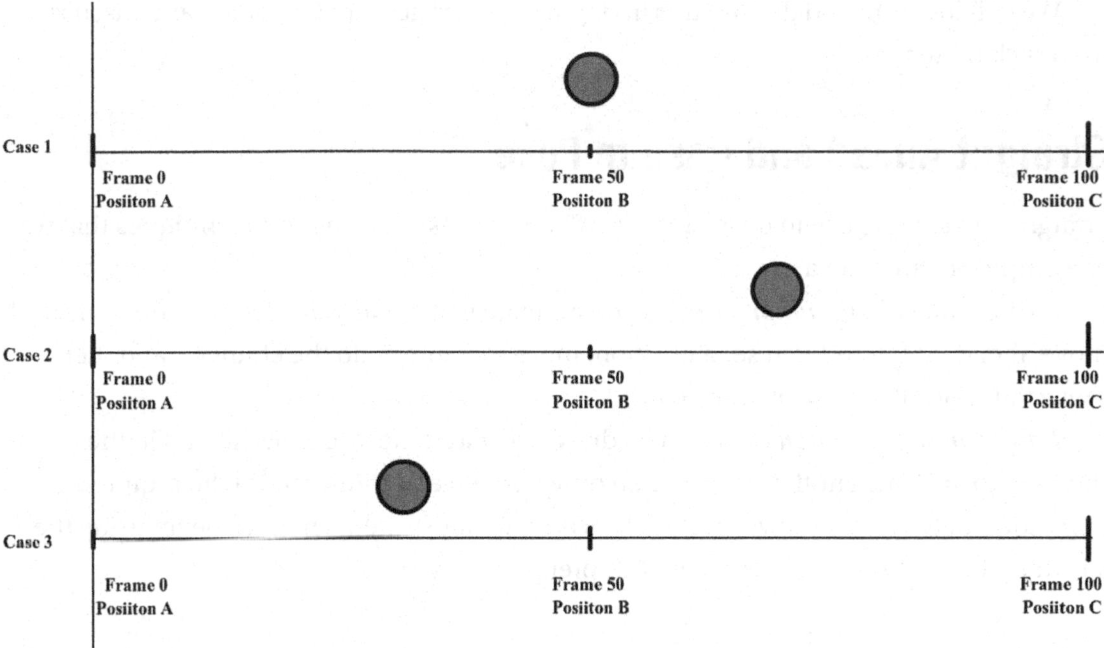

Figure 1-12. *Spacing*

If you analyze all the cases, in case 1, the ball goes at a steady speed all the way. In case 2, the ball speeds up to B and then slows down to C. In case 3, the ball is very slow to reach B, but gains speed to reach C. The middle keyframe controls the variations in animation. We will work more on this as an exercise in Chapter 2.

Note We altered the speed of the ball by using an in-between keyframe to determine the position of the ball in cases 1, 2, and 3.

Slow In and Slow Out

This topic assumes that you know and have ridden a vehicle. It doesn't matter what sort, any vehicle that moves. So when you begin driving a vehicle, it picks up at ever-increasing speed until you reach the desired constant speed. This is called *acceleration* and it is reproduced between two keyframes by applying a non-linear interpolation function, also more generally called *easing of keyframes*. This can also be done by using in-between keyframes that we used in the spacing example or by using graph editor controls. Slow in and slow out are related to acceleration and deceleration as well.

We will focus on and discuss this in depth when we get into Chapter 2 and discuss the Track Editor.

Straight Ahead and Pose to Pose

Straight ahead and pose to pose are two different forms of animation techniques that we can employ to animate a character.

Straight ahead animation is when you animate in a linear way along the timeline and move ahead. At frame 1 you set a position, move to frame 5, do the changes, and then move to frame 10, and so on and so forth.

Pose to pose animation is when you draw the first frame and move ahead in the timeline to animate another frame, then draw in-between frames to fill the required animation between these two frames. This is better illustrated when we begin using the software. I'll hold on to this one until Chapter 2.

Staging

Staging is a mix of many techniques, such as timing, spacing, composition, and framing, rather than just animation. Without proper staging, your animations aren't going to be effective.

One point to keep in mind in relation to animation is to not have too many actions happening at the same time. Take the time to research composition and framing techniques as applied to photography or cinematography. You are going to be framing and animating a virtual camera that has controls and emulates real-world cameras.

I have omitted solid drawing for the sole reason that it applies to 2D animation and not 3D. Again, I would like to reiterate that these principles are not ordered in any fashion. With all these principles revisited, we've had enough of the theoretical. Let's get into the software and bring things to life!

Summary

Let's summarize what we have learned so far. We learned about the principles of animation, with examples in a theoretical manner. These serve as a foundation and are must-knows for anyone who is venturing into animation. We will be applying these principles in the upcoming exercises using 3ds Max animation tools.

In the next chapter, you learn about keyframing tools and techniques. You will also learn how to use the Curve Editor, the Dope Editor, and the graph controls to refine your animations. As an animator, you will be spending much of your time here, so it is imperative that you become familiarized with them before going in depth with other techniques.

CHAPTER 2

Creating and Refining Animation

In the previous chapter, we learned about the principles of animation. In this and the following chapters, we will apply those principles to guide us in refining our animations. Take the time to copy all the files in the content directory to an accessible location on your computer so that you can follow along.

In this chapter, we look at setting up a project for organized workflow. We also learn about keyframing and modifying the keyframes using 3ds Max tools such as Curve Editor and Dope Sheet.

Preparing for Animation

Before you begin any project, it's a must to set it up. It helps to keep the supporting files required for the project in an organized folder, rather than pulling files from multiple locations from your drive. This helps when the project needs to be migrated to another computer or given to another person to work on.

Setting Up the Project

Let's begin by setting up our project, which is a good and structured way to begin. To create a new project, choose File ➤ Project ➤ Create Default (see Figure 2-1). (Choosing this option allows you to browse a folder and select it. Create a folder in a convenient location and select -. Choosing this option creates all the associated folders required for the project.)

Note This is not the only way to set a project; there are multiple ways to do so.

P. Raju, *Character Rigging and Advanced Animation*, https://doi.org/10.1007/978-1-4842-5037-2_2

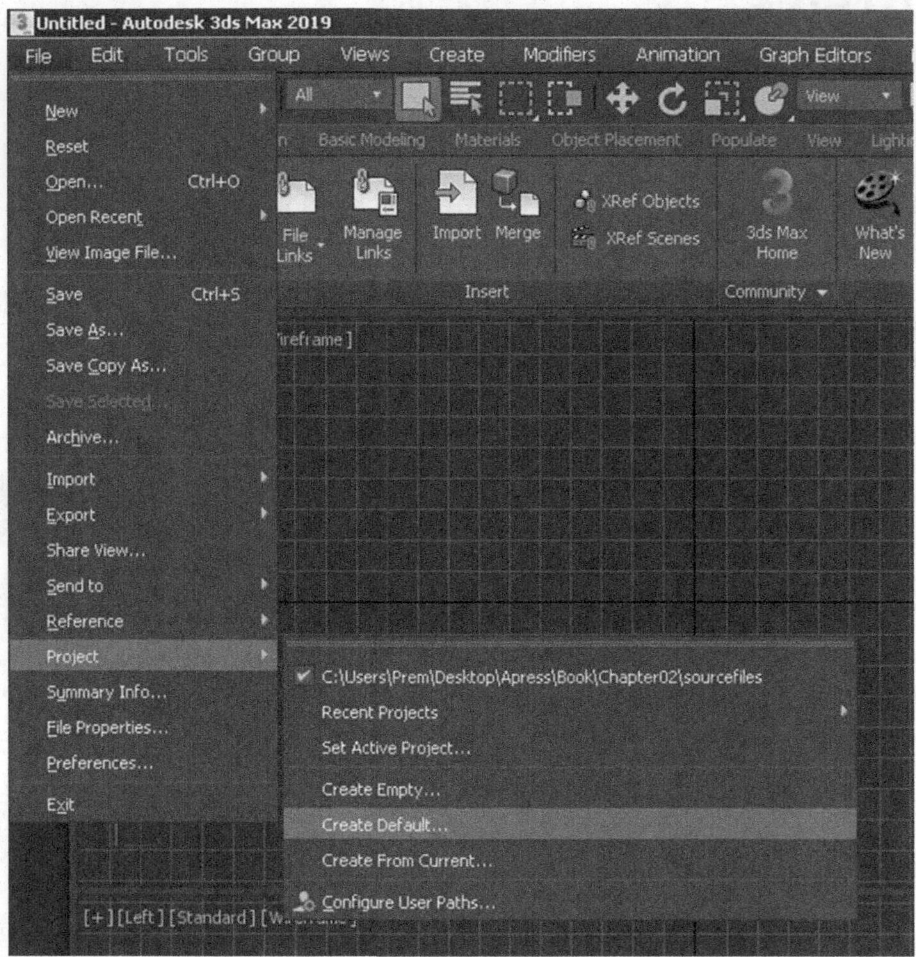

Figure 2-1. *Creating a project in 3ds Max*

When you save a file from this point on, it will default to your `scenes` folder that was created for you. If you notice the project folder in your folder explorer, you should see something like Figure 2-2. All these folders are created for organizing your project. We will not be going into what each folder is for, but you should be aware that the `scenes` folder is where the `.max` files are saved. When you download the source files for this chapter, you will see the same directory structure as follows (see Figure 2-2):

- Archives: These are for zipping a folder structure to send it to someone else.
- Autoback: This is where the software saves backup copies at regular intervals, as set in preferences.

- Downloads: This is where the files are saved when you download from the Asset Library.
- Export: This is the default location when you export anything from your scene express.
- Import: Browse to this directory to show files for import.
- Material libraries: You can save your materials into this folder for organizing purposes.
- Previews: This is where your animation previews are saved.
- Proxies: You don't always need to work with high-resolution mesh and textures; you can swap them on the fly during render time.
- Render output: This is where you should save your renders for an organized workflow.
- Render presets: Save different presets of render to load them for later use on a different file.
- Scene assets: Other scene assets created from other packages can be stored here for easy accessibility.
- Scenes: Raw 3ds Max scene files should be saved here.
- Vpost: Post-production effects that are done using video posts inside 3ds Max can be saved here for later use.
- `projectname.mxp` file: This file holds the project settings and path.

▾ Apress ▾ Book ▾ Chapter02 ▾ chapter02_sourcefiles ▾

Include in library ▾ Share with ▾ New folder

Name	Date modified	Type	Size
archives	12/15/2018 11:19 PM	File folder	
autoback	12/15/2018 11:21 PM	File folder	
downloads	12/15/2018 11:19 PM	File folder	
export	12/15/2018 11:19 PM	File folder	
express	12/15/2018 11:19 PM	File folder	
import	12/15/2018 11:19 PM	File folder	
materiallibraries	12/15/2018 11:19 PM	File folder	
previews	12/15/2018 11:19 PM	File folder	
proxies	12/15/2018 11:19 PM	File folder	
renderoutput	12/15/2018 11:19 PM	File folder	
renderPresets	12/15/2018 11:19 PM	File folder	
sceneassets	12/15/2018 11:19 PM	File folder	
scenes	1/21/2019 4:37 AM	File folder	
vpost	12/15/2018 11:19 PM	File folder	
chapter02_sourcefiles.mxp	12/15/2018 11:29 PM	3dsMax path config...	3 KB

Figure 2-2. *Directory structure*

Now that our project is set (in my case I called this project `Chapter02_sourcefiles`), let's look at another important thing that we need to address before we begin.

Setting Up Duration and Frame Rates

Before you begin working on an animation, you should have an idea as to how long your animation is going to be and the desired frame rate you want the animation to play at. This should be adhered to and set in the initial stages of the project to avoid further headaches later on during the project. Otherwise, you might need to retime keys in order to change the frame rate and animation duration.

You can change the frame rate and animation duration using the time configuration button located in the bottom-right part of 3ds Max, as outlined in Figure 2-3.

Figure 2-3. *Time configuration button*

Once you click on the Time Configuration button, a popup window, as shown in Figure 2-4, will open. The top box highlighted determines the frame speed and can be set according to TV broadcast standards, such as NTSC, PAL, Film, or custom speeds. The second highlighted area is used to determine the number of frames of your current file.

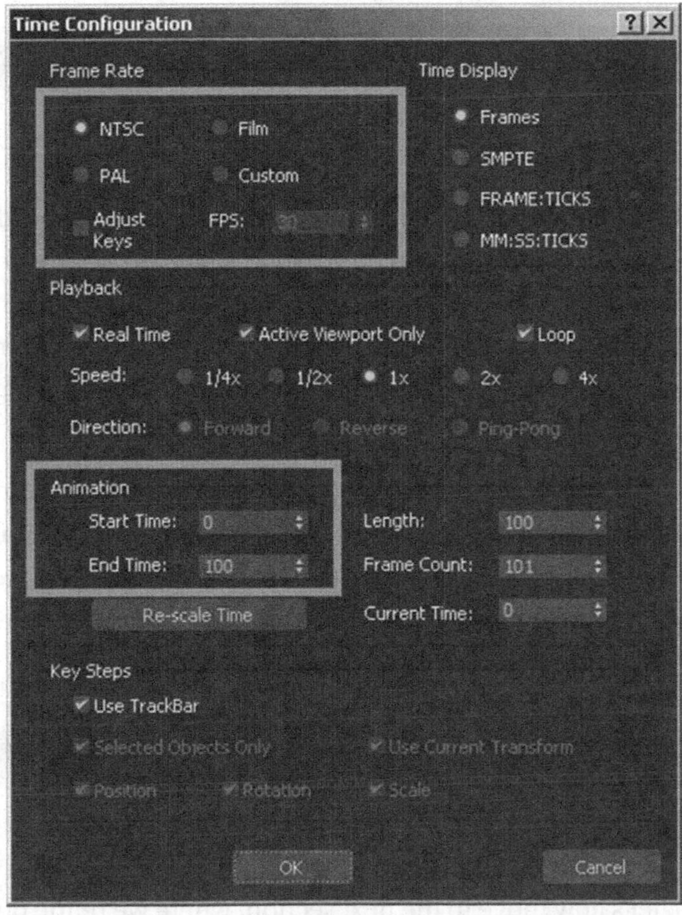

Figure 2-4. *Time Configuration window*

Creating Animations

In the digital medium, animations are created using keyframes. Keyframes hold the parameters of an object. For example, position x and position y could be scale, rotation, or any other parameter that can be animated as per the software. An animation happens when there is a change of parameters that are keyed over different frames.

Creating Keyframes

Keyframes can be created in multiple ways in 3ds Max. Let's look at two common methods—Auto Key and Set Key—which are located below the time slider, as shown in Figure 2-5.

Figure 2-5. *Auto Key and Set Key*

- Auto Key: With Auto Key enabled/turned on, the viewport borders turn red. During this time, any change of an object's parameters will get keyframed for that particular frame. Now, with this turned on, we can change the current frame by dragging the time slider and moving the object. Since auto key is on, our new position of the object gets keyframed automatically.
- Set Key: With Set Key on, the viewport border turns red again except for the keyframes not getting recorded as you move objects over time. In order to register a keyframe for a particular object and its parameters, the Set Key icon (the plus button next to auto key and set key) needs to clicked (or you can press K to use the shortcut). See Figure 2-6.

Figure 2-6. *Set Key and Key button*

With that clear, let's now move to the next section, where we refine our keyframes for varied motion using tangents.

Understanding Keyframes and Tangents

Tangents are a way of setting how a keyframe interpolates adjacent keyframes. By controlling the tangents, we can provide varied motion. Take the time to view the video located at `< INSERT PATH/Chaoter02/Reference videos/Tangents.mp4>`. All the boxes have a keyframe at 0 and at frame 100, we can see the boxes moving around. We will look at using tangents to achieve this animation.

Fire up 3ds Max and load the `Tangent_Start_Excercise.max` file from the source folder. If you minimize the top viewport (select the top wide port and press ALT+W), you'll see something like Figure 2-7.

Figure 2-7. *Tangent_start_Excercise*

In this scene I created seven boxes. There are no animations applied whatsoever just yet. Let's begin by setting keyframes to create the animation.

1. Select all the boxes by doing a box selection and setting a keyframe to lock the boxes in position at frame 0. (You can use any way as described in the previous section to create a key.)

2. Move to frame 50. Move the boxes to the right edge of the viewport and set a keyframe using any techniques that you learned earlier. If you click on play from the play controls, the boxes should move from left to right all at the same pace. You can interactively drag the current time indicator (located between the timeline frames and the viewport) to simulate playback. This is also known as *scrubbing*.

3. Now at frame 100 we want the box to start coming to its initial position as in frame 0, so that the animation can be a perfect loop. There are multiple ways to get this done (either by manually moving them back to the coordinates, or by noting the values of the X position of the boxes and inputting the same values in frame 100). The easiest and most convenient way would be to:

    a. Move to frame 0.

    b. Select all the boxes and, in the timeline, select the keyframe at frame 0 (click to select the keyframe).

    c. Hold Shift and drag the keyframes to frame 100. This way, the box comes back to its original position.

4. Now scrub the animation or use the play bar to preview the animation. Boring, right? All the boxes move together at the same time. (Alternatively, you can load the `Tangents_Keyframed_Exercise.max` file to preview. Select box001 and note that the box has three keyframes, which we set earlier (at frames 0, 50, and 100).

Note Keyframes have a in point and out point, which control the tangents, except that the first keyframe doesn't have an in point and the last keyframe does not have an out point.

With box001 selected, open the motion panel in the control panel. You should see Figure 2-8a.

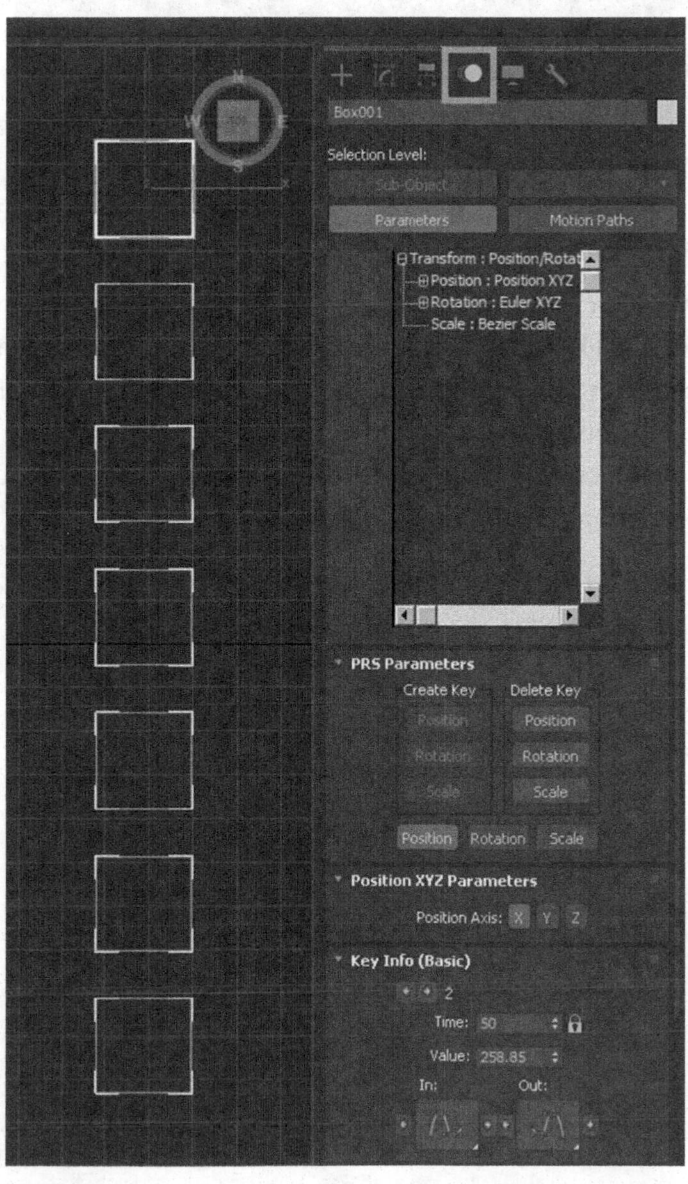

Figure 2-8a. *Motion panel*

In that panel, I would like to direct your attention toward the Key Info panel, as shown in Figure 2-8b.

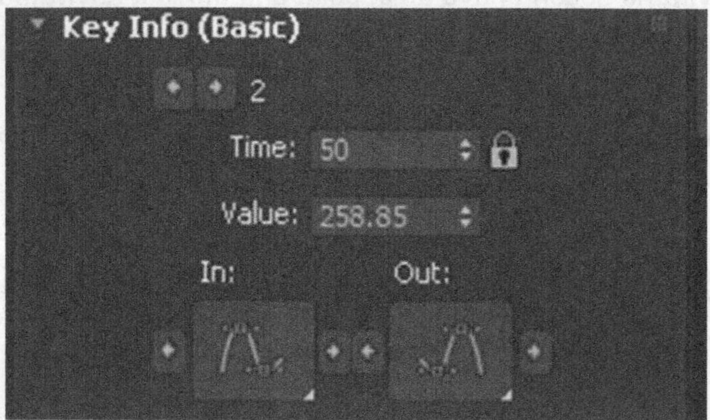

Figure 2-8b. *Key Info panel*

Note the arrows, which allow you to jump between keyframes. We have a total of three keyframes for box001, so we should be able to move among them using this instead of using the slider. If your current time is not on any active keyframe, all the values will be grayed out and no edits can be performed.

Note that the in and out categories have arrows on both sides of the icon. Clicking on a graph loads a few options for us. See Figure 2-9.

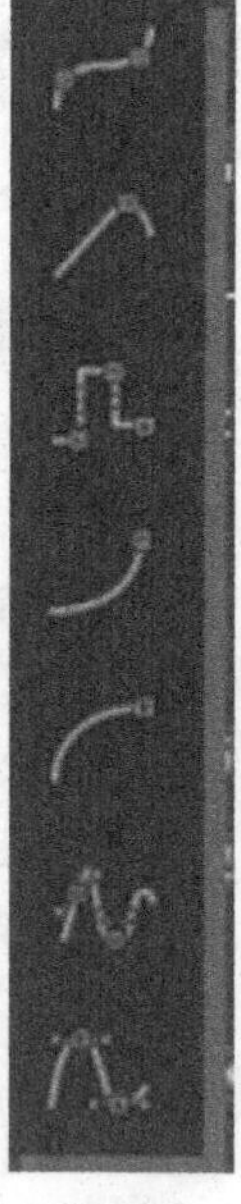

Figure 2-9. *Key info tangent types*

The keys are named Smooth, Linear, Step, Slow, Fast, Spline, and Auto Tangent. Let's apply/modify this keyframe in/out type to all the boxes at keyframe 50 to see what it does.

Before we apply the graph to an in or out point, there's one more thing we need to understand. The arrows on either side of the graphs that are visible along the in and out graphs are also known as a copiers, as shown in Figure 2-10.

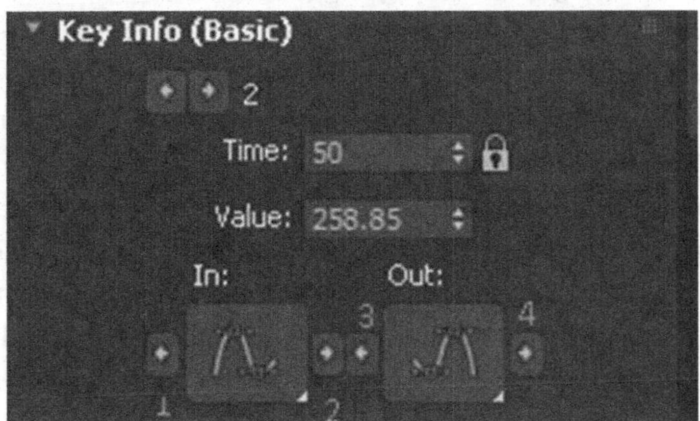

Figure 2-10. *Key Info copiers*

This is how it works. If you set an animation graph of a particular type in the in point of frame 50 (key 2) and click on the

- Arrow labeled 1, it will copy the graph type to the previous keyframes out animation type.
- Arrow labeled 2, it will copy the graph type to the animation graph to the same keyframes output animation type. In this case, if keyframe 50 is selected, the in tangent type will be copied to the out of the same frame.
- Arrow labeled 3, it will copy the out graph type to the in graph to the same keyframes input animation type. In this case, if keyframe 50 is selected, the out tangent type will be copied to the in tangent type of the same frame.
- Arrow labeled 4, it will copy the graph type to the next keyframe's out animation type. In this case, it copies to the in of the next keyframe, which is 100.

Set the Animation graph of the in/out type of each box's frame 50 keyframe to Smooth, Linear, Step, Slow, Fast, Spline, and Auto Tangent.

If you notice we get varied motion by just setting the graph type for one keyframe, and also you might wonder why boxes 005, 006, 007 still move uniformly. (They have the basic animation graph set to Fast, Spline, and Auto Tangent.) When we get into the next chapter, we discuss tweaking these handles using advanced editors.

You can load the `Tangents_FinishedExercise.max` file to preview the animation or alternatively load the rendered video in the video folder (`Tangents.mp4`). If you are wondering why we are learning this in a character animation book, the answer is that your default keyframe types are not going to cut it... the default animation keyframes are quite boring and appear better for robotic movements. If you look at an animation of a person thumping a table, the animation speed is not going to be same when the animation has begun and the speed will not be the same when the fist contacts the table. Animations need to eased in and out to convey fluid motion and that can be achieved using the previous techniques used. What we used are the basic version of them, and now let's take this a step further and move to tweaking this for further refinement.

Curve Editor

The Curve Editor allows you to see animations as curves on a 2D graph and allows you to create and tweak animations without having to handle the object in the viewport.

Invoking the Curve Editor

There are two variations of Curve Editors that can be opened. One is the mini Curve Editor that can be opened by clicking on the icon, as shown in Figure 2-11.

***Figure 2-11.** Mini Curve Editor timeline*

You can also go to the ribbon menu and click the Curve Editor icon, as shown in Figure 2-12.

Figure 2-12. *Curve Editor ribbon button*

Or you can right-click on any viewport and choose Curve Editor, as shown in Figure 2-13.

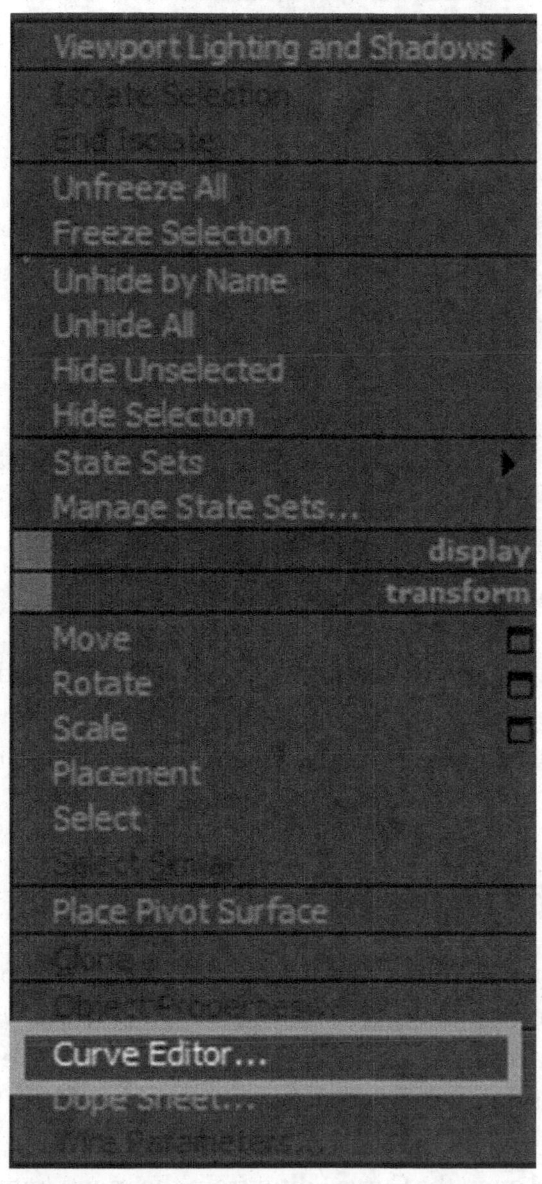

Figure 2-13. *Curve Editor's Viewport menu*

You can also use the Graph Editors ➤ Trackview - Curve Editor menu option, as shown in Figure 2-14.

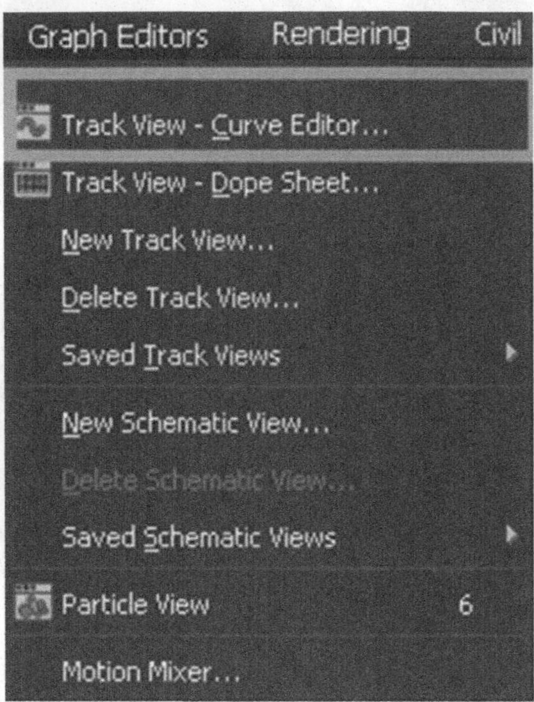

Figure 2-14. *Main menu of the Curve Editor*

Let's take a look at the Curve Editor first and move ahead with the other one. Note that we will not be covering the Curve Editor as a whole, rather we will be focusing on the most used and relevant tools that ease an animator's job. I recommend that you get familiar with the Curve Editor navigation and menus.

Working with the Curve Editor

In earlier pages we learned about using animation graphs to control the animation by applying easing to keyframes using the animation graph icon. What exactly is the graph, you might have asked? Or, can I plot my own graph to create a more customized animation? All these questions could have popped into your head. We'll answer those here.

Fire up 3ds Max and open the Curve Editor from the menu option or from the ribbon bar. See Figure 2-15.

Figure 2-15. *Curve Editor Pane, new file*

The editor menu in the Curve Editor allows you to switch between Curve Editor and Dope Sheet. Currently we are looking at understanding what a Curve Editor is, so let's stick with Curve Editor. If you changed it to the Dope Sheet, switch back to Curve Editor. If your scene is empty, you might notice the list below World ➤ Object is empty too. Add a cube or a single object and notice that the list populates. See Figure 2-16.

Figure 2-16. *Curve Editor pane with a box in the scene*

Note that if you have multiple objects in the scene, the Curve Editor will show all the selected objects parameters in it. Try adding a sphere and a box in an empty scene and load the Curve Editor. Alternate and select the objects to see the Curve Editor populate the details of the object. If you select multiple objects, you should be able to see the list of objects and parameters on the left pane.

Before we move on, let's look the right pane the graph viewer. The double vertical yellow line is your current time indicator. Scrub the timeline and it should update here. Or, if you drag the double yellow line, you the track bar updates as well. We said this is the Graph Editor, so what are the dimensions or readings of X and Y? The answer is that X is denoted by time, and Y is denoted by value.

Open the `CurveEditor_BoxStart.max` file. The scene is pretty simple with just a box at the 0, 0, 0 coordinates. Open the Curve Editor and follow along.

Pay attention to the line that is marked in Figure 2-17.

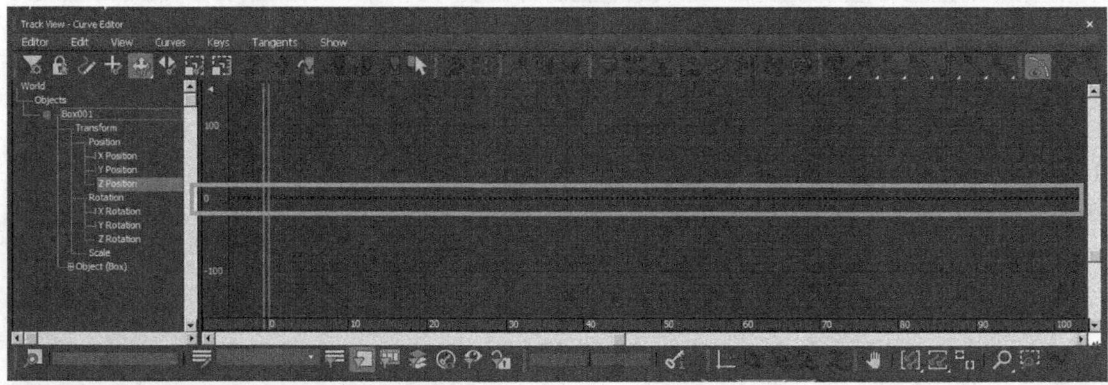

Figure 2-17. *Curve Editor pane, graph*

Since our box is on 0, 0, 0 and our selected axis on the left pane is Z, you see the line in blue at 0. Selecting a different axis will show the corresponding axis color. Now let's move the box up by 100 units and observe the changes. See Figure 2-18.

Figure 2-18. *Curve Editor pane, graph and coordinates*

Notice that the blue line is moved up overall to the reading of 100. So far we have not animated anything. The value is constant so the line is pretty straight. Now let's animate it to see what we can do.

Understanding Graph View: Curve Editor

Fire up 3ds Max and load `CurveEditor_Sphere.max` or create a new file with a sphere. Set the coordinates of the sphere to 0, 0, 0.

Open Curve Editor and observe the changes as you do the following steps:

1. At frame 0, set a keyframe so that the ball is locked at 0, 0, 0.
2. At frame 50, make the ball go up 0, 0, 100 and set a keyframe.
3. At frame 100, make the ball come back to 0, 0, 0.

Basically what we have done is make the ball go up and come back down to its initial position. If you notice the graph in the Curve Editor, it should look something like Figure 2-19.

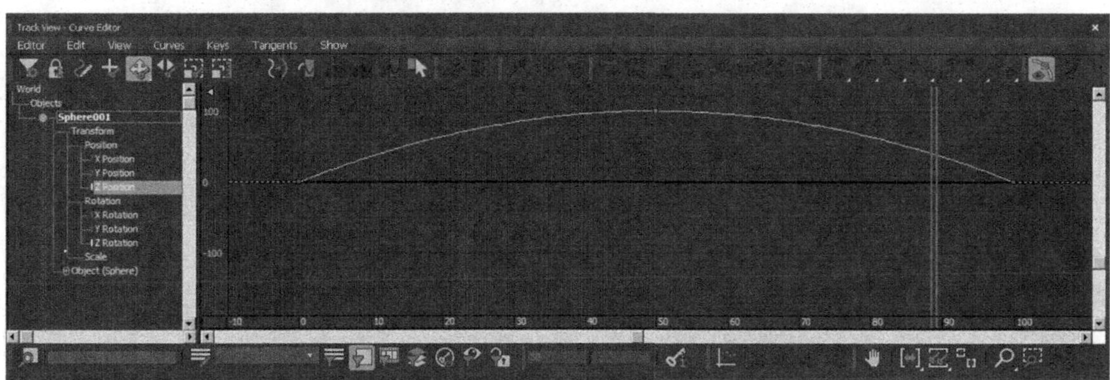

***Figure 2-19.** Curve Editor pane: Understanding Graph View*

Play the animation and preview the file. Notice that the ball is increasing its altitude at a smooth pace. Once it hits the peak, it reaches back to 0 at the inverse speed. I hope the graph viewer makes sense. We haven't gotten into the power of it yet; we just got our feet wet!

Creating Keys Manually in the Curve Editor

In this section we are going to create an animation of a sphere moving up and down using the Curve Editor.

1. Fire up 3ds Max and create a sphere with its pivot at its base or load the `CurveEditor_Spherestart.max` file. If you are creating a new file manually, ensure your animation is 100 frames in duration in the Time Configuration window.

2. With the sphere selected, open the Curve Editor.

   (Note: If the time range scale starts at from 0 and moves to a larger value than our project is set to, follow the next step. If not, there is no need to worry about it.)

   To fix it, go to the Curve Editor Menu and choose View ➤ Frame ➤ Frame Horizontal Extents. This will frame your animation time range to fit and you should be able to see the key and curves.

3. We want the ball to be in its current position, so we need to create a keyframe for its current position with the Z axis selected. To create a keyframe in the Curve Editor, click on the highlighted icon on the toolbar of Curve Editor and click on the blue line at a frame where you want the keyframe to be on the graph area. See Figure 2-20.

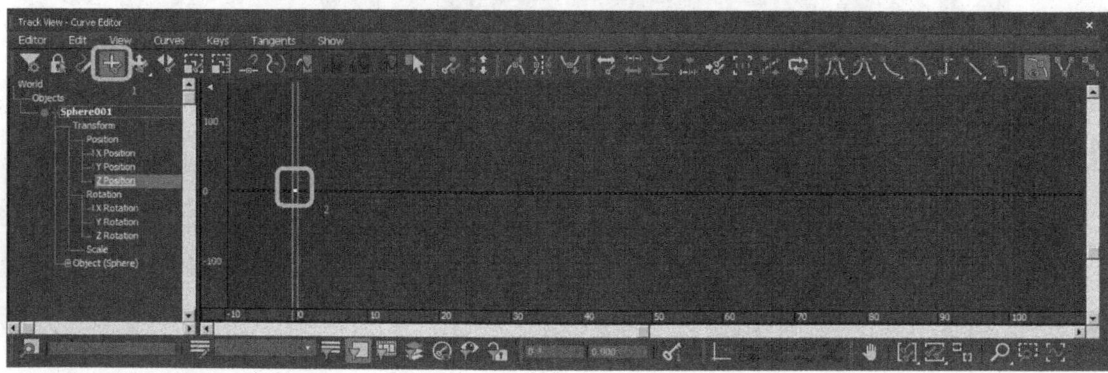

Figure 2-20. *Curve Editor pane, creating keyframes, frame 0*

4. Create a keyframe ((50,100) coordinates of the graph view). Use the same steps to create a keyframe in the Graph Editor.

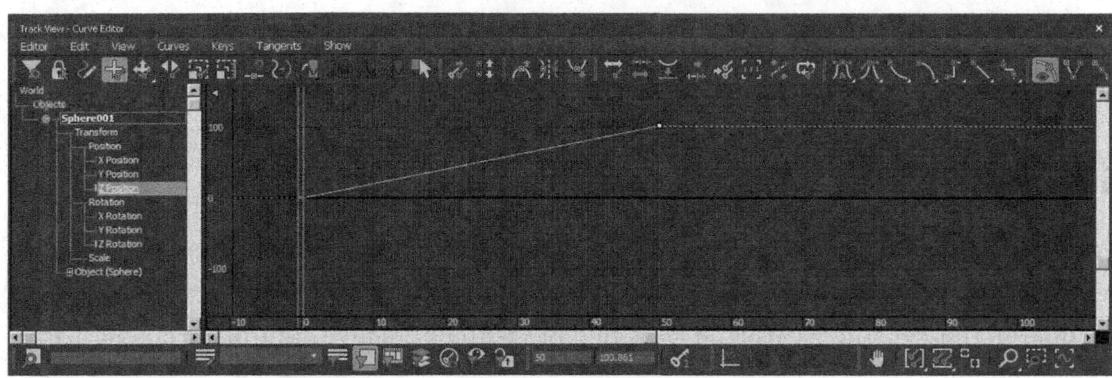

Figure 2-21. *Curve Editor pane, creating keyframes, frame 50*

5. Now for the final keyframe. Create another keyframe ((100, 0) coordinates of the graph view). Use the same steps to create a keyframe in the Graph Editor.

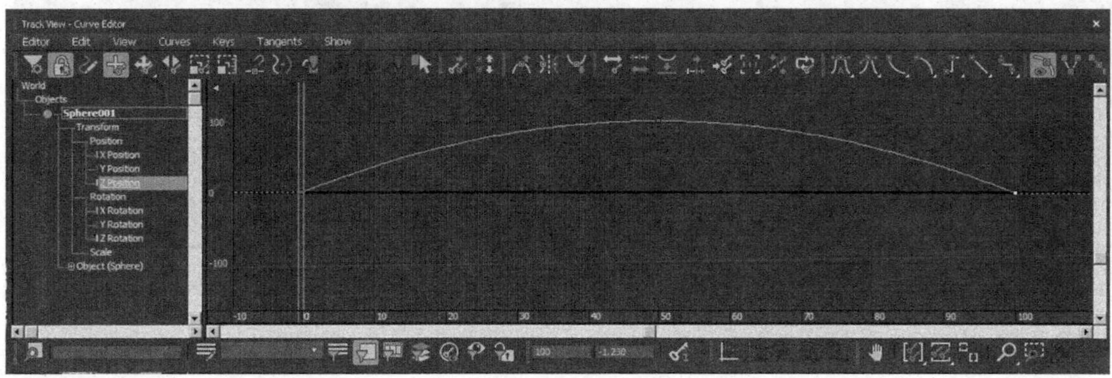

Figure 2-22. *Curve Editor pane, creating keyframes, frame 100*

6. At any point you want, you can use Add Keyframes to click anywhere on the graph in the axis line to add more keyframes and click and drag on a keyframe to translate the object to a new position.

Note To delete a keyframe, with the Add Keyframe Option enabled, hold the Shift key and click the keyframe you want to delete. Holding down Control while dragging a keyframe will constrain the movement of the keyframe to that axis.

Tweaking the Graphs

For this exercise, let's use the `CurveEditor_SphereKey.max` file. At this point, you should revisit the tangent types that we learned in the "Understanding Keyframes and Tangents" section. In this section, we use the tangent types with interactive controls to customize the animation.

Open the Curve Editor and observe the section marked.

The default type of tangent that is applied is a smooth tangent to all keyframes. As a test, select the keyframe at 50. Selected keyframes will look like white dot. See Figure 2-23.

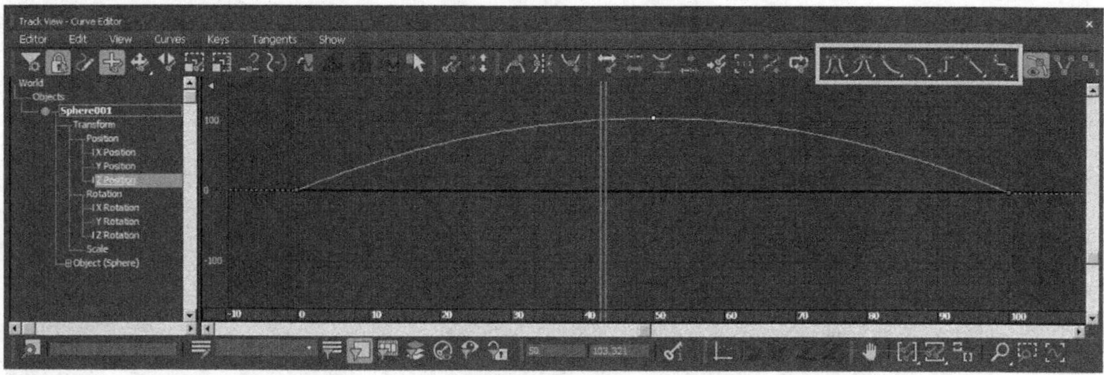

Figure 2-23. *Curve Editor pane, tangent types*

Apply the tangent to only the keyframe at 50 and preview the animation to see what is happening.

Tangent _Auto

When an auto tangent is selected as a keyframe option, a Bezier flowing curve is created from the incoming keyframe to the outgoing keyframe. It's a smooth interpolation with the exception that the Bezier handle can be controlled and manipulated using the handles. See Figure 2-24.

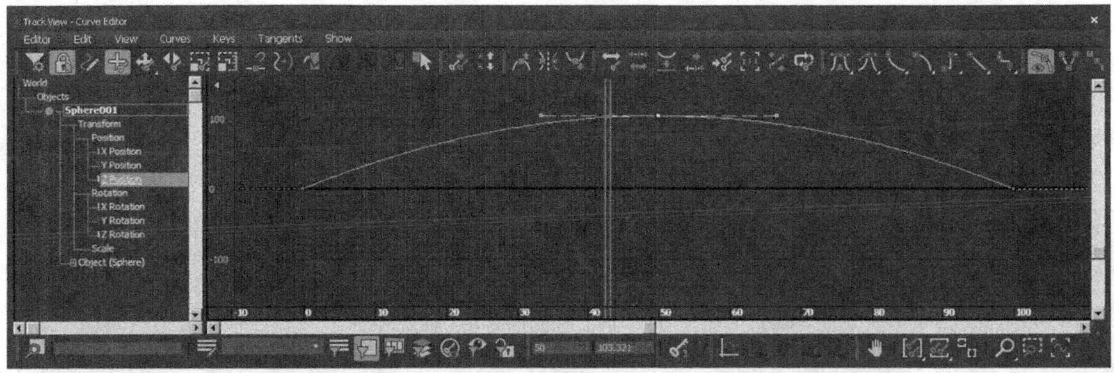

__Figure 2-24.__ Curve Editor pane, tangent handles

By holding Alt+Shift, the individual handles can be broken and controlled for interesting results, which turn the keyframe type to Tangent_spline. See Figure 2-25.

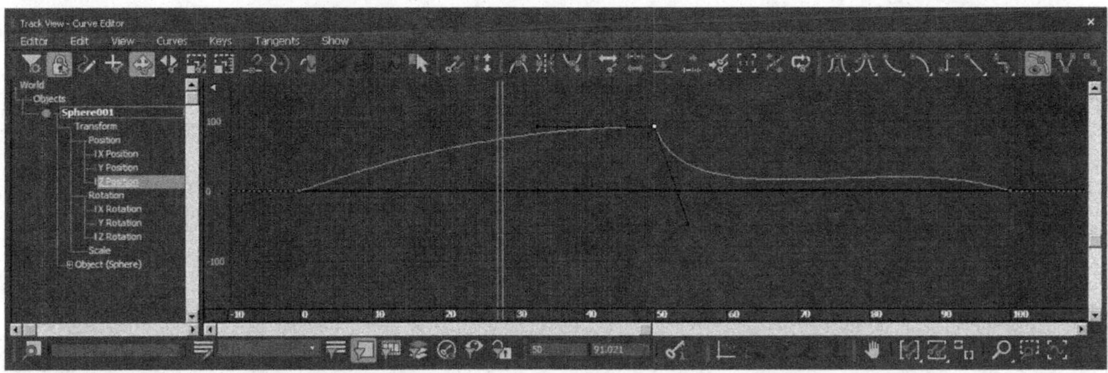

__Figure 2-25.__ Curve Editor pane, tangent spline

Tangent _Spline

The Tangent Spline option gives you adjustable tangents so that you can refine the animation. The handles can be moved independently using the Alt+Shift key drag option. Holding Control while dragging restricts a particular axis. Tangent splines are an enhanced version of Tangent_Auto.

Tangents can be unified again using the Tangent menu in the Curve Editor and then choosing Unify Tangents. This feature links the handles after a break so that moving one end keeps the other end of the handle in an unbroken line.

Tangent_Fast

In a fast tangent, the animation is faster when it's closer to the keyframe and gets slower as it recedes away. See Figure 2-26.

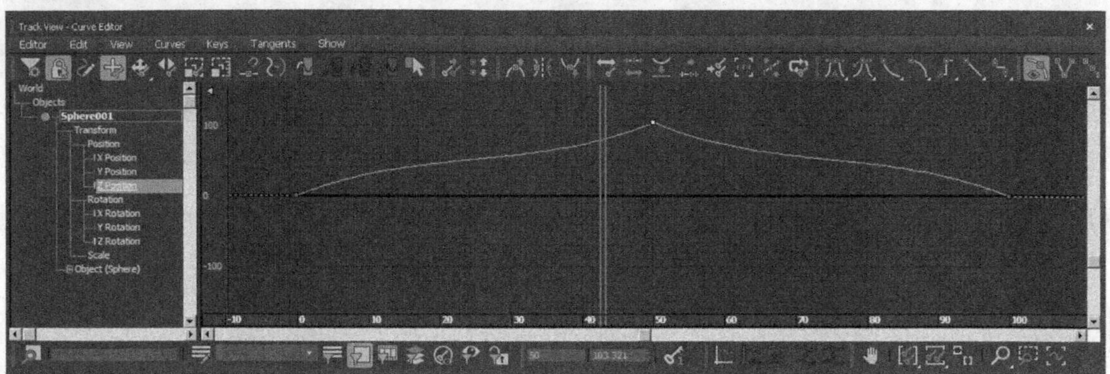

Figure 2-26. *Curve Editor pane, tangent fast*

Tangent_Slow

In a slow tangent, the animation rapidly decreases the closer to the keyframe it becomes and it accelerates as it recedes away. See Figure 2-27.

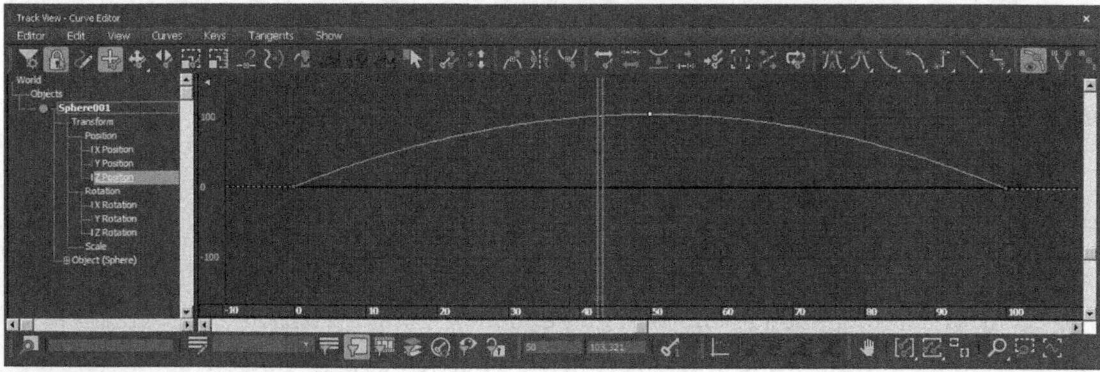

Figure 2-27. *Curve Editor pane, tangent slow*

Tangent_Stepped

In a stepped tangent, the animation value is held until there is another keyframe to change it. In this scenario, the ball would just be warping to three different positions. This tangent type is very useful when blocking out animation.

Blocking out animation is a workflow used in animation, wherein you decide where a particular object has to be on various time intervals and then later decide on the type of easing or speed of the animation you want by choosing the right tangent type. With a stepped tangent set, you will see the object warping from place to place. See Figure 2-28.

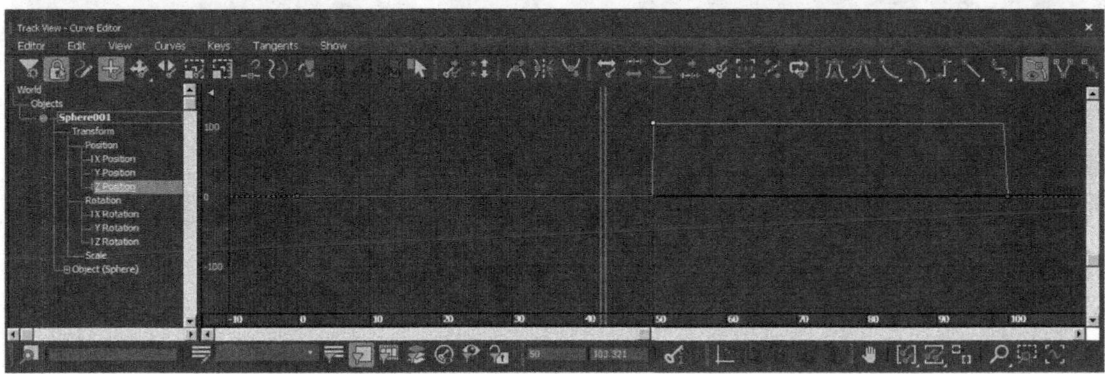

Figure 2-28. Curve Editor pane, tangent stepped

Tangent_Linear

A linear tangent works best when the adjacent keyframes are set to linear as well in this case frame 0 and 100. The ball will travel at a constant speed overall through the animation. Linear tangents are better suited for mechanical motion. See Figure 2-29.

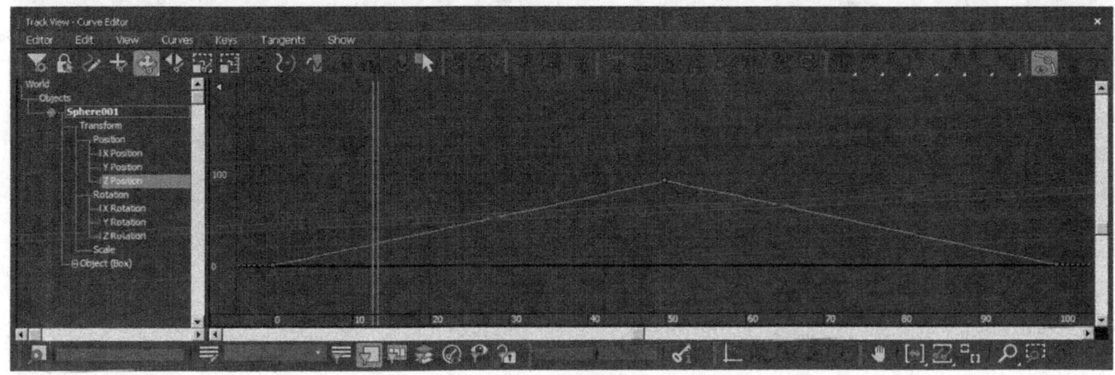

Figure 2-29. Curve Editor pane, tangent linear

Tangent_Smooth

Smooth tangent eases in and out of the keyframe to create a smooth motion, more like a blend of fast and slow. Apply the tangent to only the keyframe 50 and preview the animation to visually understand what is happening, as shown in Figure 2-30a.

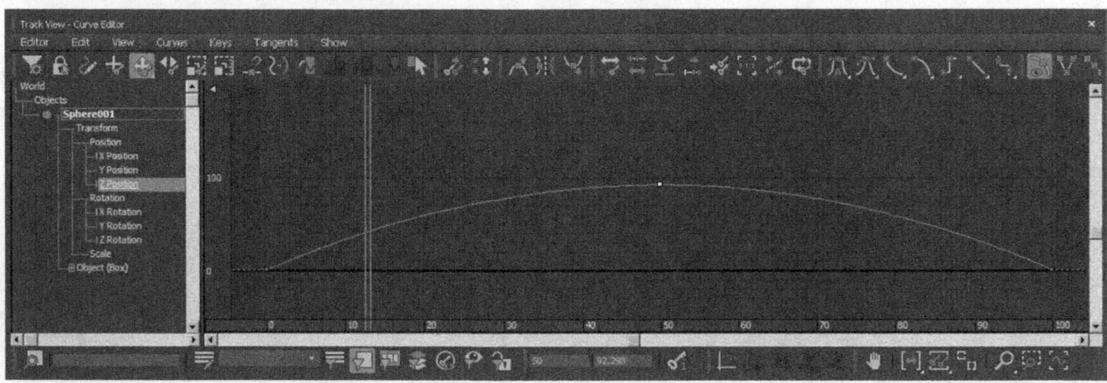

Figure 2-30a. Curve Editor pane, smooth tangent

Now that you know what tangents are and how to use and modify them, open the `Tangents_FinishedExercise.max` file and view it in the Curve Editor.

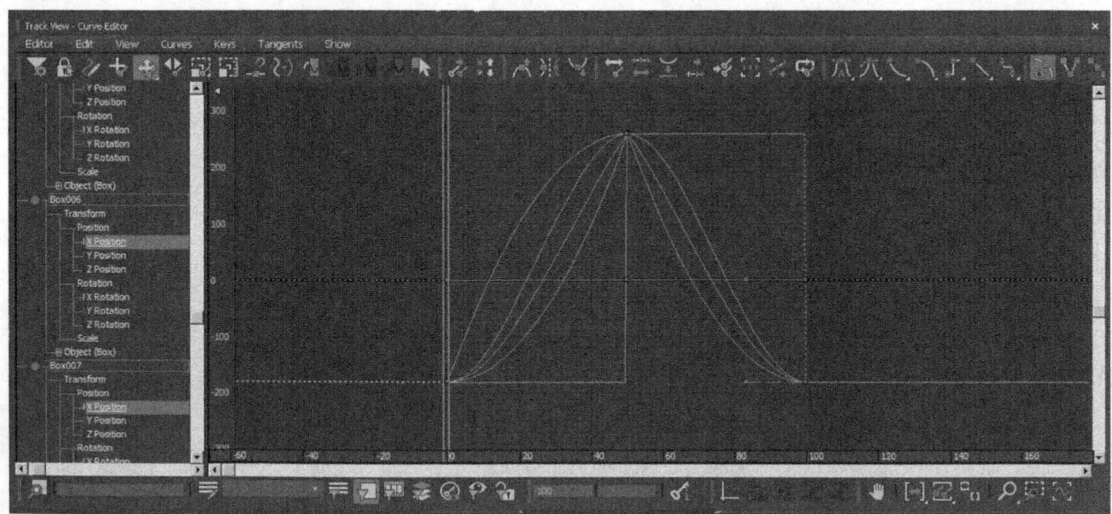

Figure 2-30b. Curve Editor pane, boxes 004, 006, and 007

Recall that boxes 004, 006, and 007 were moving the same way. If you analyze the graph, you will understand why. If you followed along with the tangents, tweak the animation graphs and you should get interesting results. For now, let's stop with the Curve Editor at this point and look at the other untouched options as we move ahead in the chapters.

Mini Curve Editor

The mini Curve Editor can be opened by clicking on its icon, as shown in Figure 2-31.

***Figure 2-31.** Mini Curve Editor button*

Once the mini Curve Editor is open, the UI will look like Figure 2-32.

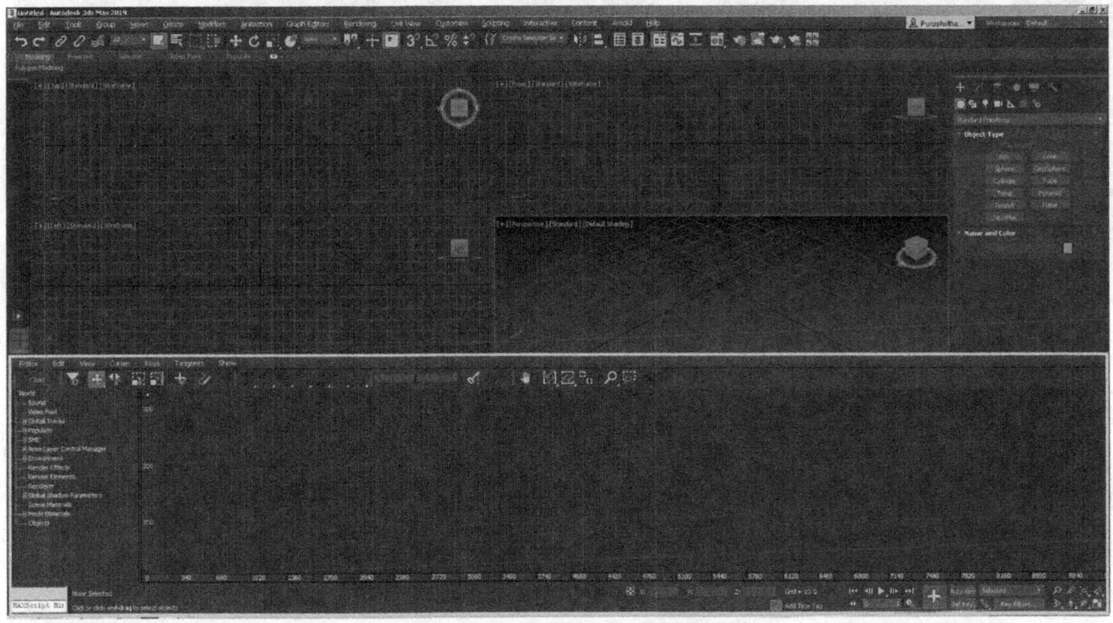

***Figure 2-32.** 3ds Max UI with the mini Curve Editor open*

The Mini Curve Editor has a lot more options in the left pane compared to our normal Curve Editor. This editor includes every feature that can be manipulated for a given 3ds Max file, such as sound, materials, and any other data that can be animated. The last in the list is the objects, under which your objects will be populated. As in the normal Curve Editor, your objects need to be selected for them to be viewable in the list.

Let's open the `CurveEditor_SphereKey.max` file and view the graph in the Curve Editor. In fact, I recommend that you look at both and identify what makes this mini Curve Editor a mini over the other one. See Figure 2-33.

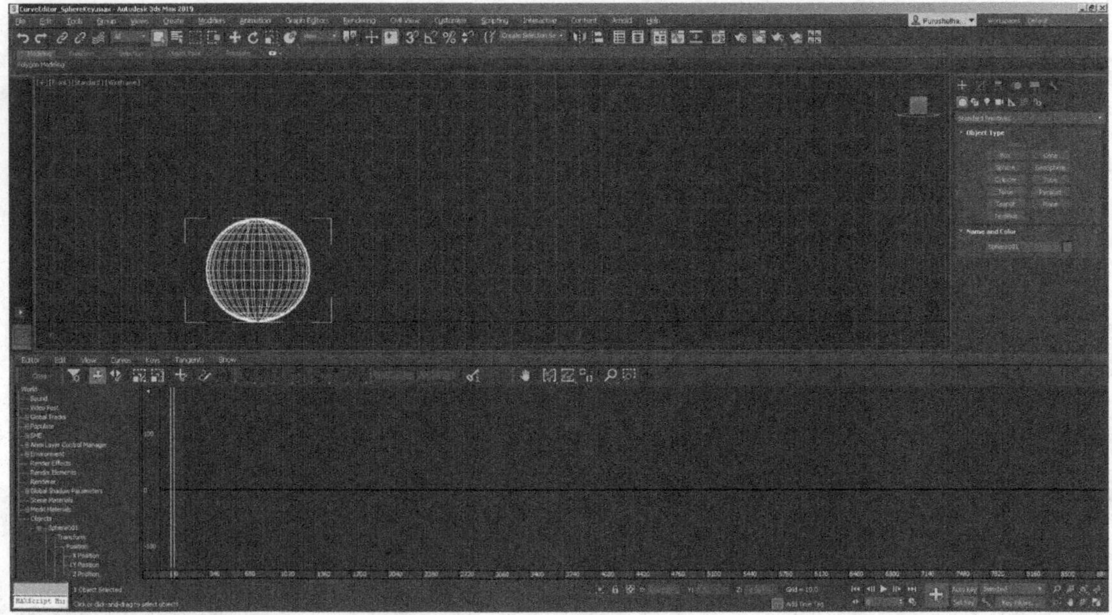

Figure 2-33. *3ds Max UI with mini Curve Editor file open with animation*

A couple of things you'll notice when you view the file:

- The animation is there but we are not able to see the keys in the graph view even though our sphere is selected
- The time range scale shows from 0 to a higher value than our project is set to

Let's fix that. To do so, go to the mini Curve Editor menu bar and choose Menu ➤ Frame ➤ Frame Horizontal Extents. This will frame your animation time range to fit and you should be able to see the key and curves. See Figure 2-34.

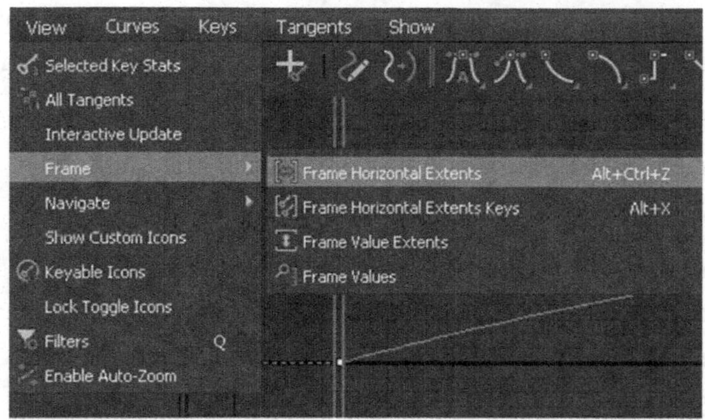

Figure 2-34. *Mini Curve Editor, frame extents*

The tangents for the mini Curve Editor are located as marked in Figure 2-35.

Figure 2-35. *Mini Curve Editor, tangent types*

One other feature of the mini Curve Editor is that it allows you to freehand sketch curves. See Figure 2-36.

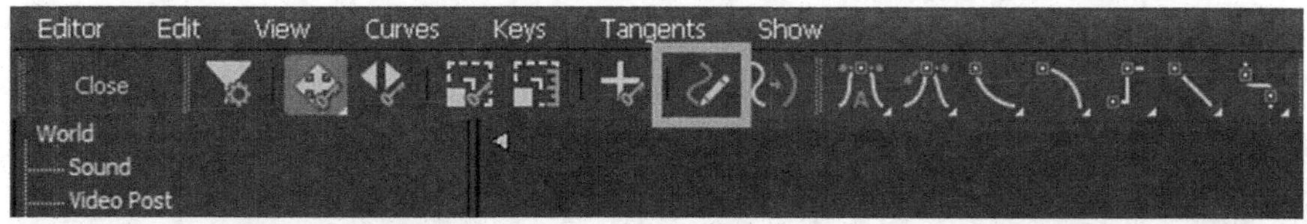

Figure 2-36. *Mini Curve Editor, draw curves*

Once you have selected the Draw Curve tool, you can select an object and choose any axis and then freehand sketch a curve on the graph viewer. Let's take a quick look at having a ball animation using the mini Curve Editor and the Draw Curve tool.

1. Launch 3ds Max and create a sphere with its pivot at the base at the 0, 0, 0 coordinates.

2. Move it up on the Z axis so that it falls and moves over.

3. For this purpose, we are going to assume the perspective grid as our ground. Or you could create a cube to mimic a ground plane.

4. Open the Mini Curve Editor and frame your animation in the Graph view by pressing Ctrl+Alt+Z or choosing the Menu ➤ Frame ➤ Frame Horizontal Extents menu option.

5. Keep in mind that the ball is going to be animated in two axes. One is the Z axis where the ball gradually loses its height every bounce and the second is the X axis as the ball moves forward after every bounce. Refer to Figure 2-37.

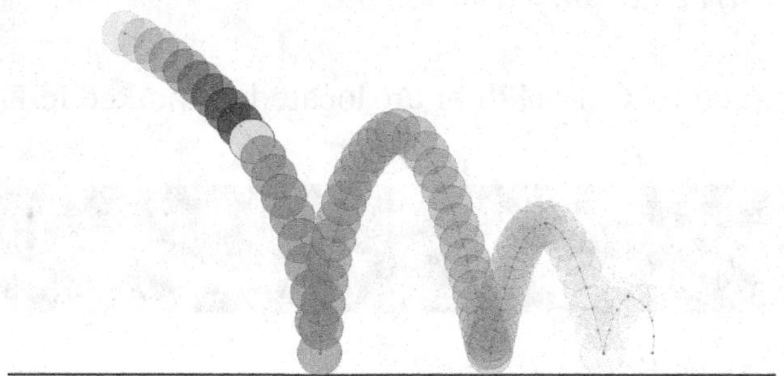

***Figure 2-37.** Ball bounce reference image*

6. Let's create an animation for the bounce. Select the Z axis of the sphere and choose the Draw Curves tool from the toolbar of the mini Curve Editor. See Figure 2-38.

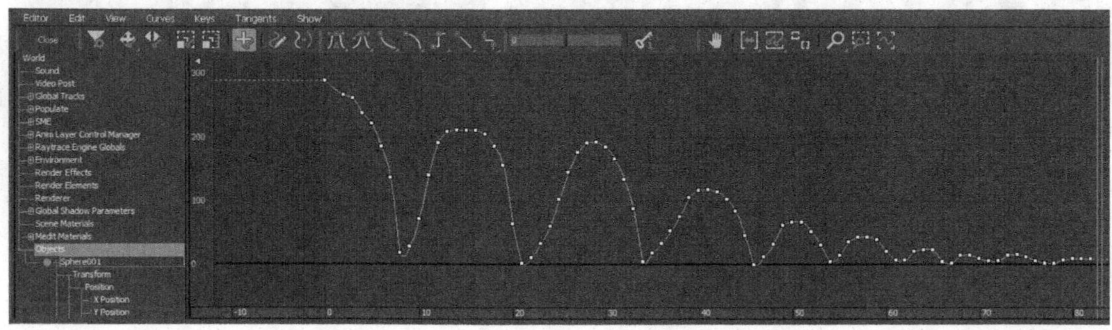

***Figure 2-38.** Ball bounce pattern drawn using Draw Curve tool, Z axis*

7. Redraw until you are happy with the curve. Play and preview the animation to see how the ball moves up and down. You can load the `MiniCurveEdtior_SphereDrawCurve.max` file as well.

8. Now let's move to the X axis, where the ball has to move forward after it hits the ground. I would like you to check until which frame you have drawn the curve (on the Z axis). In my case, it's at frame 82.

9. For the X axis animation, we can just move the ball over two frames and create keyframes where they need to be. See Figure 2-39.

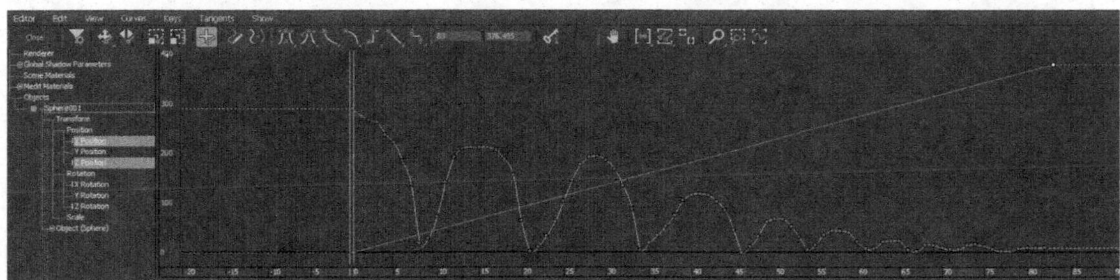

Figure 2-39. *Ball movement pattern drawn using the Draw Curve tool, X axis*

10. Preview the animation. Voila, the ball is bouncing around. What is missing? The squash and stretch. If you animate the scale parameter, you will have a ball bounce animation complete.

Dope Sheet

The Dope Sheet lets you to work with keys on a one-dimensional graph (time), instead of curves like in Curve Editor. Note: We adjusted the position value in the previous examples, but value can be anything you want to animate (rotation, size, colors, etc.).

The Dope Sheet is used to retime your keyframes and offset your animation so that it begins at a different frame. Let's say, for example, we have a ball rocket taking off at frame 50 and exploding at frame 100. What you could do with the Dope Sheet is have the rocket start at any other frame of your choice and play the animation from there. This helps us reposition our animation keys without having to redo it altogether.

Like the Curve Editor, there are two variations of the Dope Sheet. One is the mini Dope Sheet, which can be opened by clicking on the icon, as shown in Figure 2-40, and then choosing Dope Sheet from the Editor menu. If you notice in your mini Curve Editor, there is a close button to close the editor, but if you change your Curve Editor to the Dope Sheet, you lose the ability to close the editor. Even switching back to the Curve Editor will not bring back the close button. The only way to close it this way is to undock the panel and close it. Click and drag the left-most border of the Graph Editor to undock. This undocking method works for any panel in 3ds Max.

Figure 2-40. *Mini Curve Editor/Dope Sheet button*

Alternative method 1: Right-click on any viewport and choose Dope Sheet from the menu, as shown in Figure 2-41.

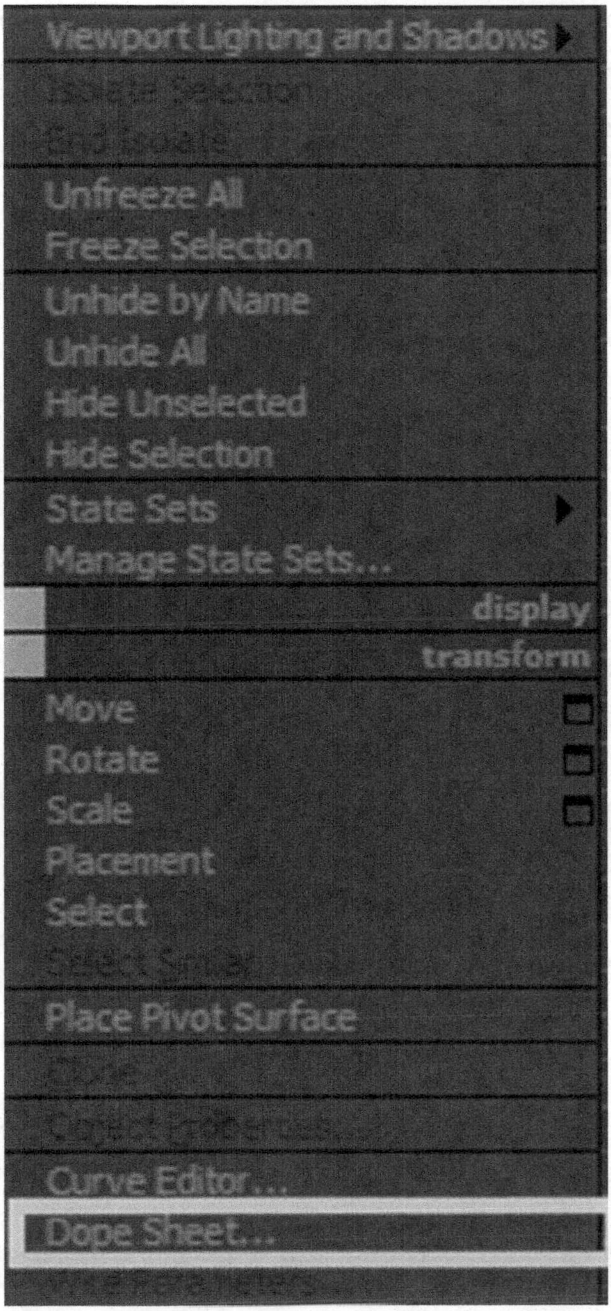

***Figure 2-41.** Viewport menu, Dope Sheet*

Alternative method 2: Go to the Graph Editor ➤ Trackview - Dope Sheet menu, as shown in Figure 2-42.

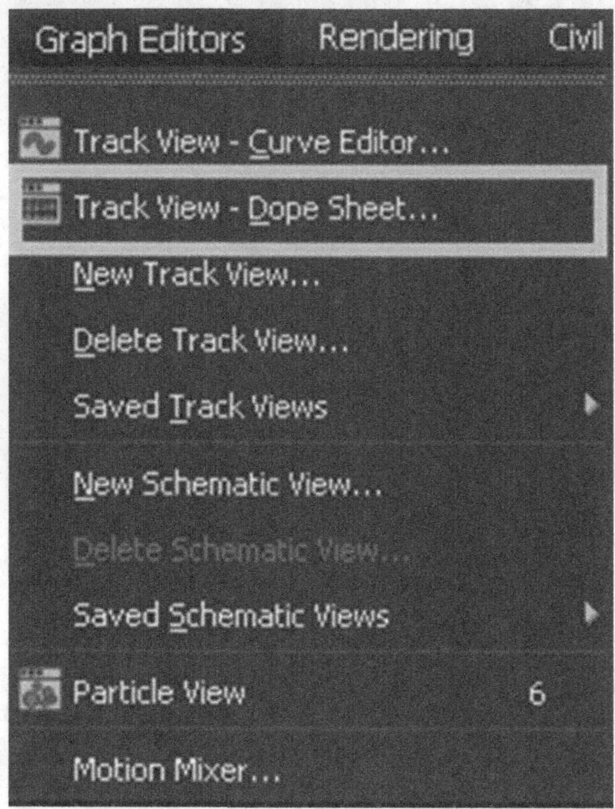

Figure 2-42. *Dope Sheet from main menu bar*

Load `DopeSheet_BallAnimation.max` and open the Dope Sheet to see what we can do with it.

By default, you are in Edit Ranges, as shown in the toolbar in Figure 2-43. Edit Ranges and Edit Keys are the first two buttons in the toolbar of the Dope Sheet.

Figure 2-43. *Dope Sheet toolbar Edit Ranges mode*

In Edit Ranges mode, the animations are shown as bars. You will not be able to see how many keyframes there are in the object. The range will show where the animation is starting and where it is ending. When you hover your mouse over an animation range, the cursor changes into three types. See Figure 2-44.

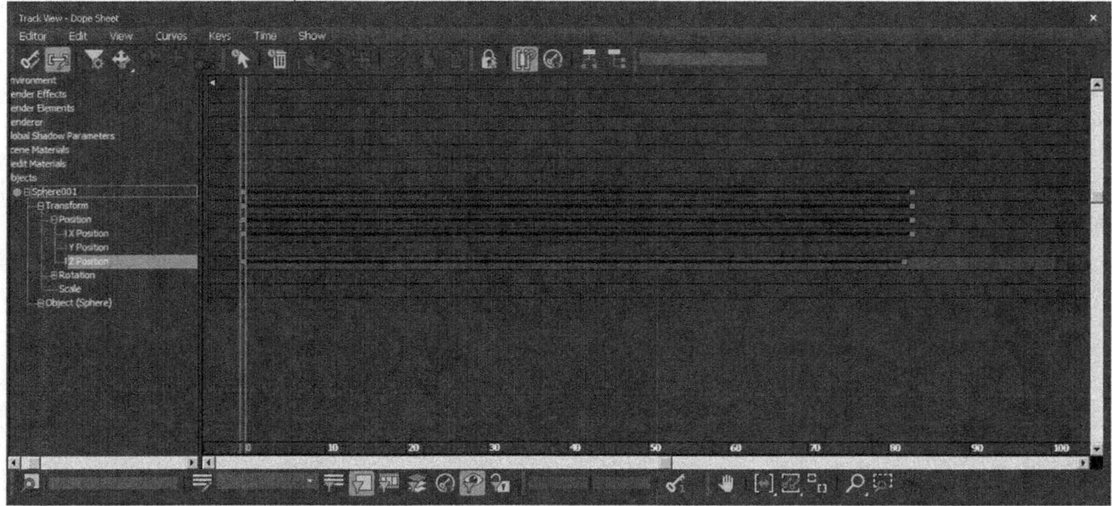

Figure 2-44. *Dope Sheet range bars*

- When you hover over the starting point of an animation and click and drag the start point, you can scale the animation. In this case if you select the start point and move it toward the end point, you will be scaling down the duration so the animation will play faster. Think of it this way—the size of the range bars' scale from initial to altered state will determine the speed.
- When you hover the mouse over to the right side, the same thing happens.
- Alternatively, you can hover over the middle of a range and will be able to slide the animation without altering its speed. Let's say we have a robot jumping from frame 50 to 100 but we want the animation to play at frame 220. Simply select the range and drag its new starting point to 220.

The Curve Editor and Dope Sheet are very powerful tools to aid animators.

Summary

If you have followed along, you should by now have an idea of the principles of animation, keyframes, tangents, and tangent types, as well as the typical uses for the animation editors (Curve Editor and Dope Sheet). This concludes the foundation module.

We use the advanced controllers and constraints in the next chapters and then move ahead to character animation.

CHAPTER 3

Advanced Animation Tools

In the previous chapters, we learned about the principles of animation and how to create animation within 3ds Max. We learned how to tweak our animations using animation editors such as the Curve Editor and the Dope Sheet. In this chapter, we look at using advanced animation tools to animate in a desired and procedural way. We look at animations using constraints and controllers as well. We begin by setting up hierarchy, pivots, and layers to geometric objects and then move into learning and using various types of constraints for advanced animation.

Getting Started with Hierarchy

To begin, let's look at what hierarchy is. *Hierarchy* is a software technique used to create parent/child relationships. Hierarchies ease the workload of an animator. For example, when you lift your thigh up, your knee, ankle, and feet bones also rise up because they are linked to each other. Without this hierarchy, the animator would need to animate all the bone parts individually. Follow along and you will understand this better as I guide you through an example.

Setting Up a Hierarchy

Hierarchy for objects/geometries needs to be set up before you begin any animation that has multiple parts. As an example, load `Hierarchy_Start.max` from the source files folder. A simple robotic arm has been created with basic primitive shapes (probably not the best modeling you have seen, but this should suffice for now). See Figure 3-1. At this point, see if you can move the robotic arm from its default pose to a different pose.

P. Raju, *Character Rigging and Advanced Animation*, https://doi.org/10.1007/978-1-4842-5037-2_3

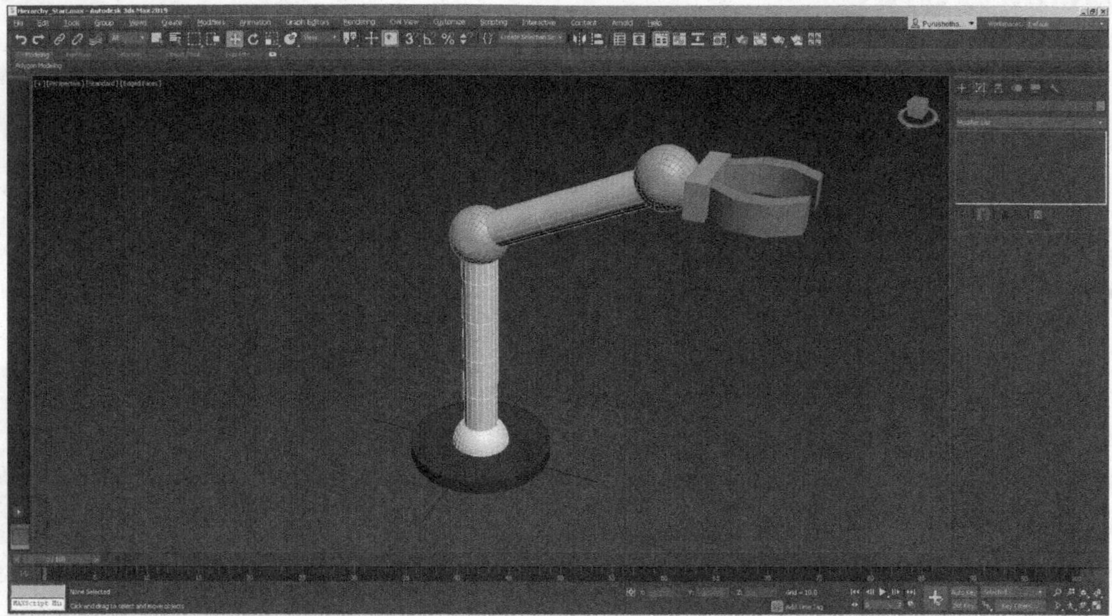

Figure 3-1. *Simple robotic arm setup*

If you try to pose the arm in a different way, you will notice that the arm is made of multiple parts. That means that posing it is tedious. Now go ahead and swivel the arm 360 degrees on its base or have the claw pick up and play the animation. This is tough and you might end with animations where the parts move away from each other. The purpose of this section is to show how to address these problems.

Reset your workspace by selecting standard design so that the Scene Explorer is docked on the left view. Alternatively, you can open Scene Explorer by choosing Tools menu ➤ All Global Explorers ➤ Scene Explorer. (Refer to Figure 3-2.)

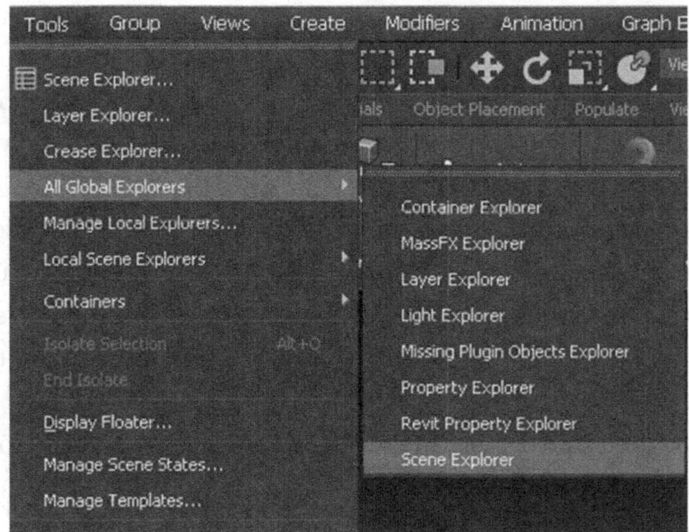

***Figure 3-2.** Scene Explorer menu*

Once you open the Scene Explorer, you should see the Scene Explorer panel with the hierarchy of the robotic arm, as shown in Figure 3-3.

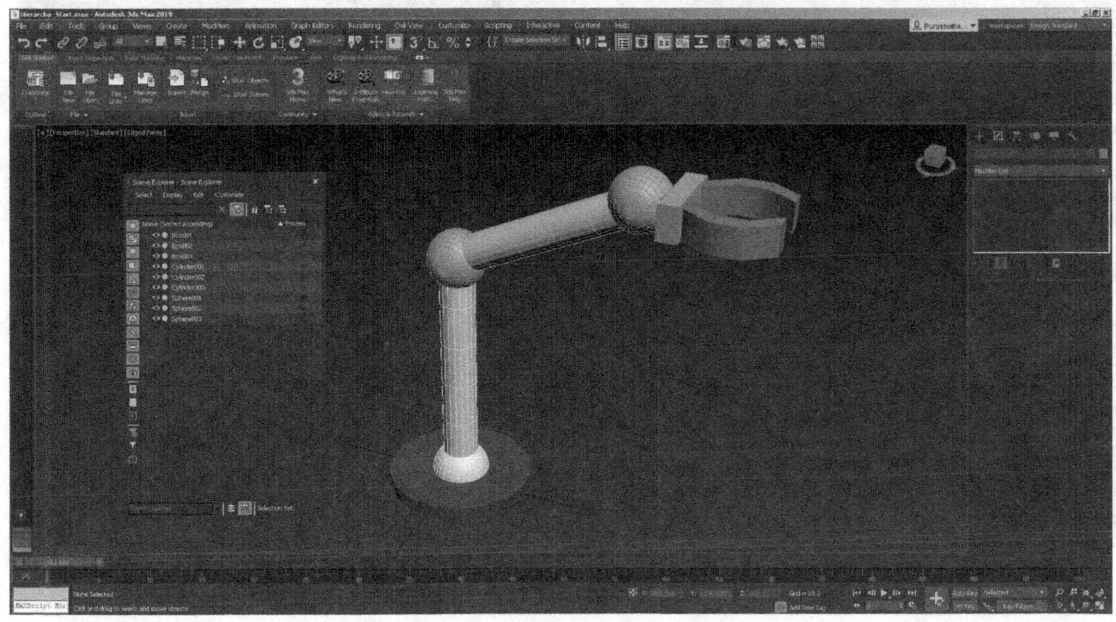

***Figure 3-3.** Scene Explorer panel*

Once the Scene Explorer is open, you can see that there are many primitive shapes that make up the robotic arm. As you can see, my naming conventions for mesh are nonexistent and this is for a reason. To rename the primitives, select one in the Scene Explorer, right-click, and choose the Rename option. Once you have given it an appropriate name, save it and proceed.

If you look before each primitive name, there is an eye icon that toggles the visibility of the object and a snowflake icon on the right, which freezes the mesh but leaves visibility so that you don't accidently select it in the viewport. As you can see, except for the segment in pink, every other primitive is frozen and the claws are set to invisible (note the eye icon).

The leftmost column shows the switches used to toggle the visibility of objects based on type (see Figure 3-4).

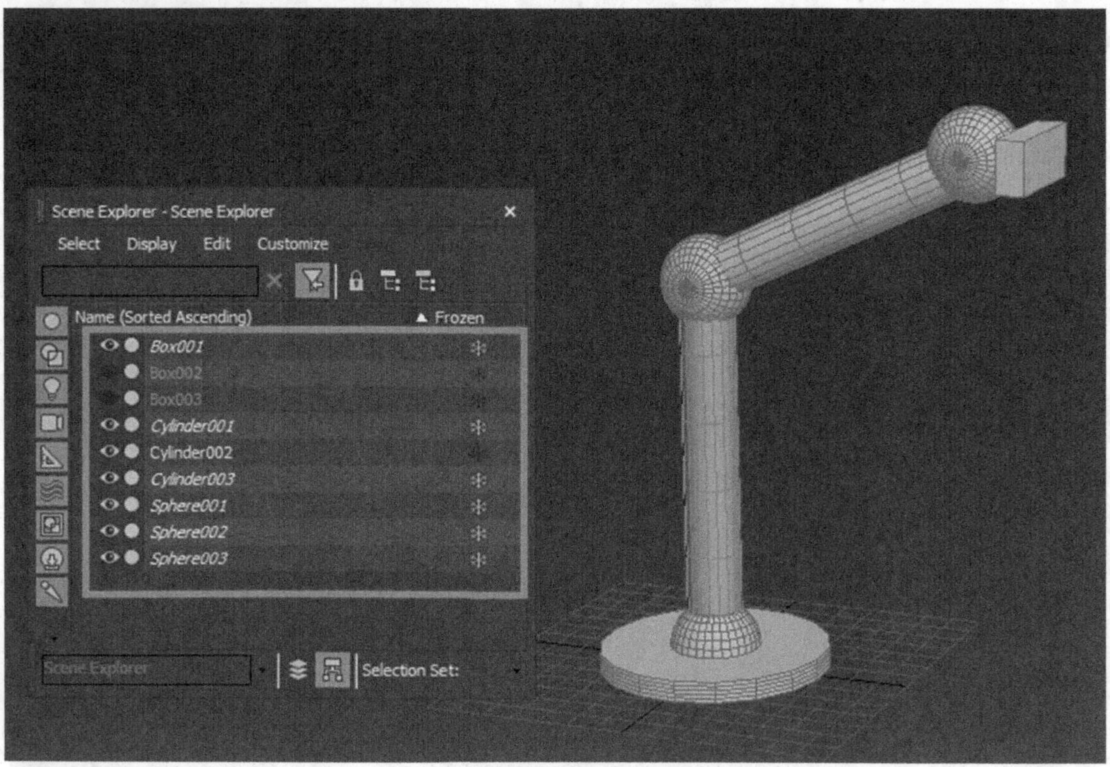

Figure 3-4. *Scene Explorer: visibility and frozen toggles*

Once you have renamed the files the way you want, you need to set up a hierarchy so that rotating sphere001 reorients all the others as well. Hierarchy can be set by dragging objects and dropping them below the one you want them to be a child of. In essence, the topmost object is the parent and the ones under it are the children.

Load `Hierarchy_Structured.max` and see what I have set up. Note that box002 and box003 are children of box001. Use the Rotate tool from the toolbar or press E shortcut for rotate and try rotating any joints. You should see that the children follow their parent's rotation. By dragging and dropping items in the Scene Explorer, we have set up hierarchy so that animating this hand is a lot easier. We should be able to pose and animate the robotic arm in a much easier way. See Figure 3-5.

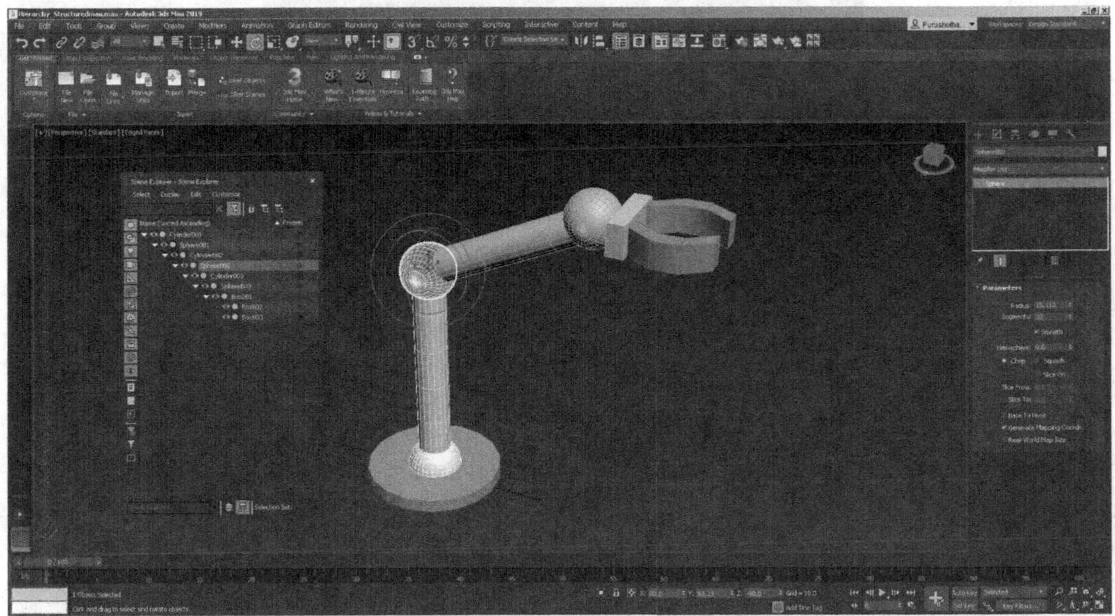

Figure 3-5. *Object rotated using rotation tool*

Go ahead and animate the hand by trying to pick an imaginary object. You will notice that the claws won't rotate to give the crab-claw kind of motion.

Objects rotate around their pivot and a pivot by default is located at the center of the mass of an object, but this can be relocated as needed. Spheres have the pivot in the center by default, as they are symmetrical on all axes. The box in its current state cannot be animated like a claw hand since it needs to have the pivot at the base for it to have a claw motion. How do we fix this?

Setting Up a Pivot

When you select the claws that make up box002 or box003, you'll notice that the pivots are in the center. We need to change them to the base so that the clawing motion can be achieved.

Notice the claw and the rotation pivot in the middle. Open the hierarchy panel open by clicking on the Hierarchy tab from the control panel. See Figure 3-6.

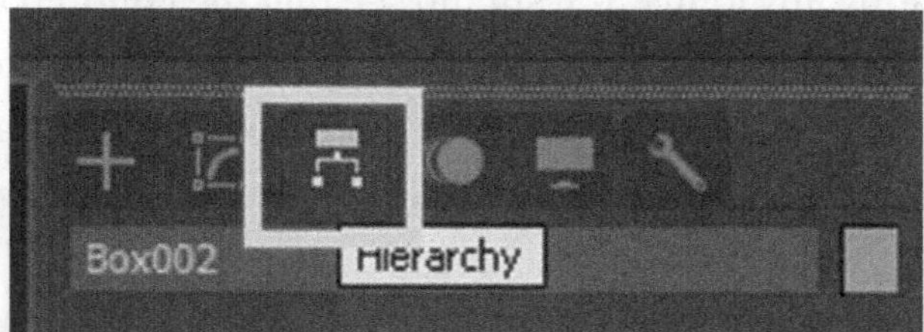

***Figure 3-6.** Command panel: Hierarchy tab*

Clicking on the Hierarchy tab from the command panel will populate the tab with hierarchy data and give us options to tweak to our liking. See Figure 3-7.

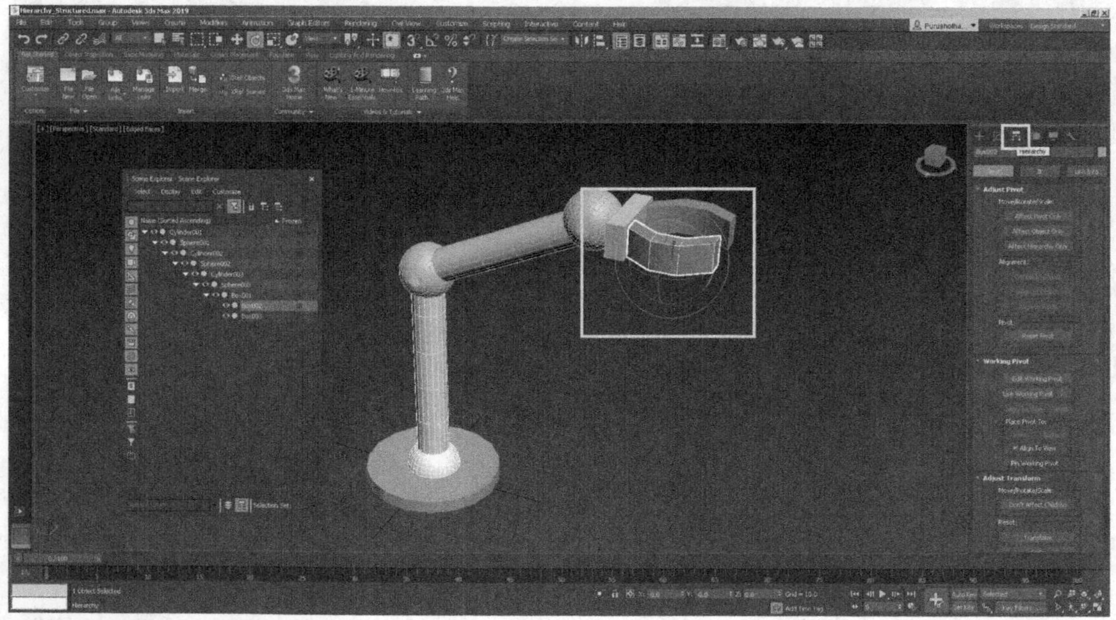

***Figure 3-7.** Hierarchy tab options*

Once you have selected the object box002 and have the Hierarchy panel open, choose Affect Pivots Only from the Hierarchy tab (see Figure 3-8). You will be able to reposition the pivot to the desired location.

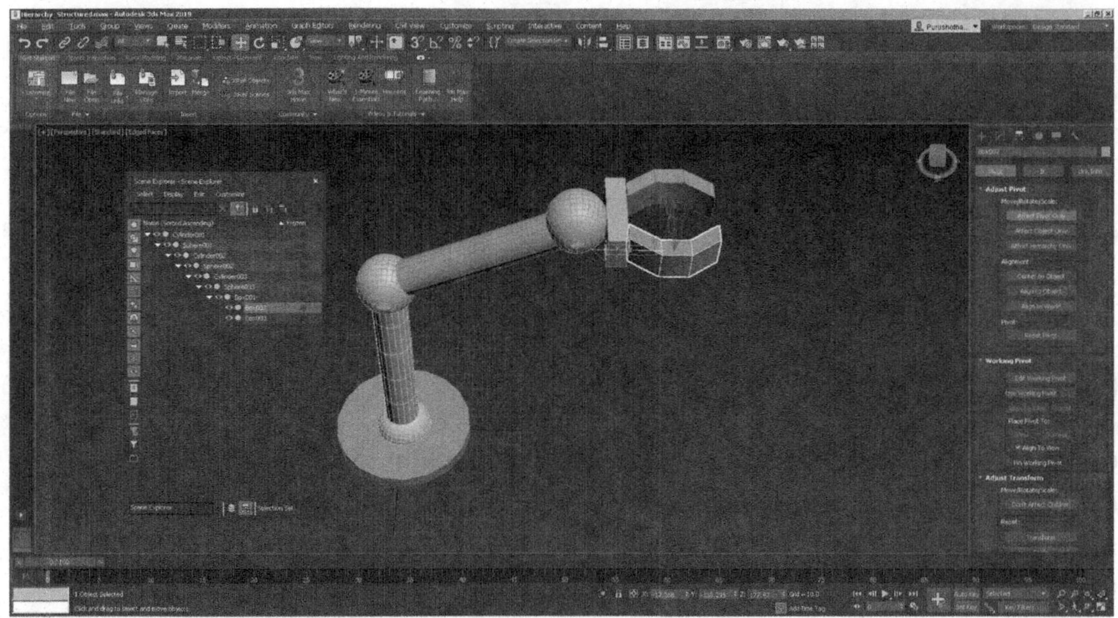

Figure 3-8. *Viewport pivot repositioning, before*

In this case, I recommend you go to the top viewport and orient it, as shown in Figure 3-9, for both claws.

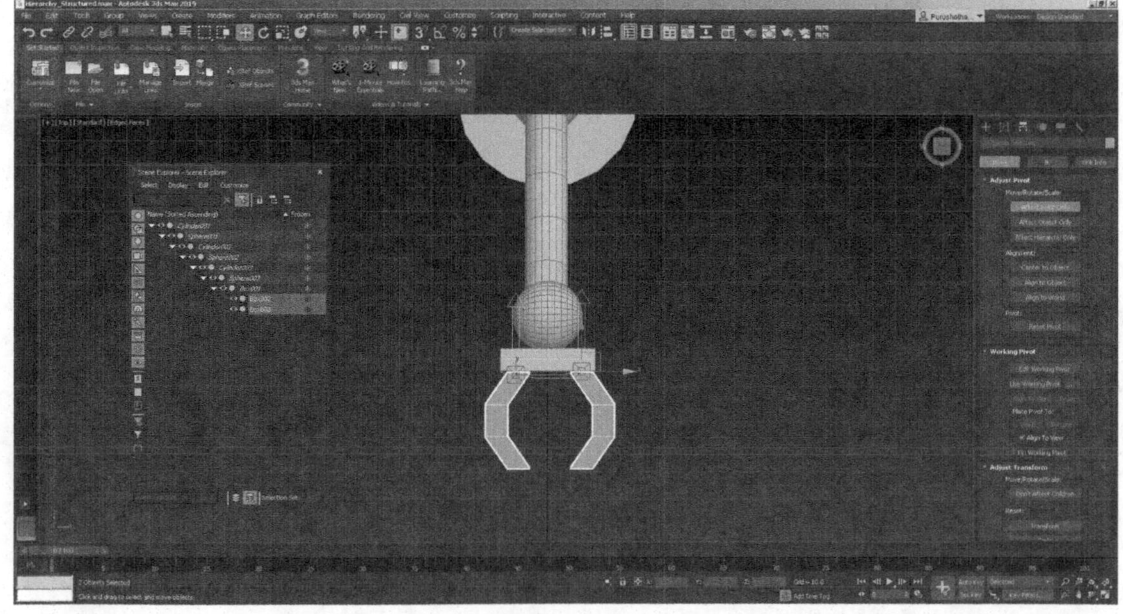

Figure 3-9. *Viewport pivot repositioning, after*

Once the pivots are set, click on the Affect Pivot Only button to exit pivot editing mode and rotate the claws. Voila! The animation works correctly. Load the `Hierarchy_StructuredwithPivots.max` file. Animate and experiment.

Note Keep in mind that all the animation keys you create can be tweaked in the Graph Editor for smooth motion.

Constraints

Constraints allow us to animate an object's transformations to another object based on the type of constraint used. There are a couple of constraint options available in the menu. Choose Animation ➤ Constraints. Let's look at each one and see how we they function and help us with animation. See Figure 3-10.

Figure 3-10. *Constraints menu*

Attachment Constraint

The Attachment constraint is used to attach one object to another. With this constraint, we can animate a relationship. Let's load the `roboticarm_start.max` file and animate it to pick up a ball. Follow these steps:

1. Create a box named `helper` from the Create tab on the command panel. It's located on the right side of the screen. Position the helper box where the ball will be held.
2. In the Scene Explorer make the helper a child of box001 so that box002 and box003 are children of the dummy. (A checkpoint file has been created called `Roboticarm_helper.max`.)
3. Animate the robotic arm in a way so that, at frame 30, it reaches the ball on the ground and, at frame 70, it goes to a different position.
4. Play the animation and refine the keys as applicable (reference the checkpoint file called `Roboticarm_Keyframed.max`).

If we are not using the constraint, we would animate the ball to match the movement of the arm, but if someone were to change the arm's animation path, the ball would need tweaking as well. The Attachment constraint comes to our rescue here.

Let's have the robotic arm pick up the ball and place it on the table.

1. Select the ball that needs to move with the arm and choose Constraints and Attachment constraint from the Animation menu. Your cursor will change to a ribbon dotted line. The software waits for you tell it what object it is attached to, with the ribbon line clicked on the helper box that we created. See Figure 3-11.

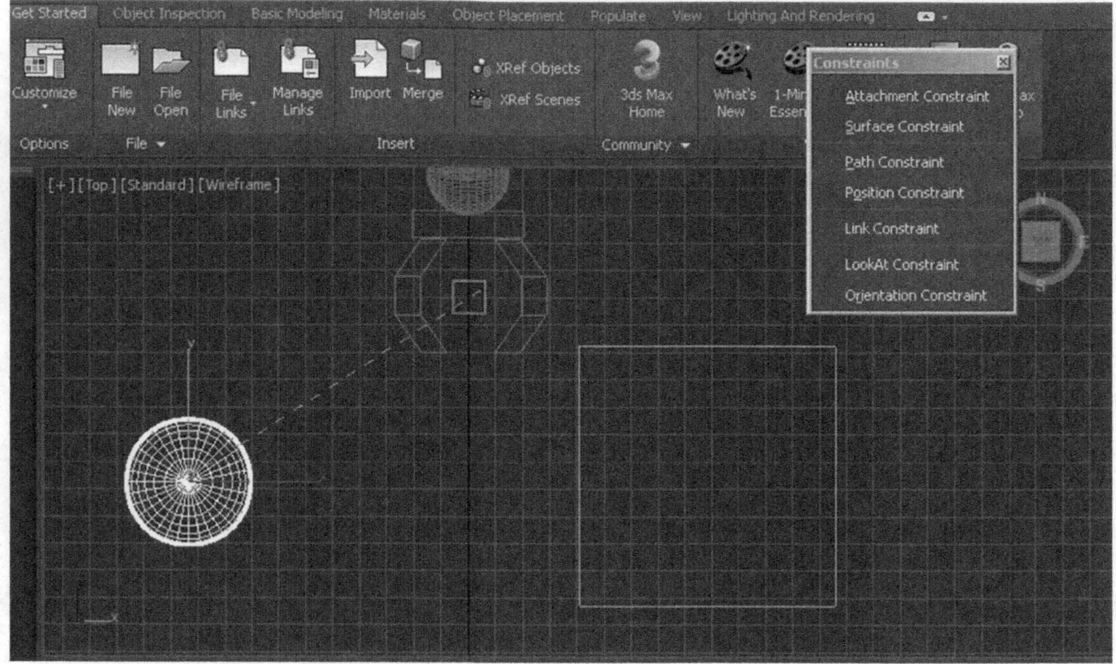

***Figure 3-11.** Constraint wiring, ball to helper*

2. Once you choose the Attachment constraint, the ball moves to the helper object and sticks there. This is not what we want. We want the ball to be picked up and placed. We need one more step to achieve that effect.

   With the ball still selected, go to the motion panel in the control panel. See Figure 3-12.

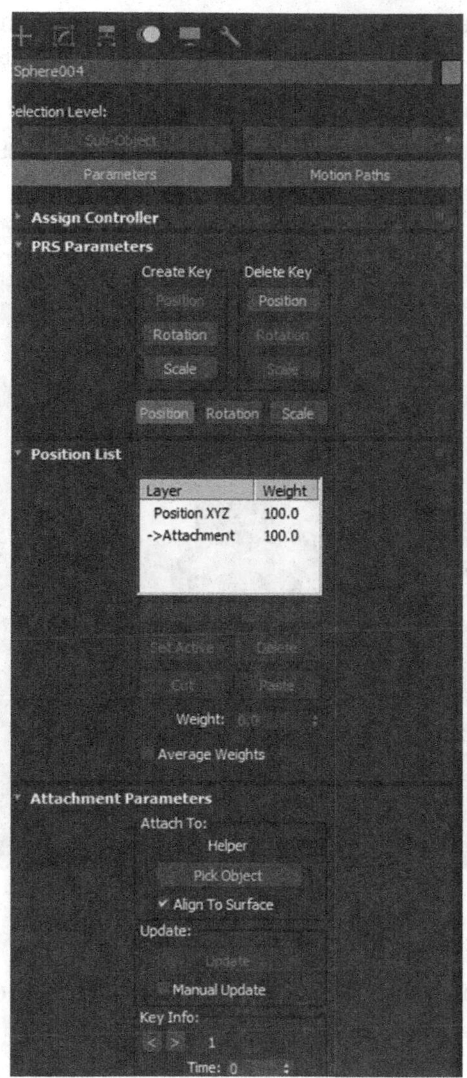

Figure 3-12. *Motion panel*

3. Select the Attachment constraint in the position list pane of the motion panel and animate the weight so that it is 0 from frames 0 to 29 and set to 100 at frame 30. Weight can be locked by turning on the auto key and changing the value to 0 at frame 0. At frame 29, change the value to 1 and 0 back again so that a key is created. At frame 30, change the weight value to 100.

4. You might notice the ball moving from frame 0 to frame 29 in an unexpected way, as seen in the checkpoint file called `RoboticArm_Attachment_Constraint_Curve.max`. Open the Curve Editor and set both keys to linear for the weight for frame 0 and 29 and that should fix it. See Figure 3-13.

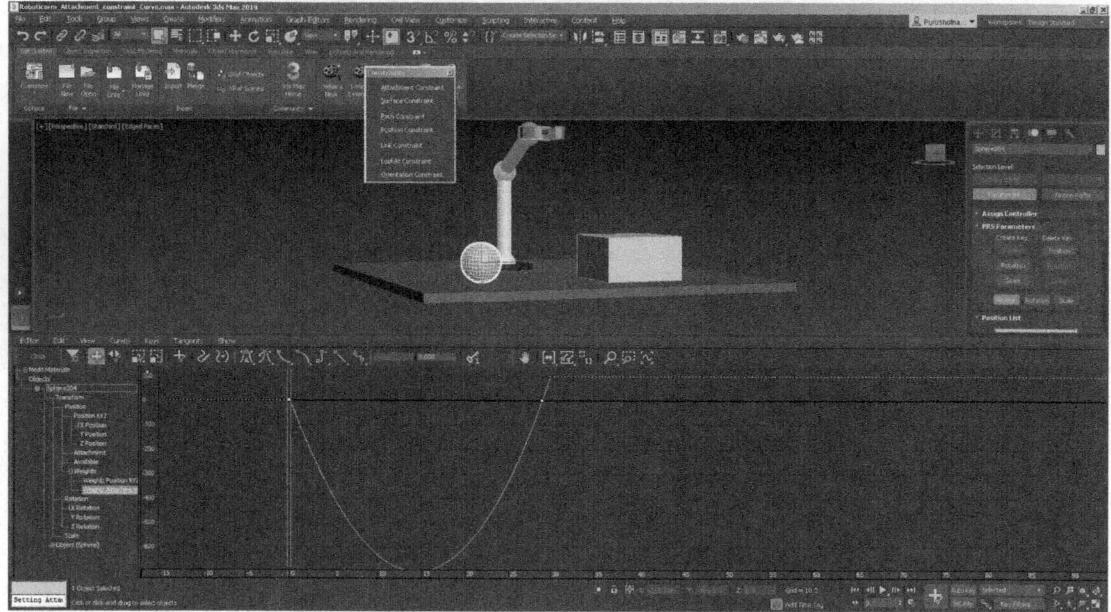

***Figure 3-13.** Graph of ball before keys are set to linear*

5. Tweak the graph as shown in Figure 3-14 by setting the keys 0 and 29 to linear. Then play the animation.

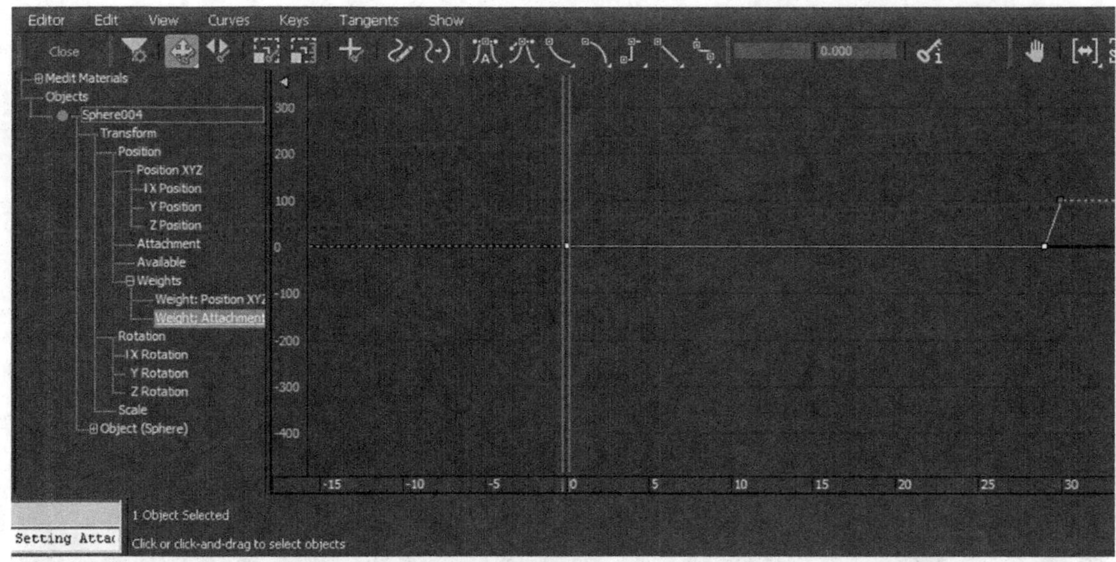

***Figure 3-14.** Graph of ball after keys are set to linear*

Taking this a step ahead, if you want the robotic arm to place the ball on the box named `table`, you need to add another Attachment constraint to the sphere and choose the table. Animate the weight to 100 only when the ball needs to be kept on the table. The same technique can be applied to character animation, when a character has to pick up and place something.

Surface Constraint

The Surface constraint is used when you want to conform an object to stick to the surface of another object. This constraint works only for parametric objects, thus limiting the scope of how we can use them freely.

Here's a simple example to show you how it works. Load `surfaceconstraints.max`.

1. Select the cylinder and choose Animation ➤ Constraints ➤ Surface Constraints and then select the sphere.

2. In the motion panel, go below to the surface controller parameter and use the U and V sliders to manipulate the cylinder on the sphere geometry. See Figure 3-15.

Reference the `SurfaceConstraintComplete.max` file, which has been provided in the source folder.

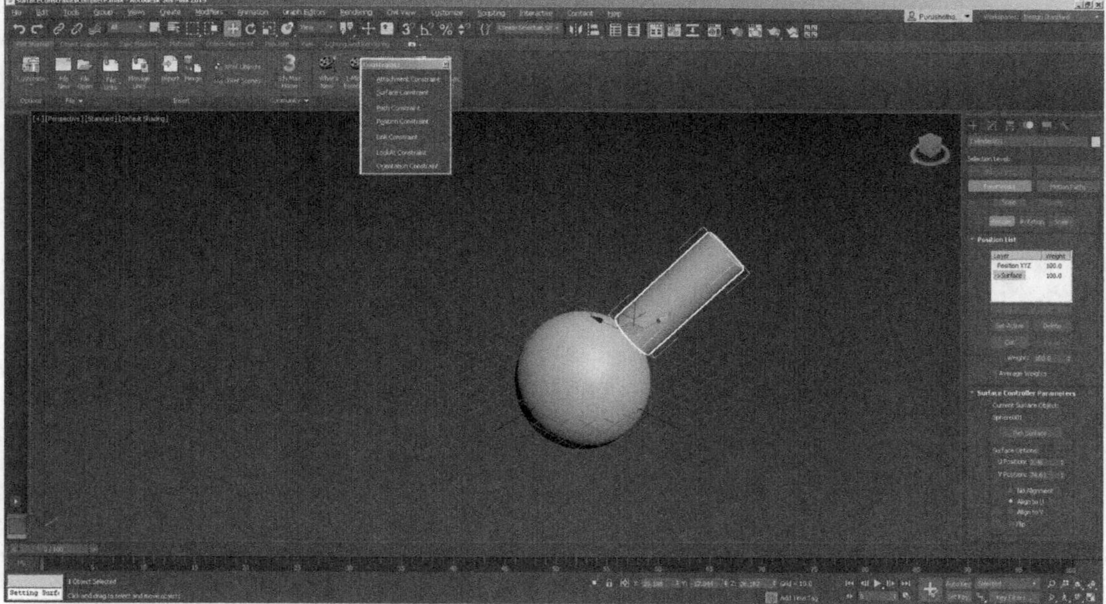

Figure 3-15. Surface constraints, motion options

Path Constraint

The Path constraint is used when you want an object to follow along a specific path. It not only allows the object to follow the path, but also orients and tilts it according to the change in the path's direction. A typical example is to have a skater move along the path and then later manually animate his hands for balance based on twist and turns.

1. Open the `pathconstarint_Start.max` file.
2. A teapot and a line drawn through shape tools are the only two objects.
3. Select the teapot and choose Animation ➤ Constraints and Path Constraint. See Figure 3-16.

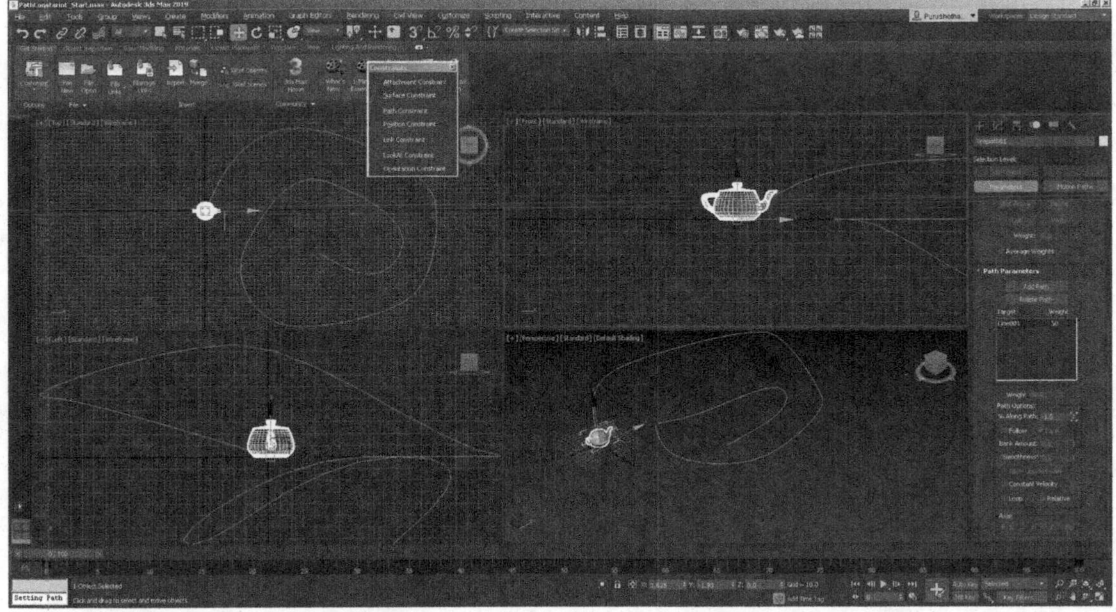

***Figure 3-16.** Path constraint*

4. The Path constraint puts the object at the beginning of the line. The amount of distance the object covers is based on the percentage along the path.

5. Orient and Bank allow the object to face the path's direction and lean in on the curves as the object turns.

6. Loop keeps looping on the path if that is the kind of animation we seek.

Another typical example is to animate a bird flapping its wings endlessly and then put it on a path to fly.

Position Constraint

When you apply the Position constraint for object A to object B, the position of A is locked to B. That means you can no longer change the position of A manually. If you move object B, object A will move along.

Load the `positionconstraint.max` file:

1. If you notice, we have three objects in the scene: two boxes and a sphere.
2. Select the sphere and choose Animation ➤ Constraint ➤ Position Constraint.
3. With the wiring enabled, select one of the cubes.
4. Your sphere now immediately moves to the cube's location.
5. Go into the sphere's motion panel and choose Keep Initial Offset. This keeps the sphere where it is.
6. Now try moving the sphere using the Move tool. It is locked in position, as it is deriving its position from another object.
7. Select the sphere again and choose the Position constraint. Choose the other cube. When you have more than one position controller applied, you can control the weight. Play around with the values to see how we can influence the sphere's position by moving the two cube geometries in the scene.
8. Note that the sphere can be rotated and scaled regardless of the position of the cubes. See Figure 3-17.

Reference file `Positionconstarint_Complete.max` is available in the source files folder.

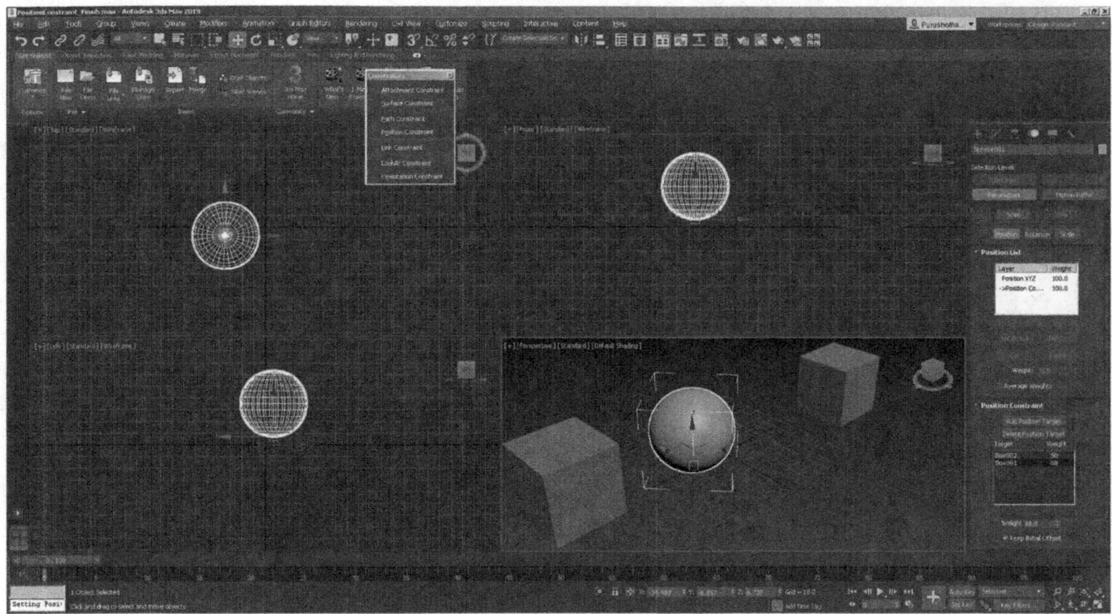

Figure 3-17. *Position constraint motion panel*

Link Constraint

The Link constraint allows you to dynamically change the parent as and when needed. The Link constraint works like the Attachment constraint, but with the addition of having the parent/child relationship animated, which is not available otherwise.

If you look back at the previous section where we discussed the Attachment constraint, we had the robot pick up the ball and move it. If we were to have another robot receive the ball, we would need the Link constraint. The Link constraint lets you animate the link.

Load `LinkConstraint_Start.max` and play the animation to see what we have. Notice we have two boxes and a sphere, and everything is animated.

I want you to pay attention to the way they are positioned. Note at frame 15 that box001 and the sphere come into contact and the ball and sphere move in their animated direction. At frame 24, we have both boxes converging and moving on after that frame.

The Link constraint enables us, at frame 15, to make the ball begin moving along with the green box. At frame 24, the ball will begin moving with box002. We also want the sphere to stop following any box after frame 46 (this is the frame where box002 comes back). Follow these steps:

1. Select the sphere and choose the Animation ➤ Constraints ➤ Link Constraint menu option.
2. Select any box. It doesn't matter at this point; you just need two objects to create a link constraint.
3. Once you've established a link, select the sphere, go to the motion options, and delete the link by selecting the Link Params from the motion panel and clicking on the Delete Link button. See Figure 3-18.

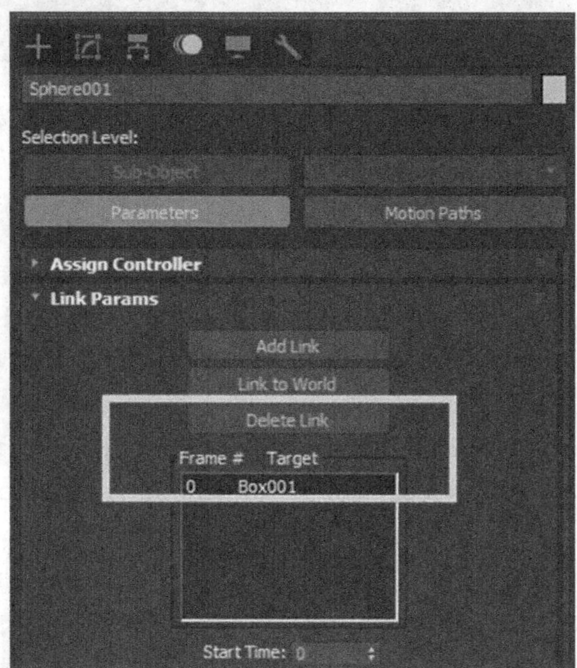

***Figure 3-18.** Link constraint, Delete Link motion panel*

4. Once you have deleted the link, ensure you are in frame 0 and click on Link to World.
5. Move to frame 15 and click Add Link. Then choose box001.
6. Move to frame 24 and click on Add Link. Choose box002.

7. Finally at frame 46, click on Link to World again. Link Params in the motion panel will look like Figure 3-19.

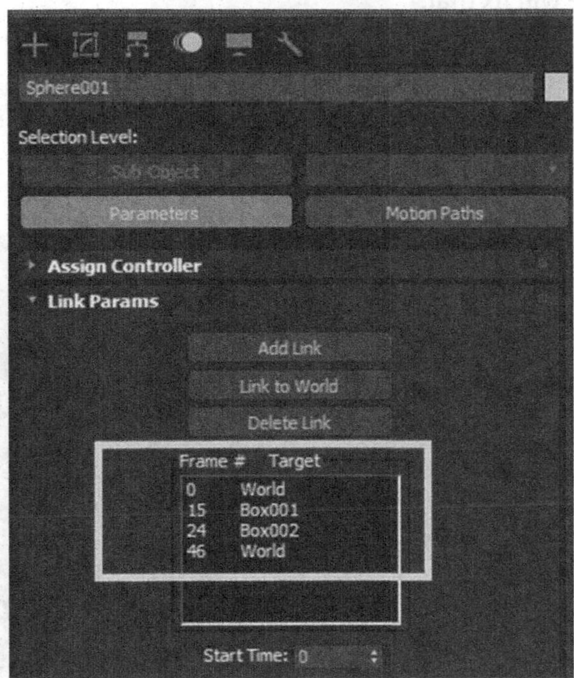

***Figure 3-19.** Dynamic linking over time with the Link constraint*

8. Now play back the animation and see how the sphere moves.

We used the Link constraint to create a dynamic parent for the sphere at various points of time. This was not possible otherwise. A checkpoint reference file is created for you to preview called `LinkConstraint_Completed.max`.

LookAt Constraint

The LookAt constraint creates quick and efficient eye rigs for characters. The object is oriented along the axis of the target. This is done by locking an axis to always face the target.

Load 3ds Max and open `Lookatconstraint_Start.max`. Then follow these steps:

1. The scene file is pretty simple. We have two eye-shaped primitives and a target box.

2. Select one eye and choose Animation ➤ Constraint ➤ LookAt Constraint.

3. Choose the target box.
4. At this point, the sphere might reorient itself. Nothing to worry about, as we will fix that.
5. Repeat the steps on the other eye.
6. You should see a line drawn from the eyes to the target, as shown in Figure 3-20.

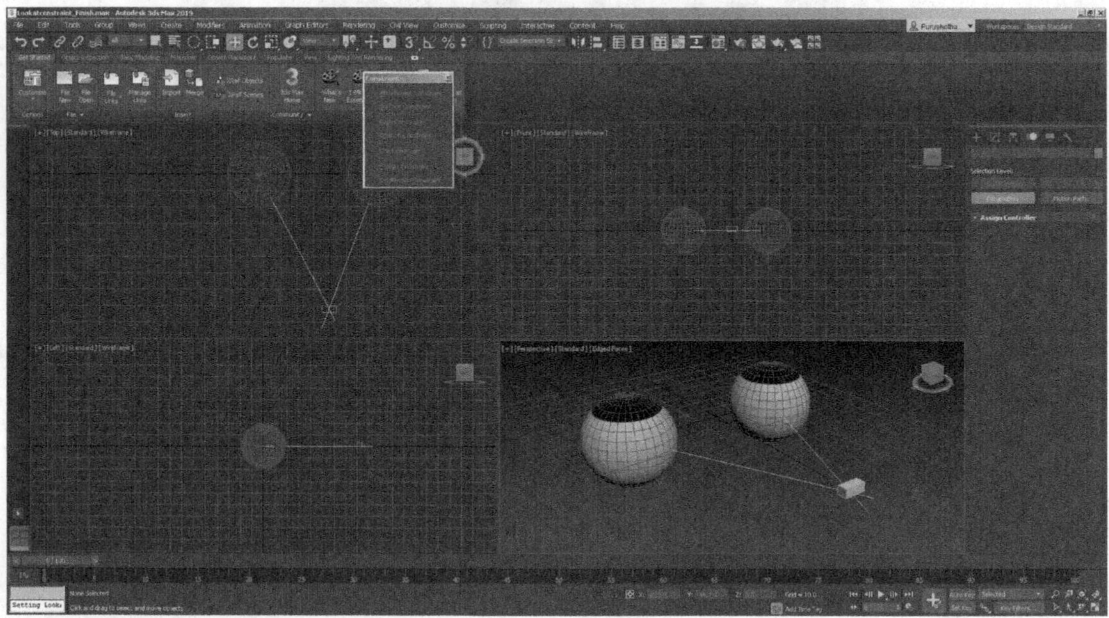

***Figure 3-20.** Link constraint for a pair of eyes*

7. Now select one sphere and go into the motion options.
8. In the PRS parameter rollout, click on the rotation button. PRS rollout stands for position, rotation, and scale.
9. With rotation clicked, you should see the LookAt constraint rollout right below the Rotation list.
10. Choose the LookAt constraint and set Keep Initial Offset to on. That should bring the eye back to its original rotation. See Figure 3-21.

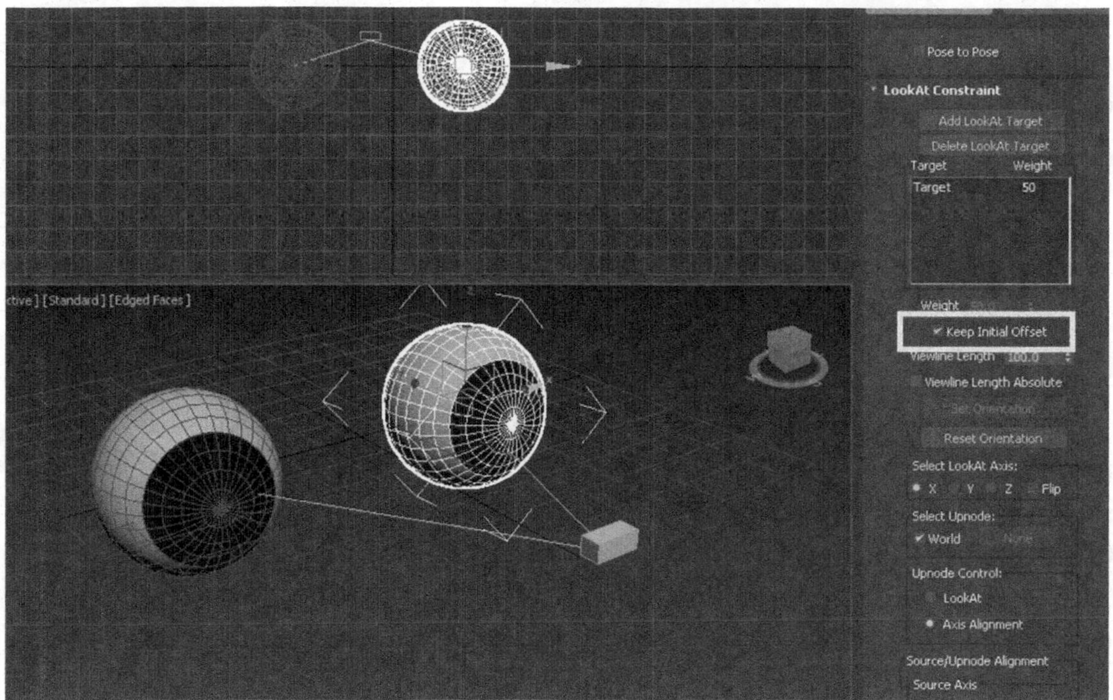

***Figure 3-21.** LookAt constraint, initial offset toggle*

11. If you move the box now, you will see that the eye tracks the object.

This technique can be used for anything that needs to track another object, such as a surface to air missile launcher tracking a fighter jet in the air, or a predator keeping its prey in sight. A checkpoint file called `Lookatconstraint_Finish.max` has been created for you to see the final result.

Orientation Constraint

The Orientation constraint is similar to the Position constraint. The difference is that the Orientation constraint will lock the rotation of the object, although the object can be scaled or repositioned. Having multiple Orientation constraints allows for average rotations applied based on the weight of each target.

A typical use case for this constraint would be for window blinds. Instead of manually animating each blind, a single main object can be animated and other pieces that make the windows blind can replicate the rotation.

Load `OrientationConstraint_Start.max`. If you notice in the file, I did a rough modeling of a window frame and 22 boxes to emulate them as window blinds. I also created a box called `control`.

1. Select all the objects that are blinds.
2. Go to the Animation menu and choose Constraints ➤ Orientation Constraint and choose the control.
3. If you rotate the control now, you will notice that the blinds rotate as well.

We used the Orientation control to rotate the window blinds. This will save a lot of time, when you don't want to select each one and rotate. Position and scale are not locked in this constraint, so you are free to manipulate them. (The `OrientationConstraint_finish.max` file has been added for your reference.)

We will use all these constraints to develop character animation in the upcoming chapters. In the next chapter, we look at wire parameters and advanced controllers.

Engine: Mechanical Animation Using Constraints

Let's now create a piston animation of an engine using constraints.

1. Load `MechanicalMotion_Engine_Start.max` and observe the geometry and see how each pivot rotates.
2. Let's set up a simple animation for the Crankshaft, as this rotation will drive other animations. Turn on the auto key and, at the end frame, give it a few rotations.
3. Play the animation. Only your crankshaft will be rotating at this point.
4. Make the Crankshaft_Connector a child of the crankshaft. If you play the animation now, the Crankshaft_Connector will rotate along.
5. Select the Connecting_Arm and make it a child of the crankshaft. Rotating the crankshaft now will rotate the connecting arm as well. But we have a problem. The connecting arm is supposed to always face the direction of the piston. Let's fix this issue.

6. Select the Connecting_Arm and go to the Animation menu. Choose Constraints ➤ LookAt Constraints and choose the piston the arm will look at in the other axis.

7. The arm will look in a different direction. With the Connecting_Arm selected, go to the motion panel, PRS parameters, and ensure you have Rotation selected. With Rotation selected, you should see a LookAt constraint rollout.

8. In the LookAt constraint rollout, choose the Z axis, as the object needs to point up in the Z space. The object should revert to its initial position.

9. Play the animation now. You should see the Connecting_Arm point at the piston.

For the next challenge, we need the piston to move up and down as the arm goes up and down. We are going to use helpers to restrict the movement of the piston so it can't move sideways.

1. From the command panel, go to Create ➤ Helpers ➤ Standard and create a dummy. A dummy is nothing but a null; it's simply an tool that cannot be rendered.

2. Align the newly created dummy to the pivot of Connecting_Arm.

3. Select the newly created dummy and make it a child of crankshaft. Play the animation. You should see the dummy rotating along with the crankshaft.

4. Ensure you are at frame 0 and select the dummy. With the dummy selected, go to the Hierarchy tab in the control panel and choose the Link Info tab. See Figure 3-22.

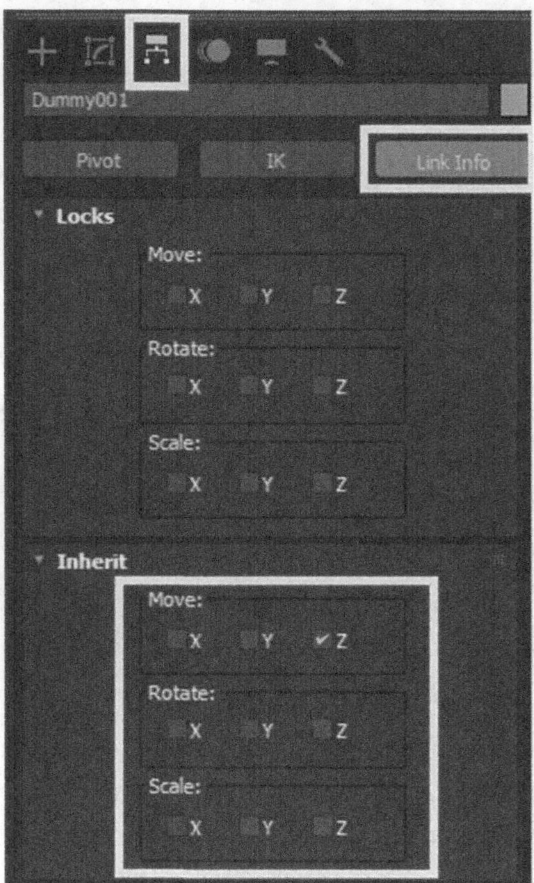

***Figure 3-22.** The Link Info tab*

5. In the Link Info tab of the dummy, we want the dummy to use the parents' Z position only. By default, all the options will be checked in the Inherit section, which would mean that the object would follow along on all axes in position, rotation, and scale. Check only the Z axis of Move. Uncheck everything else. Now the link will work only on the Z axis of Move. This makes the current object follow the parent only on the Z axis. Play the animation to see the result.

6. We need to move the piston up and down as the crankshaft rotates. To do this, make the piston a child of Piston_Connector.

7. Select the Piston_Connector and make it a child of the dummy that we created. Voila! We have a working engine mockup ready.

A checkpoint file up to this point has been saved for your reference at `MechanicalMotion_Engine_Complete.max`. Load it and see if you are running into any difficulties.

Summary

In this chapter, we learned about setting hierarchy and about the various types of constraints available. In the upcoming chapters, we use these constraints to drive character rigs for animation.

CHAPTER 4

Bones Rigging

In the previous chapters, we learned about the principles of animation and animation tools in 3ds Max, and we looked at advanced animation using constraints. In this chapter, we look at creating custom rigs to drive our animation using bones. We will begin by understanding how bones are deployed in 3D and then look at setting up a structure of a human using them. We will then learn to drive a human mesh and skin animation using this rig of bones. Although Chapters 5 and 6 revolve around preset rigs that are shipped with 3ds Max (Bipeds and CAT), this chapter will give you a foundation of how a rig structure works and how to set one up using a guided approach.

Bones

In essence, *bones* are deformation tools. They are used to drive and deform the mesh attached to it. For instance, think about your hand. Your bones and bone joints determine where the hand bends and twists. We will emulate that in 3D using bones. Bones can be created from the Create panel, by choosing Systems ➤ Standard Rollout ➤ Bones. Alternatively, bones can also be created by accessing the Bones tool in the Animation menu and choosing Bone tools. See Figure 4-1.

P. Raju, *Character Rigging and Advanced Animation*, https://doi.org/10.1007/978-1-4842-5037-2_4

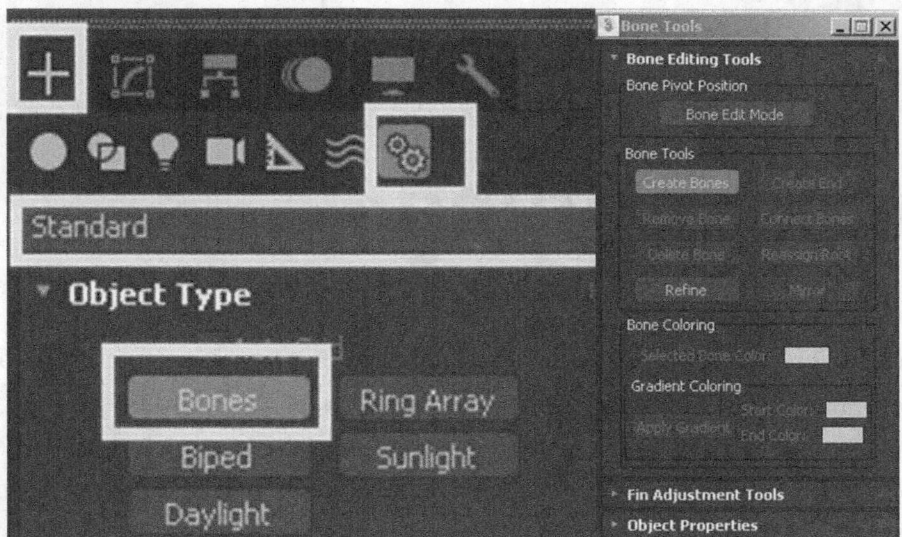

Figure 4-1. *Create panel's System tools (left) and Bone tools (right)*

It is always best to create bones in orthographic viewports and not in perspective view. Once you click on bones in the rollout, you can switch your view to any orthographic viewport. Orthographic viewports are the top, bottom, front, back, left, right viewports.

1. Click and move your mouse to create your first bone (in my case, I use the left viewport).
2. Now move your mouse again and click to form the second bone. Note that the bones are created as a chain. Clicking further and drawing bones makes them the child of the previous bone.
3. End the bone creation mode by right-clicking. When you're done, a bone end is created.
4. Create a simple leg setup (as shown in Figure 4-2) and notice the hierarchy in the Scene Explorer. The first bone you created is a root and the subsequent bones are child bones of the previous one.

5. You can load the `Bonechain_Start.max` file from the scene files provided with this chapter. Scene Explorer can be opened by going to the Tools menu and choosing All Global Explorers ➤ Scene Explorer.

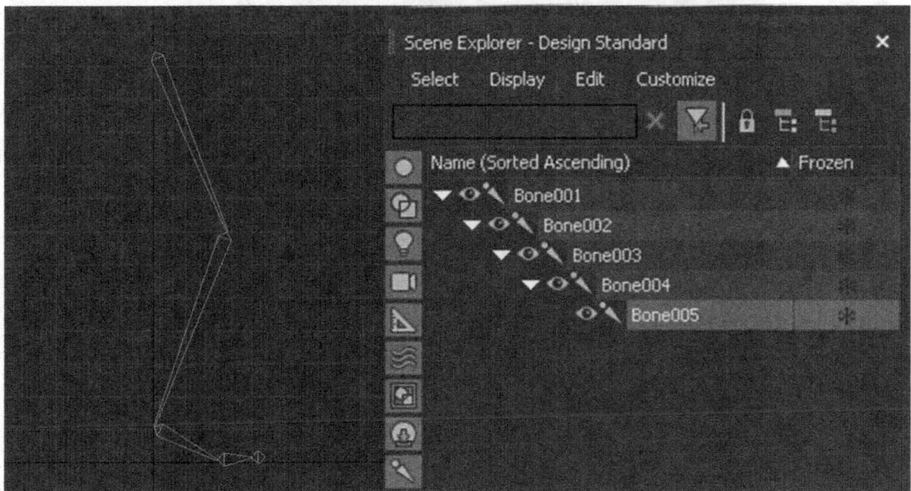

Figure 4-2. *Bone chain and hierarchy*

Note Bones are not renderable by default, as their primary use is to deform an object. But they can be made renderable if need be.

Now let's look the options available while creating the bones.

When you click on Bones in the creation rollout, you have these options:

- Bone Color: This will determine the color of the bone in the viewport. This is for organizational or aesthetic purposes, when you want a bone to be rendered in a different color. When you begin creating a bone, you can assign it a color, or you can select each bone and go into Modify and color them later according to your needs or wishes.
- IK Chain Assignment: We will not be covering this option at this point, but will in later chapters.
- Bone Parameters: These parameters determine how your bone is going to be in terms of size, shape, etc. The same parameters are available for each bone in the Modify panel.

Let's use the `BoneChain_Start.max` file and look at the properties that we can manipulate. Load `Bonechain_Start.max` and select the top bone. Go into the Modify panel, which is the second tab in the control panel on the right side of your screen. See Figure 4-3.

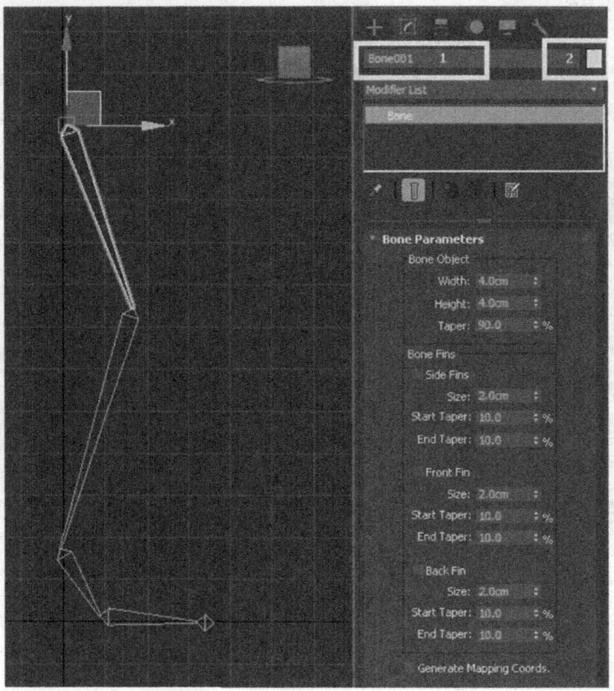

Figure 4-3. *Bone parameters*

Note that you can rename a bone by typing the name of your choice to identify the bone for ease of use. It is always good practice to rename bones and you can also change the color of the selected bone in the Modify panel. (Refer to Figure 4-3.)

Let's get into the bone parameters now. Select the top-most bone and name it thigh_bone:

- Now with the thigh_bone selected, adjust the width, height, and taper to see the difference. The width and height make the bone wider and the taper (when set to 0) makes the ends of a bone the same size. The start of the bone is currently wider and it tapers out as it ends.
- Fins help you create variations in bone types.
- Load `BoneChain_boneparameters.max` to see some variations done to each bone.

The thigh_bone is our root parent and the other bones are child. You can select all the bones at once by double-clicking on a bone. In this case, double-clicking on thigh_bone will help you select all the bones.

Creating a Skeletal Structure

In this chapter, I provide you with a scene called `Human_Start.max`. This file has a model generated from free software called *Makehuman*. You can use this file to continue or use another model downloaded from the Internet or other character generator software. We will be using this model as a reference to lay out our bones. See Figure 4-4.

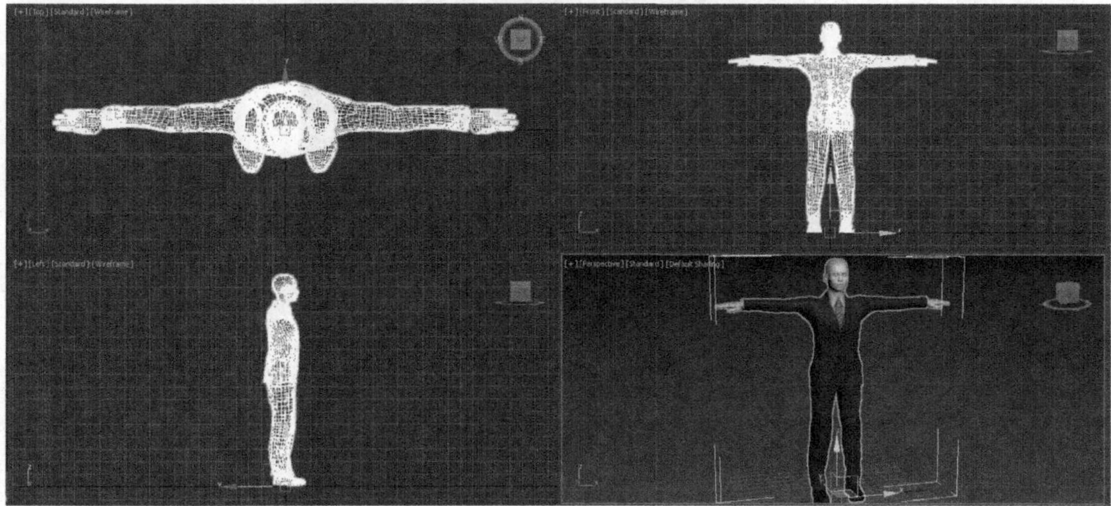

Figure 4-4. *Character in a t-pose*

Note I want to direct your attention to a couple of things. It is good practice to follow these guidelines. The character is in a pose called a t pose, and it's ideal to have your model posed in this manner. It helps in setting up weights and makes the rigger easier. Once rigged, the character can be posed any way you like. The character is symmetrical, which helps a lot. You can set up structure on one side and mirror it.

Let's begin rigging a character with bones from scratch:

1. Fire up 3ds Max and load `Human_Start.max`.
2. Go to the Tools menu and choose All Global Explorer and Layer Explorer. See Figure 4-5.

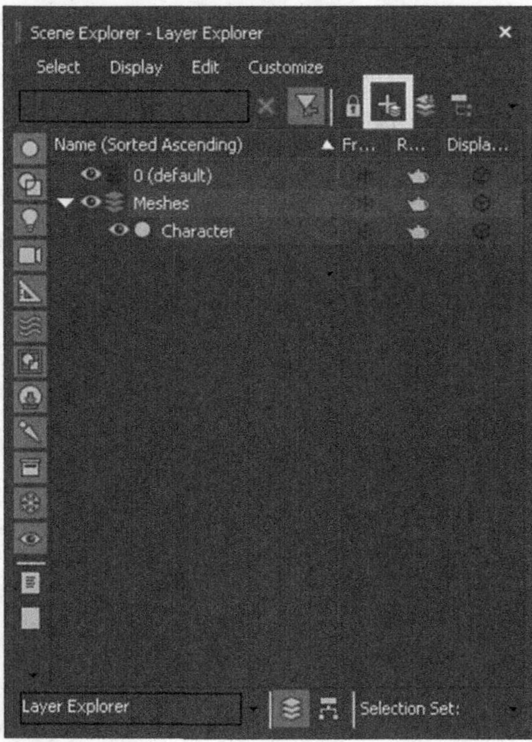

Figure 4-5. *Scene Explorer*

3. First select your character in the viewport and click on the new layer. Call it meshes. If your model was selected, as it should be, it will be moved to the new layer named meshes. If not, drag the character mesh from the layer into the newly created mesh layer. We will not be doing anything to the mesh at this point so let's freeze this. You can do this in the layer, where there are three options—Freeze, Renderable, and Display. Click on Freeze for the meshes layer. Your mesh should no longer be selectable.

4. Create a new layer called Bones. If you had another layer selected, the newly created layer will become the child of it. You can drag it below the list to "unchild" it. See Figure 4-6.

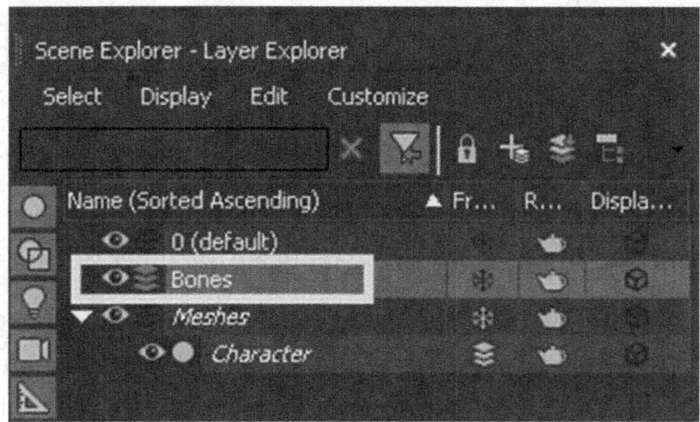

***Figure 4-6.** Scene Explorer, layer management*

5. With the Bones layer selected and active, go into the side viewport and draw the bones for the leg, starting from the hip to the foot. See Figure 4-7.

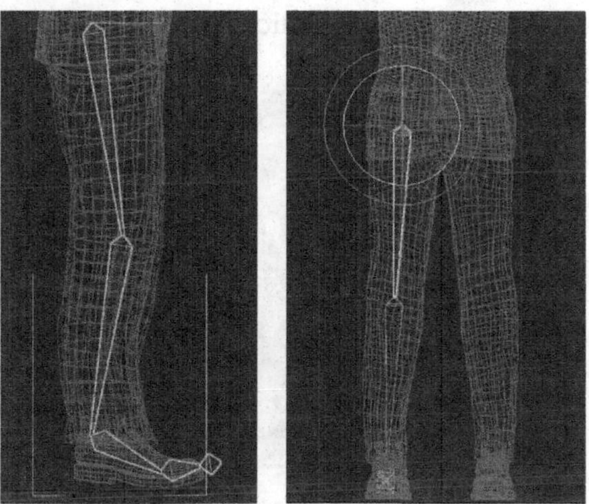

***Figure 4-7.** Leg Bones reference*

6. Be sure to add a bend in the knee, as this will help the software calculate the rotations of the bone. If you notice in the front viewport, the bone will be in the middle. Select the thigh_bone and move it into position. Then rotate as needed.

7. Select the bones and rename them R_thigh_bone, R_ankle_bone, R_foot_bone, R_toe_bone, and R_ bone_end.

8. A checkpoint file has been created called `Human_Start01.max`.

    - You can recreate another leg using the same process, but let's use the software's built-in feature to replicate the other side for us.

9. Go to the Animation menu and open the Bones tools. If you need to realign the bones, click in Bone Edit mode and select the bones and move them. Do not move bones with the Move tool without the Bone Edit mode on. Once you're happy with the position, disable Bone Edit mode by clicking on it.

10. Select the L_thigh_bone and double-click on it to select the entire chain.

11. In the Bone tools, choose Mirror and leave the defaults. We want the mirror to happen on X. Use the offset to position the chain correctly. Once it's set in position, click OK. See Figure 4-8.

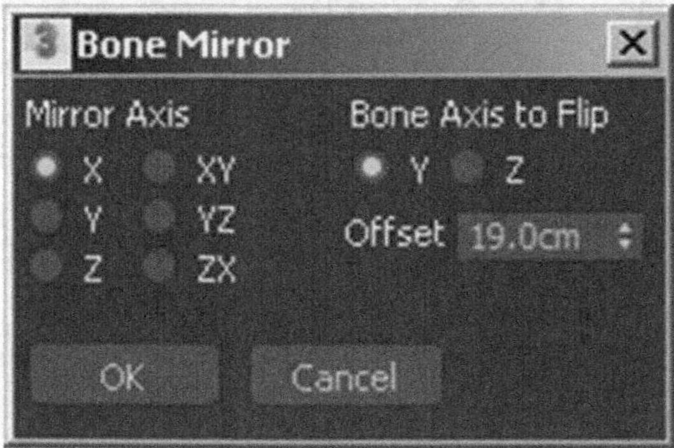

Figure 4-8. *Bone Mirror tool*

12. Notice in the Layer Explorer that the bones are named with the mirrored suffix. Don't be alarmed if you don't see the hierarchy here. We are in layer mode so we are seeing objects in layers, despite the hierarchy. See Figure 4-9.

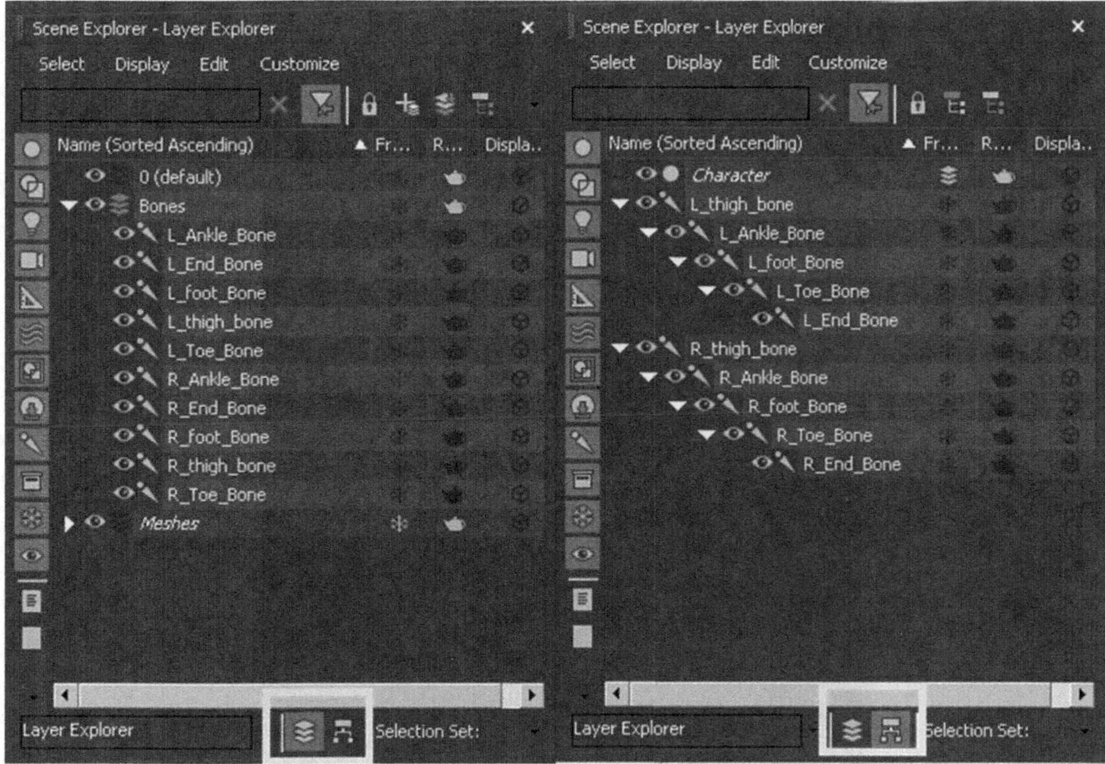

Figure 4-9. *Scene Explorer (Layer and Hierarchy view)*

13. Note in Figure 4-9 that I renamed the Left leg bone with the L_ prefix. The Bone tools has an option to do this, but that would be beyond the scope of this lesson.

14. A checkpoint file has been created called `Human_Start02.max`.

    If you have been following along, you can continue with the working file or load `Human_Start02.max` to follow along from this point. See Figure 4-10.

15. Go into the left viewport and create a bone chain from the hip to head. We are not looking at facial rigging at this point, so let's up to the head. If you're going to do facial rigging, you will stop at the neck. Also when you create a new bone, don't click too close to an existing bone, as they will become one chain. We want to keep them individual for now.

16. Rename the bones spine01_Bone, spine02_Bone, spine03_Bone, neck_Bone, head_Bone, and Head_end_Bone.

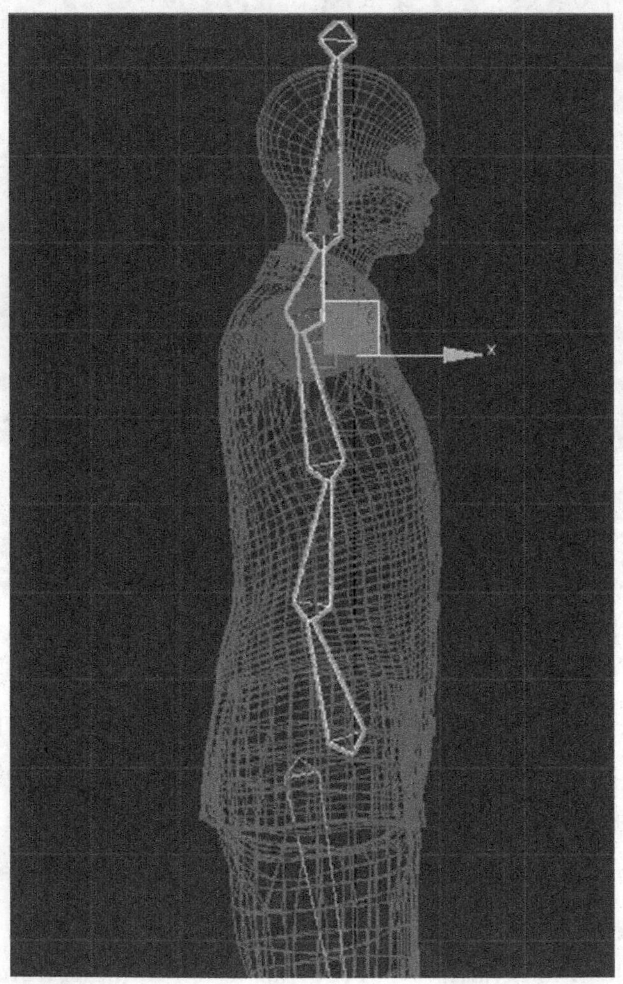

Figure 4-10. *Spine Bones reference*

17. A checkpoint file has been created called `Human_Start03.max`.

Let's move ahead and create the character's arms. Continue with the steps or load `Human_Start03.max` and follow along:

1. In the top viewport, click on the shoulder area and begin creating your arm bone setup with L_Shoulder_Bone, L_Arm_Bone, L_Forearm_Bone, L_Hand_Bone, and L_Hand_End.
2. Once you have created the front viewport, select the root bone (L_Shoulder_bone) and position it. Use the Bone Edit tool to reposition other bones as need be.
3. Now let's repeat the steps for the legs and mirror them.
4. Select the L_shoulder_bone and double-click it to select all its children bones.
5. In Bones tool, use the Mirror option to give it an offset value and position it accordingly.
6. A checkpoint file has been created called `Human_Start04.max`.

   Now let's continue creating the fingers for our hand. If you have been following along, continue the guided approach or load `Human_Start04.max`.

7. In the top viewport, begin creating the fingers for the hand, as shown in Figure 4-11, Be sure not to click near an existing bone, as they will connect. Adjust the finger bone size accordingly.
8. Once you have created the five fingers, note that they have been positioned on the World grid. Select the newly created bones and move them into position so that they are exactly inside the mesh. Tweak them using the Bone tools if need be. See Figure 4-11.

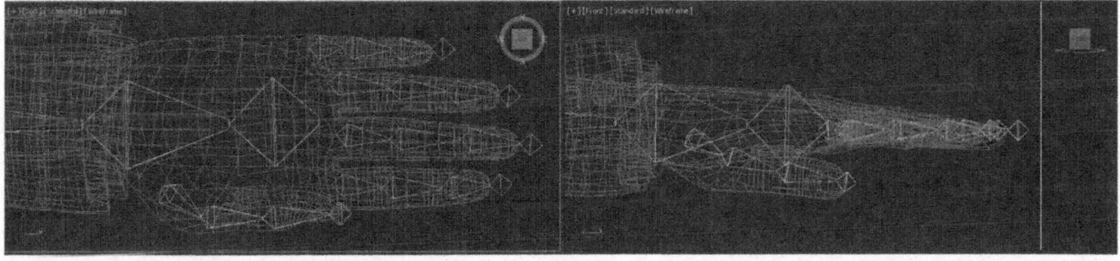

Figure 4-11. *Hand bones reference*

9. The next step is to rename the finger bones to avoid confusion. In my case, I named them as follows:
   - Thumb: L_thumb0, L_thumb1, L_thumb2, and L_thumb_end
   - Index: L_Index0, L_Index1, L_index2, and L_index_End
   - Middle: L_Middle0, L_Middle1, L_Middle2, and L_Middle_end
   - Ring: L_Ring0, L_Ring1, L_Ring2, and L_Ring_End
   - Pinky Finger: L_pinky0, L_pinky1, L_pinky2, and L_pinky_end
10. Once you're done with the left finger, select the fingers and use the Bone Mirror tool to mirror to the right side, as we did for the hands and legs. Rename the fingers with the R_<finger name> format that we used for the left hand.
11. Be sure to position the bones to match the anatomy of the human model that we are using. This will save you a lot of time later.

To summarize what we have done so far, we have created two leg chains for each leg, a spine bone chain that runs to the head, and two arm chains that start from the shoulder and end at the palms, as well as a total of 10 finger chains for the hands. If your character has feet and toes, you need to add the toe bones in a similar manner to what we did for the hands.

Proceed further once you are familiar and comfortable with what we have done so far. I recommend you redo the process by either following along and doing it again or practicing on your own.

We haven't created a hip bone yet, so let's create one and then begin linking the chain. In the side viewport, click and create a hip bone and end it. We just need one bone to serve as our hip. Use the reference image in Figure 4-12 for guidance.

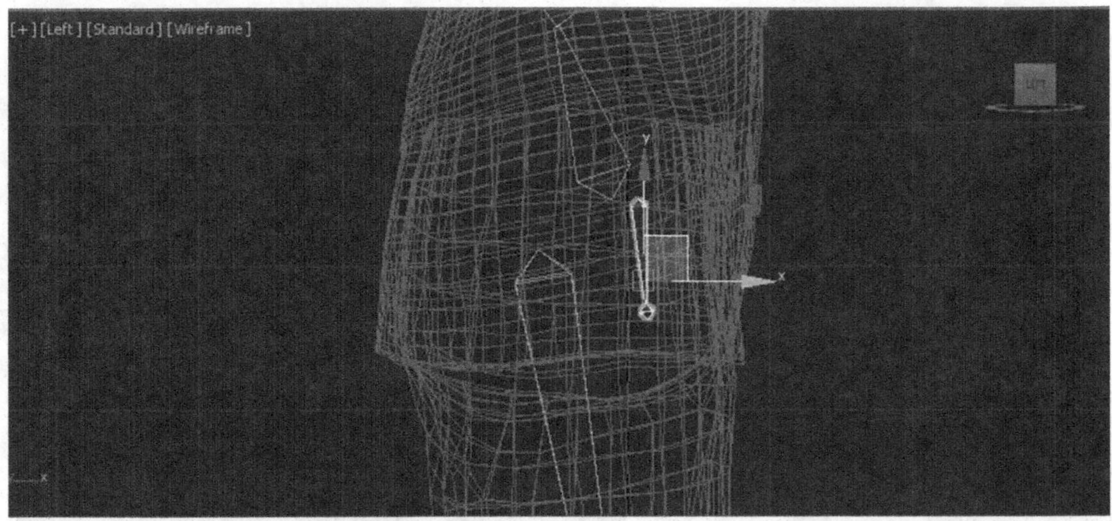

Figure 4-12. *Pelvis bone reference*

Rename the bone Hip_Bone and the end bone Hip_endbone. A checkpoint file called `Human_Start05.max` is saved in the scenes folder for your reference.

Bone Chain Hierarchy

In the previous section, we created bone chains to mimic the human anatomy. In this section, we look at taking all those individual chains and linking them. We link them so that when you animate one chain, there is an effect that is perceived to connected bones of the other chain, as in the real world.

Let's begin by linking the bone chains to one another.

1. Select the root bones of the fingers (L_thumb0, L_index0, L_middle0, L_ring0, and L_pinky0). You can hold the Ctrl key down and select bones to add to the existing selection. (The Shift key is used to duplicate objects in 3ds Max.)

2. With the bones selected, choose the Link option from the toolbar (see Figure 4-13). Your cursor will change because the software is looking for your input to choose another bone.

Figure 4-13. *Link tool*

3. Now with the bones selected, click on the Link tool and drag from any of the selected bones to the L_Hand_Bone. Release when it turns to yellow. (See Figure 4-14.)

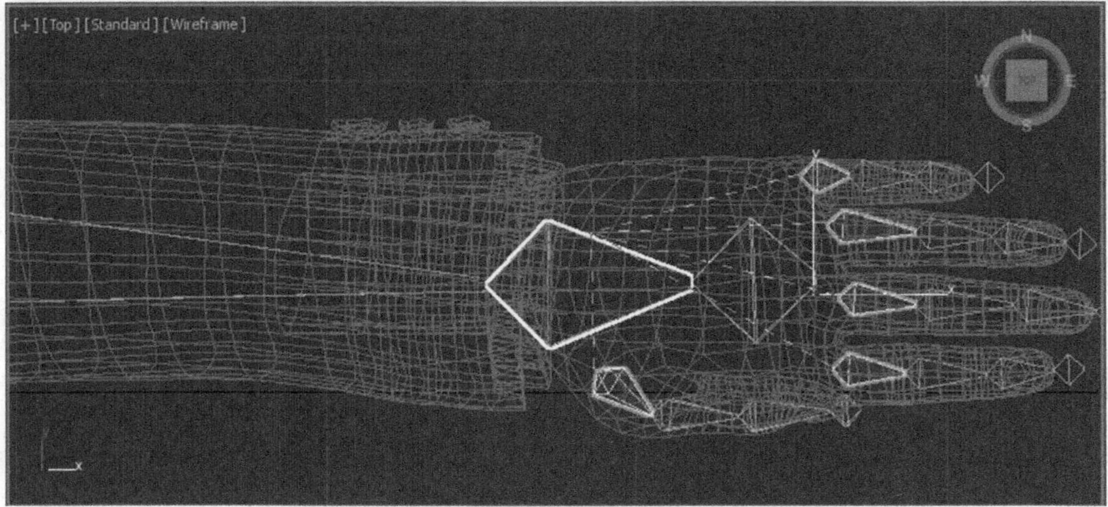

Figure 4-14. *Fingers to hand link reference*

4. If you select the L_Arm_Bone on the left side and rotate, you should see that the fingers are moving along as one chain with the left hand now. Undo any rotations you did.

5. Select the root bones of the fingers (R_thumb0, R_index0, R_middle0, R_ring0, and R_pinky0).

6. With these bones selected, choose the Link option from the toolbar. Your cursor will change because the software is looking for your input to choose another bone.

7. Now with the Link tool selected, choose the R_Hand_Bone.

8. Test the right hand and then undo any rotations you did for testing.

Note You could have also done the linking for one hand and then mirrored the entire arm, which works as well.

9. Let's link the shoulder bones to the spine. In this case, select L_Shoulder_Bone and R_Shoulder_bone and then select the Link tool from the toolbar.
10. With both bones selected and Link tool active, click on the Spine03_Bone. See Figure 4-15.

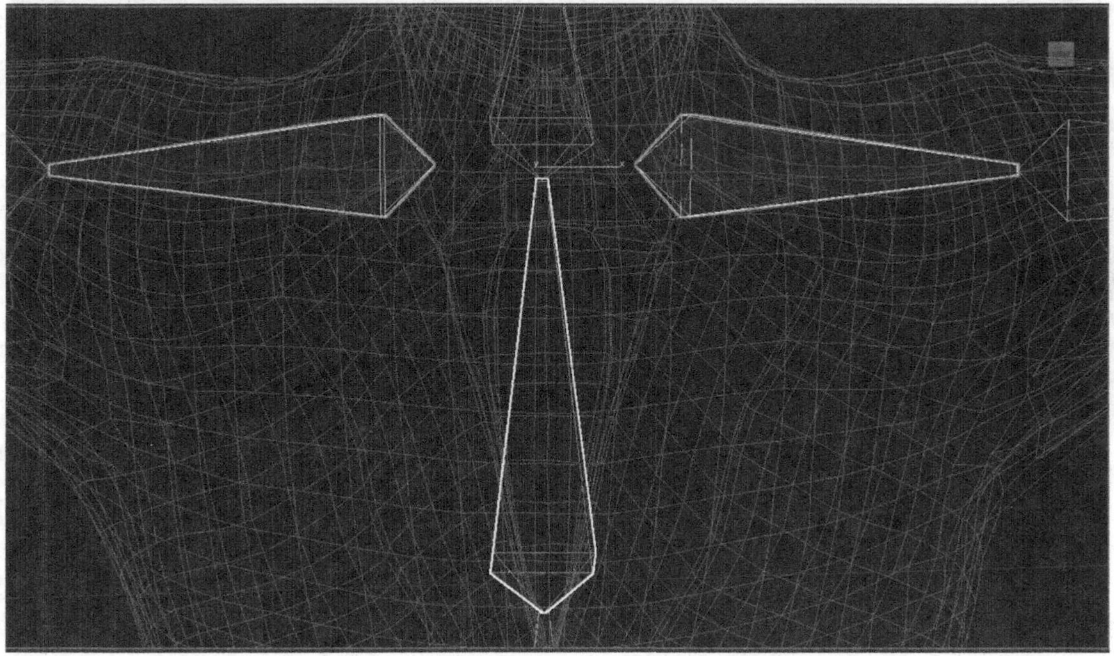

Figure 4-15. *Spine to shoulder link reference*

11. Rotate the spine03_bone. You should see that the entire arm chain follows along based on the rotation axis. Notice how we can create human poses by linking these chains. Again, as usual, undo any rotation changes you made so that the bone fits back perfectly inside the mesh.

12. Let's move ahead and connect our leg and spine chains to the hip. By now you should have an idea of which bone needs to be connected for this. Follow along to see if you are right.

13. Select L_thigh_bone, R_thigh_bone, and Spine01_Bone and use the Link tool to connect them to the Hip_bone. See Figure 4-16.

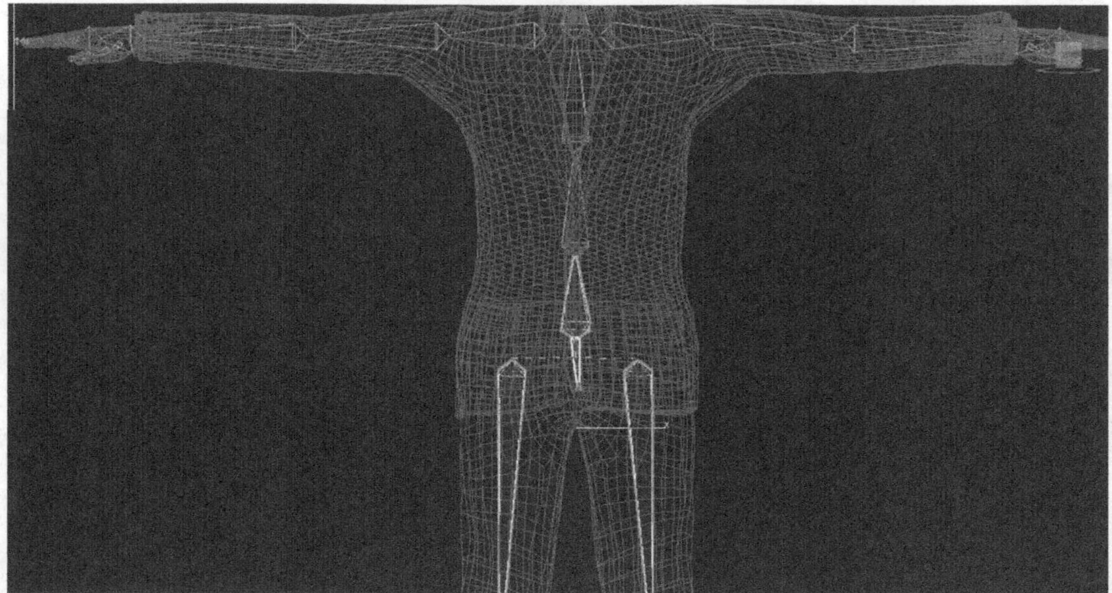

Figure 4-16. *Legs to pelvis link reference*

14. Once you have linked the bones, you should be able to reorient and reposition the entire bone chain as needed. At any point if you need to move the entire bone chain, select the Hip_bone and reorient it as needed.

15. A checkpoint file has been created called `HumanStart06.max`.

The approach of setting the bone structure is the same even if your character is a dinosaur or a dog. Mimic the bone structure and parent it as per the anatomy of the model. We have created a bone structure, but this is still not a complete rig. We need to get this animation ready using IK and FK techniques. Let's look at setting them up in the next section.

FK/IK

In this section, we look at the most common terms that animators use—FK and IK. We will begin by understanding what FK and IK are with a simple guided example, and then we look at using these techniques to create a bipedal rig part by part.

What Are IK and FK?

FK and IK are animation techniques that determine how the computer will calculate motion. FK stands for *forward kinematics* and IK for *inverse kinematics*. Let's explain these with a real-world example.

1. Load `IKFK.max`.
2. The file includes two bone chains and a sphere in the middle. The right bone chain is IK enabled, but not to worry, as we will look at setting it up later. For now, let's look at what each means.
3. If you select bone 1 and rotate it, and then move into bone 2 to rotate it, and then go to bone 3 to accommodate the reach, it will be like a robotic movement. You reorient each bone to get to the reach of the ball. To put it in simple terms, FK is where parent motion is inherited to the child. Rotating bone 1 will have bone 2 rotate as well. In order to reach the ball, we might need to animate three bone rotations. See Figure 4-17.

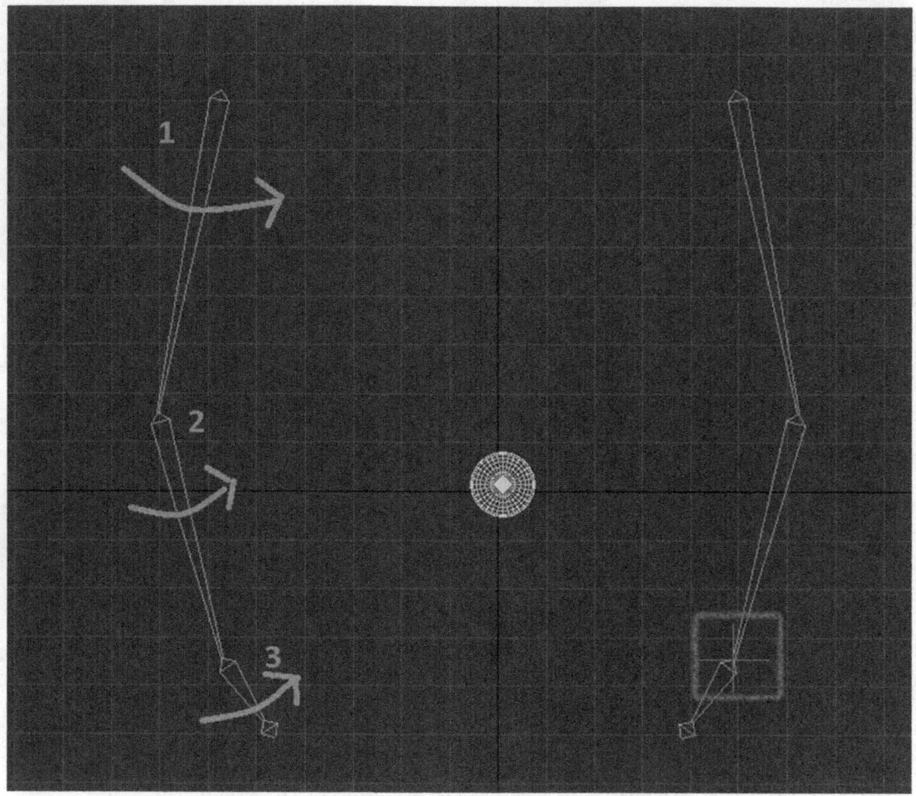

***Figure 4-17.** IK versus FK 1*

4. Let's look at IK now. Select the IK Chain001 marked green in Figure 4-17 and move it to the ball. Notice how the parent bone rotates along to accommodate the reach? This is called IK or inverse kinematics. See Figure 4-18.

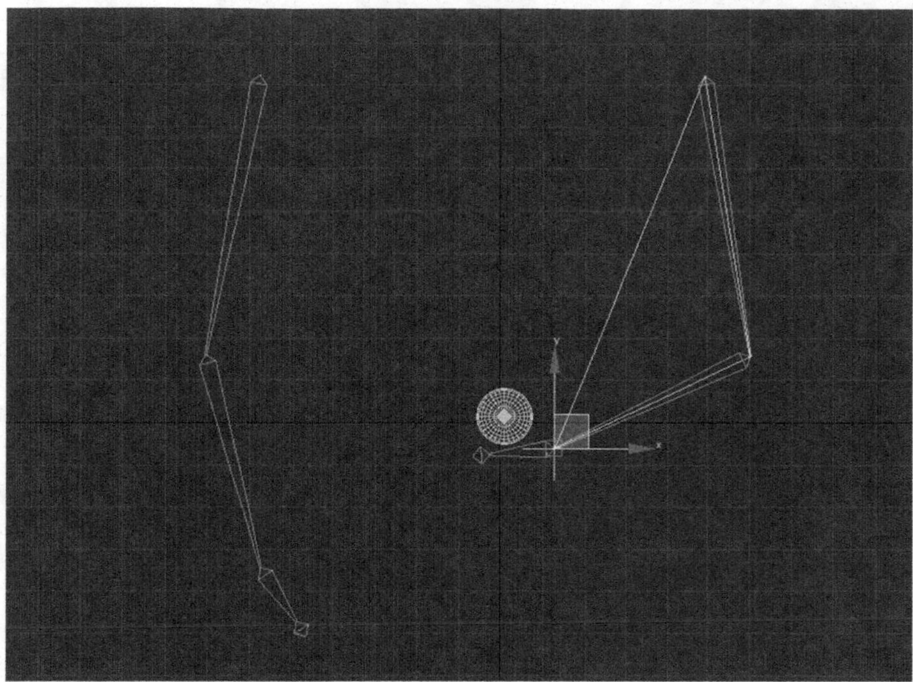

Figure 4-18. *IK versus FK 2*

To simplify it even more, remember these points

- In an FK chain, the animation is passed from parent to child. If you rotate the parent, the child will rotate along with the parent. FK is rotation based.
- In an IK chain, the parent's bones accommodate to the child's position. In the previous example, when we moved the IK Chain001, the parent bones rotated too.

IK simplifies the animation here. We just need to move one item, whereas in FK, we need all the bones to be rotated to reach the sphere. Let's now look at setting up our own IK chain.

Simple IK Chain

In this section, we create a simple IK chain. We are going to mimic a leg setup and set an IK chain to animate the leg.

1. Load `IK_Chain.max` or create a setup of a bone chain, as shown in Figure 4-19.

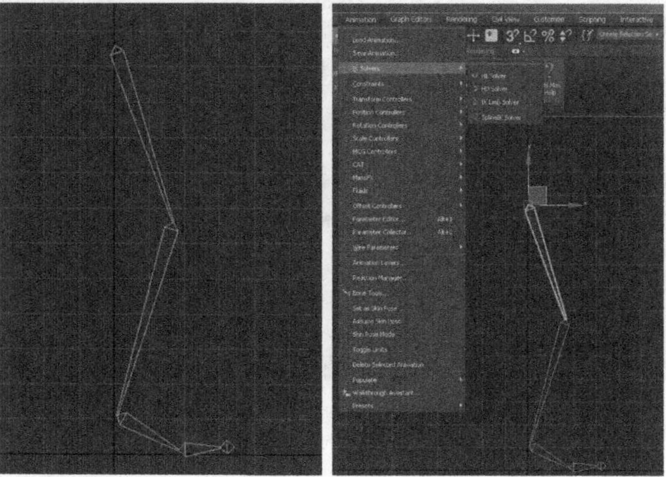

Figure 4-19. *Simple IK chain*

2. Select the top-most bone (the bone that emulates the thigh anatomy).
3. Go to the Animation menu and then the IK Solvers menu and choose HI Solver.
4. The software now expects you to choose the IK chain link, so select the feet_bone (the bone that resembles the heel anatomy).
5. An IK chain will be created for you at the beginning of the selected bone. That's it—you have created a simple IK chain. You can now move the IK Chain001 to move the leg up and down or to the side. Practice moving it to see how you can animate the bone chain. Try to get it in various poses and see how it can be done using FK.
6. A test file called `IK_Chain01.max` is available for your reference to test the IKChain.

IK Chain for a Leg

The IK leg in the previous example is able to just move the leg, There are a couple of animations that would be impossible with this setup, for instance tiptoe animation, feet swivel, and more. Let's look at how we can address them and apply them to the bone structure that we completed in the earlier exercise:

1. Load `IK_ChainAdvanced.max`. The bones have been renamed to avoid confusion.

2. Set up an IK chain from thigh_bone to ankle_bone.

3. Now our foot will be able to lift and move forward. As mentioned, we cannot enable heel rotation, swivel, or tip toe animation.

4. We will be using helpers to achieve this. Go to the Create panel and the Helpers tab. Select the Point helper and choose the Box mode in the Parameter section (see Figure 4-20). This will help us identify it easier.

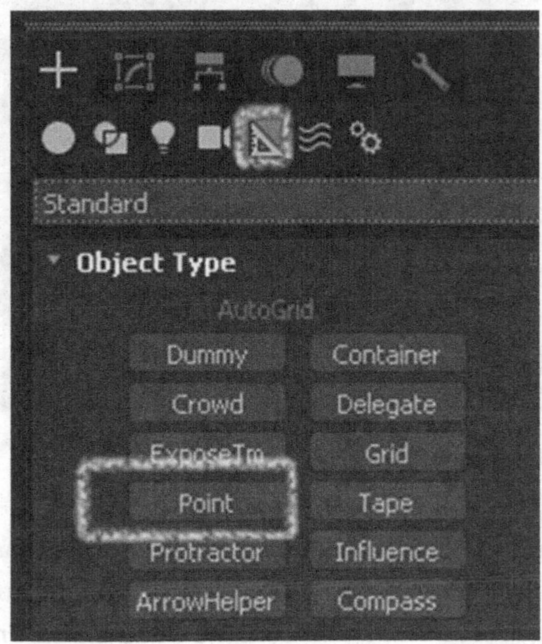

Figure 4-20. *Helpers*

5. Position the point helper in the place of the IK Chain001.

6. Create three more point helpers and position them as shown in Figure 4-21.

   Rename the helpers and color them in the Modify panel:

   - 1: Ankle_Helper
   - 2: Heel_Helper
   - 3: Toe_helper
   - 4: ToeTip_Helper

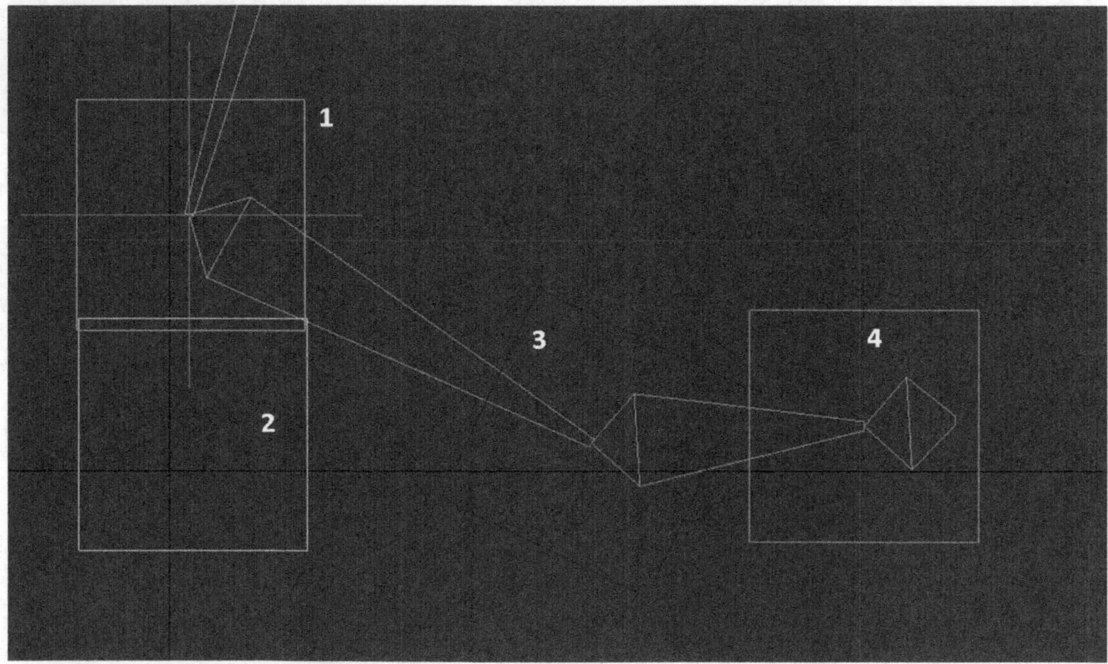

Figure 4-21. *Leg helper setup*

7. Select all the point helpers and freeze the transformations. You can freeze transforms by holding Alt and right-clicking and then choosing Freeze Transform from the Quad menu. Freeze Transform helps us zero back after any changes. In other words, the object's current position will be set to 0, 0, 0. See Figure 4-22.

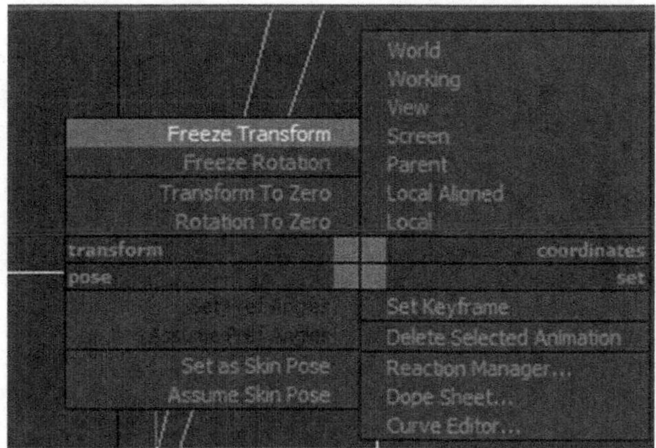

Figure 4-22. *Freeze Transform menu*

When you freeze an object or anything for that matter in 3ds Max, you will be presented with the dialog shown in Figure 4-23. Click Yes to continue freezing the object.

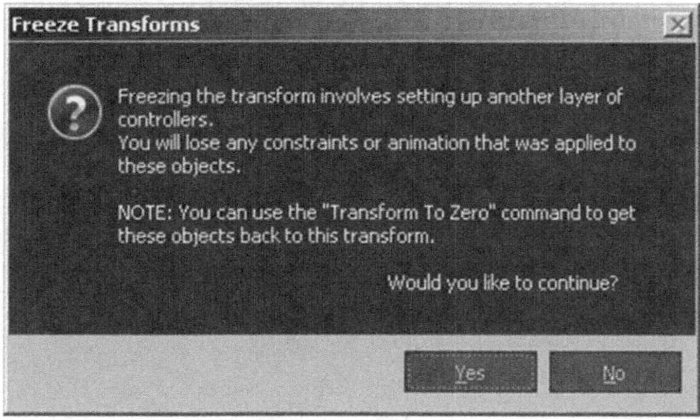

Figure 4-23. *Freeze Transforms confirmation*

8. Set your hierarchy as shown in Figure 4-24a.

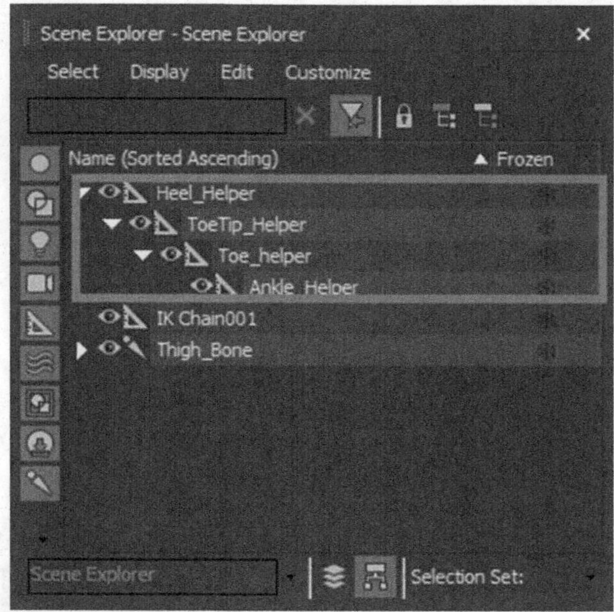

Figure 4-24a. *Leg helper hierarchy*

9. A checkpoint file is available called `IK_Chainadvanced02.max`.

IK Chain Constraints

We are going to set up constraints to the point helpers and the respective bones so that we can manipulate the helpers and bones accordingly.

1. Load `IK_ChainAdvanced02.max`.
2. Select the IK Chain001.
3. Go to the Animation menu and choose Constraints and Position Constraint. Now choose the Ankle_Helper. The constraint is set so that if you move the Ankle Helper, the IK chain moves, which directly controls the bone's position.
4. Select the ankle_Bone and go to the Animation menu. Choose Constraints ➤ Orientation Constraint. Now choose Toe_helper.

5. Do not fret if your toe is rotated. Select the Toe_Bone and go to the Animation menu and choose Constraints ➤ Orientation Constraint. Now choose ToeTip_Helper. The bones should fall back into place.

6. We need one more helper to assist us in moving the feet. This time, let's use a shape. In the top viewport, draw the shape line around the leg using the splines from the Shape tab in the Create panel. See Figure 4-24b.

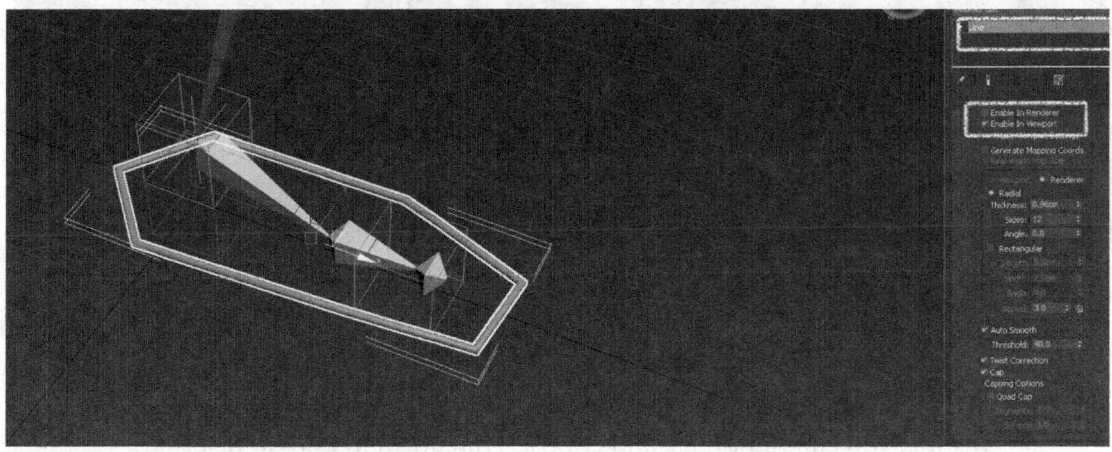

Figure 4-24b. *Leg IK controller*

7. Rename the object Leg_Control and set its pivot point to where the IKchain001 is. The pivot point can be changed by going into the Hierarchy panel and choosing Affect Pivot Only and moving it. See Figure 4-25.

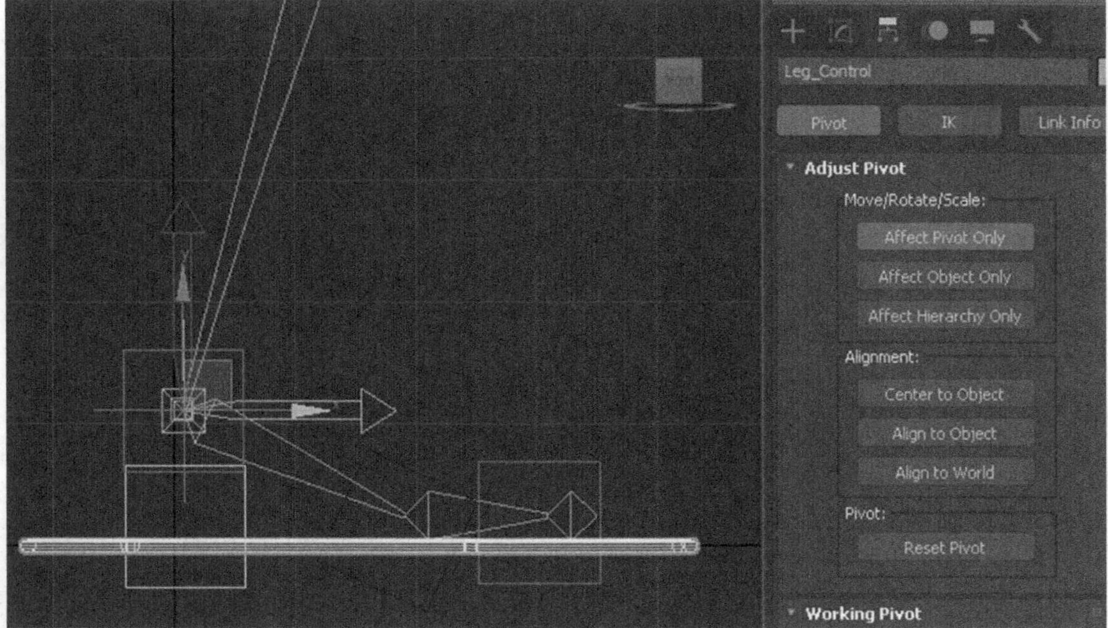

Figure 4-25. *Leg IK orthographic view*

8. Freeze the transformations by Alt+right-clicking the Leg_Control. So its current position will be read as 0, 0, 0. At any point after testing, you can right-click and choose Transform to Zero to reset it to its initial position.

9. Select the Heel_Helper and click on Link in the toolbar. Now select the Leg_Control to link it.

10. Now select the Leg_Control and rotate it on multiple axes to see the varied motion we can get.

You can now animate the foot into any pose. The animator needs to animate the leg control and the helpers to achieve motion. Try mimicking this setup into the bone structure we created in earlier sections. The reference file called `IK_ChainAdvanced03.max` has been set up in the scenes folder; experiment with it.

We will be further tweaking this rig with custom controls to give even more controls and to animate it easier. We will use wire parameters in the animation section, which we will cover in the next few chapters.

IK Chain for an Arm

We have set up a leg IK; now let's look at setting up an arm IK chain

1. Load `Hand_Rig.max`.
2. Let's set an IK chain quickly. Select L_Arm_Bone and go to the Animation menu and choose IK Solver and HI Solver. Then choose L_Hand_Bone.
3. A new IK chain is created. Select it and move it; you will be able to move the hand. We need to set up controllers and helpers like we did for the leg so that we can have grasping and wrist twisting animation).
4. Similar to the leg_control we created for the leg, let's create a hand control using shapes.
5. Rename it L_Hand_Control. Be sure to set its pivot point to the IKChains position.
6. Go to Helpers and create a point helper. Rename it L_Point_Helper.
7. Position point_handcontrol exactly where the IK Chain001 is. You can use the align tools to perfectly position it.
8. Select L_Hand_Bone and go to the Animation menu. Choose Constraints and Orientation Constraints. Then choose the L_Point_Helper. See Figure 4-26.

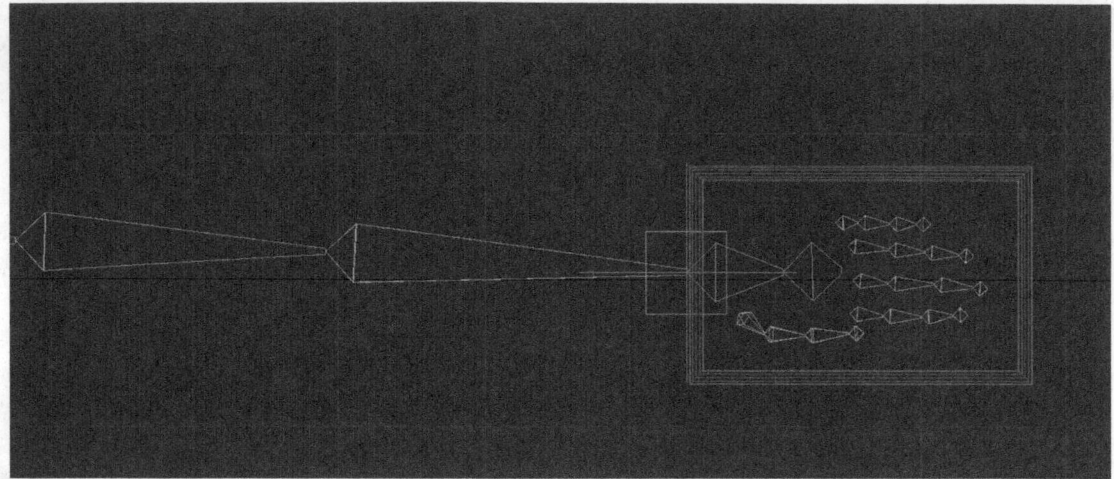

Figure 4-26. *Hand controller setup*

9. The next step is to select the point helper and use the Link tool from the toolbar to drag it to the L_Hand_Control, creating a link between the point control to the hand control.
10. Select the IK Chain001 and go to the Animation menu. Choose Constraint ➤ Position Constraint and choose the L_Point_Helper.
11. Now you can select the L_Hand_Control and rotate it to do arm twist animation. Use the Move tool to move the arm.
12. Be sure to set Freeze Transform for the L_Hand_Control from the Alt+right-click menu or for any control so that you can reset it to its initial position using the Transform to Zero option (see Figure 4-27). Alt+right-click to get the menu.

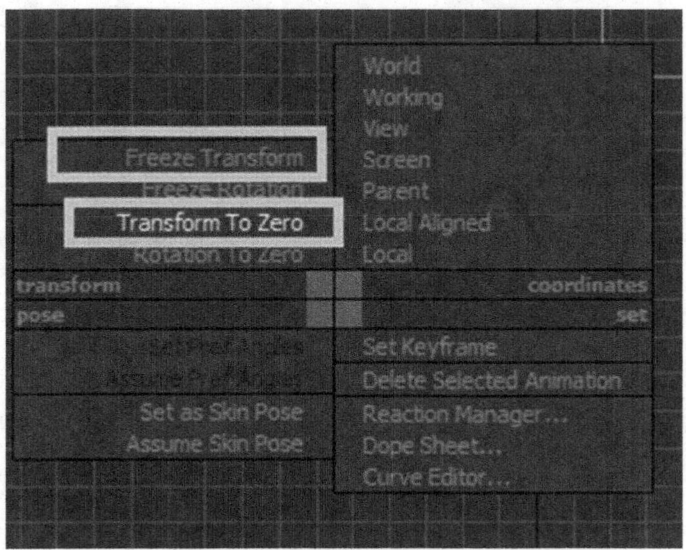

Figure 4-27. *Freeze Transformation menu*

Let's create an elbow control so we can swivel the arm.

1. Create a point helper named L_Elbow_Controller and align it to L_Forearm_Bone. (Once it's aligned, move it back to the arm a bit so that we can see it clearly.) We follow the same steps to create a point helper as we did for the leg chain in the previous section.

2. Select the IK_Chain001 and go to the Motion panel from the command panel. Choose IK_Solver rollout. See Figure 4-28.

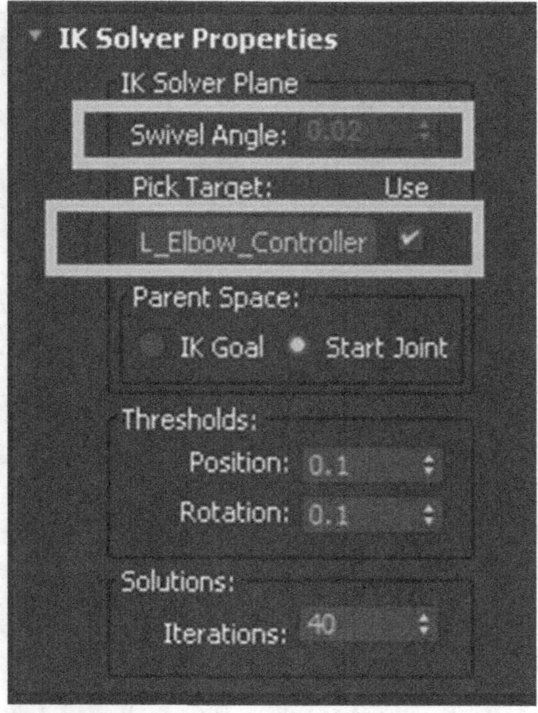

Figure 4-28. *IK Solver properties*

3. From here, the swivel angle can be tweaked/animated without using any controller to swivel the arm.

4. Alternatively, you can use pick target and choose the L_Elbow_Controller. Reposition your Hand_Control to have a bend and move the L_Elbow_Controller up and down to see the arm swivel.

A scene file has been created called `Hand_Rig01.max`.

Let's now focus on animating the fingers. You can continue if you have been following along or you can load `Hand_Rig02.max`, which has the previous steps done and saved.

1. Create a shape for your finger control. In this case, I create a rectangle, but you can create any shape.

2. Convert the newly created shape to a editable spline by right-clicking and choosing Convert To ➤ Convert To Editable Spline.

3. I am going to use this shape for the thumb finger, so I align it using the align tools so that it follows along the bone's position and rotation. See Figure 4-29.

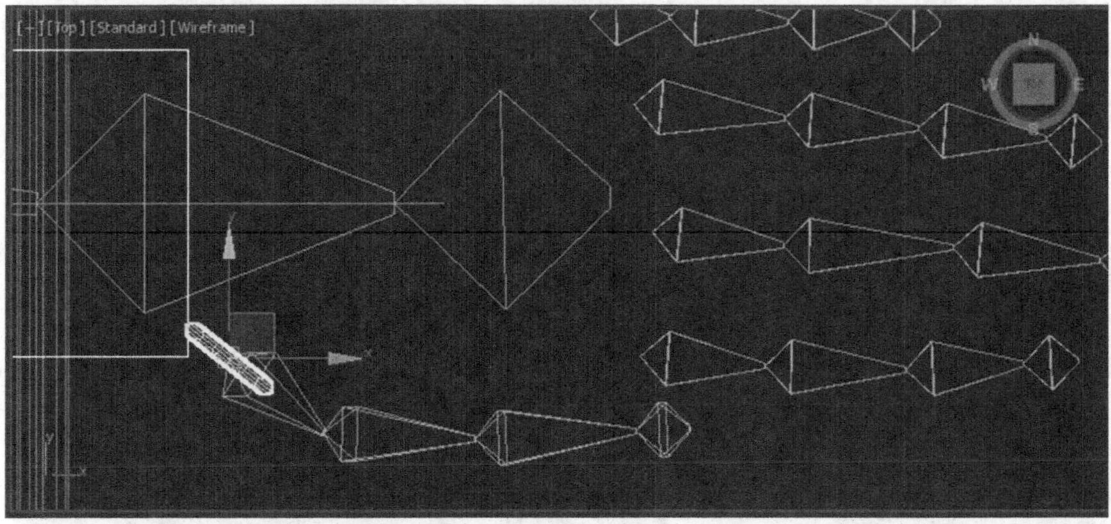

Figure 4-29. *Finger controller setup 1*

Let's clone this shape for other fingers and align them to the beginning of each finger. Rename the shapes with the appropriate names for each example, such as L_Index_Finger_Control:

Now let's set the constraints for the bones:

1. Select L_thumb0 and go to the Animation menu. Choose Constraint ➤ Orientation Constraint. Click on the L_thumb_Finger_control.

2. Select L_Index0 and go to the Animation menu. Choose Constraint ➤ Orientation Constraint and click on the L_index_Finger_control.

3. Select L_middle0 and go to the Animation menu. Choose Constraint ➤ Orientation Constraint and click on the L_middle_Finger_control.

4. Select L_ring0 and go to the Animation menu. Choose Constraint ➤ Orientation Constraint and click on the L_ring_Finger_control.

5. Select L_pinky0 and go to the Animation menu. Choose Constraint > Orientation Constraint and click on the L_pinky_ Finger_control. See Figure 4-30a.

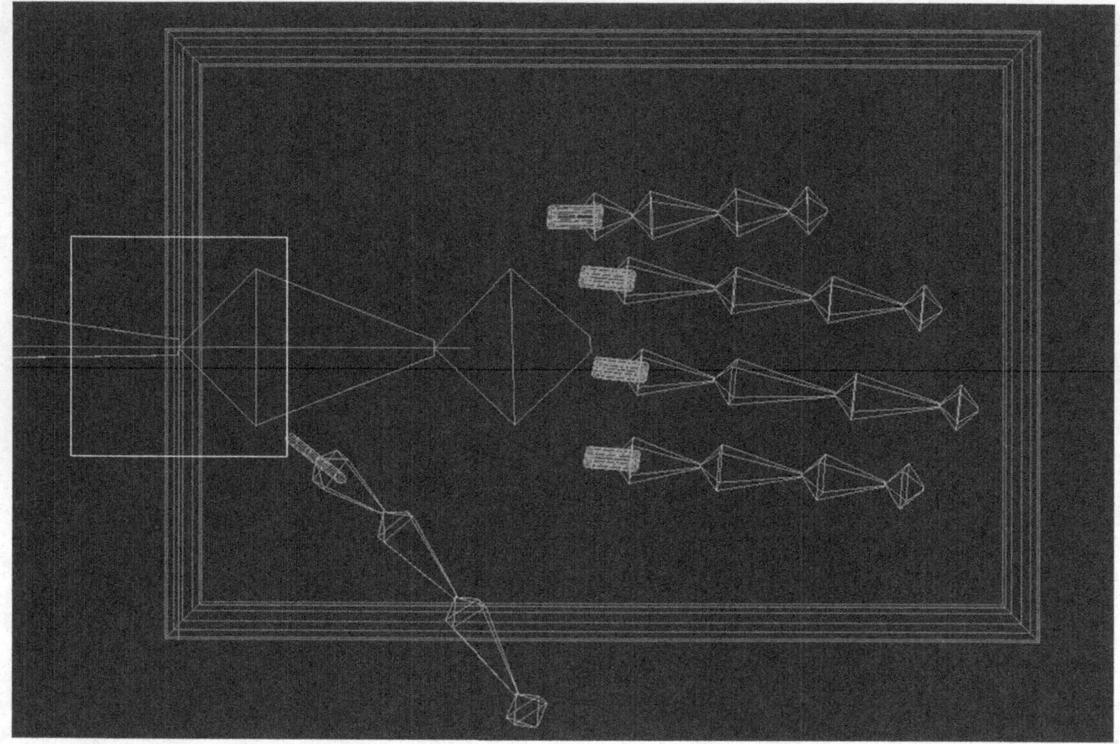

Figure 4-30a. *Finger controller setup 2*

Note in Figure 4-30a that I added the finger control for all the fingers. A checkpoint file is available called `Handrig_03.max`.

Custom Attributes and Wire Parameters

We are going to create custom attributes to mimic the finger motion. Although we could just select the beginning of the finger bone and create an IK chain and add controls. Let's use the feature of custom attributes and a wire parameter to drive the animation here.

1. We will be following along from the previous section, so fire up 3ds Max and load `Hand_Rig03.max`.

2. Select the L_index_Finger_control, go to the Modify panel, and add an Attribute holder from the Modifier list.

3. With the L_index_Finger_control still selected, go to the Animation menu and choose Parameter Editor (or press Alt+1). See Figure 4-30b.

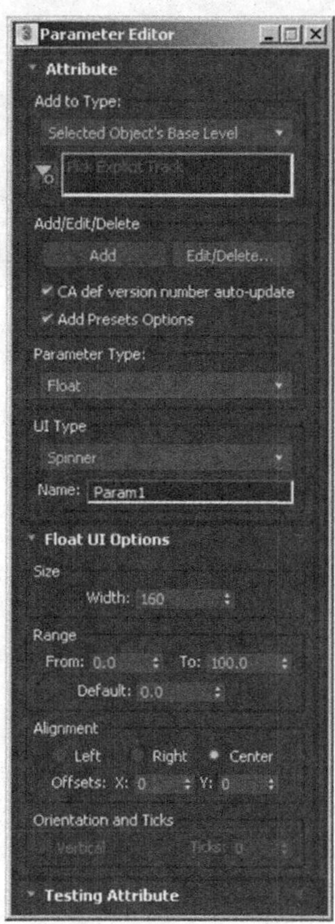

Figure 4-30b. *Parameter Editor*

4. Under UI type, call it Index_Finger and change the range from 0 to 10. Once you're done, click on Add and you should see the newly created parameter populate in the Modifier panel. See Figure 4-31.

Figure 4-31. *Attribute Holder Modifier*

5. Go to the Animation menu and choose Reaction Manager. See Figure 4-32.

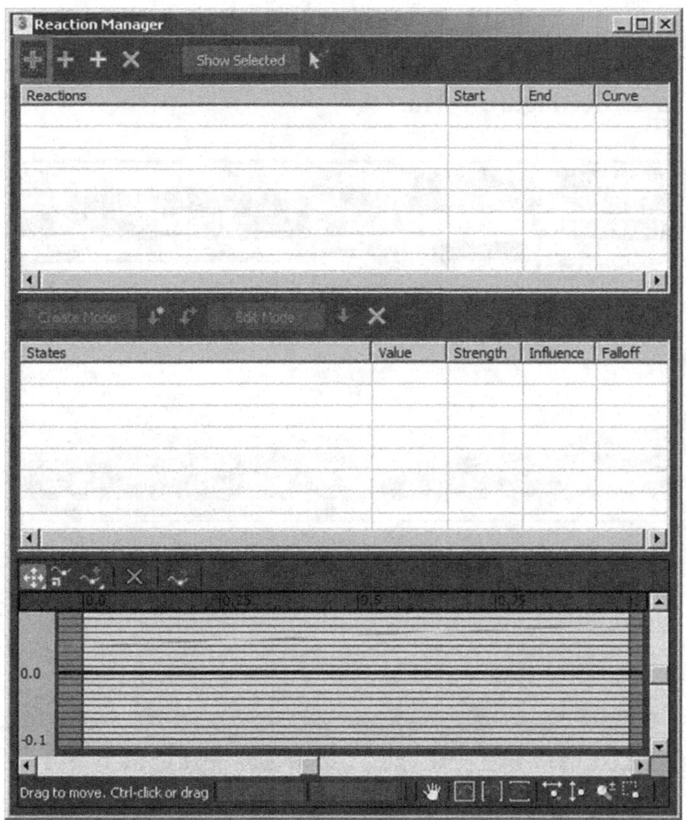

Figure 4-32. Reaction Manager

6. Click on the Add Master and, in the viewport, choose the L_index_finger_control, as shown in Figure 4-33.

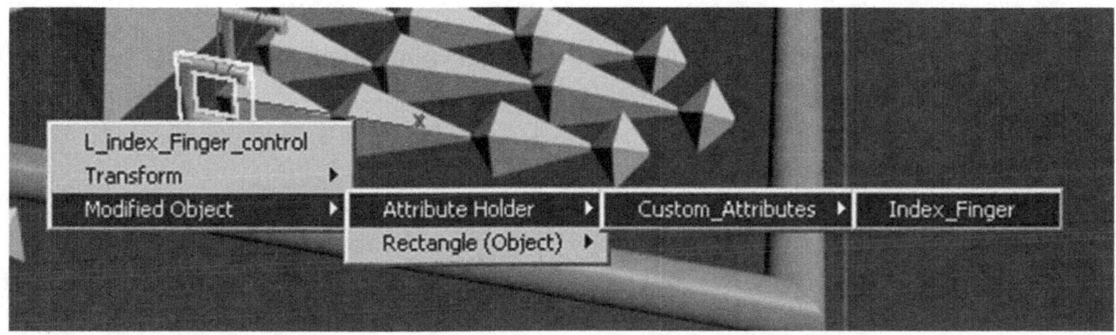

Figure 4-33. Assigning Master Control

7. Select the L_index1 and L_index2 bones and, in the Reaction Manager, click on Add Selected. From the menu, choose the Z rotation axis. See Figure 4-34a.

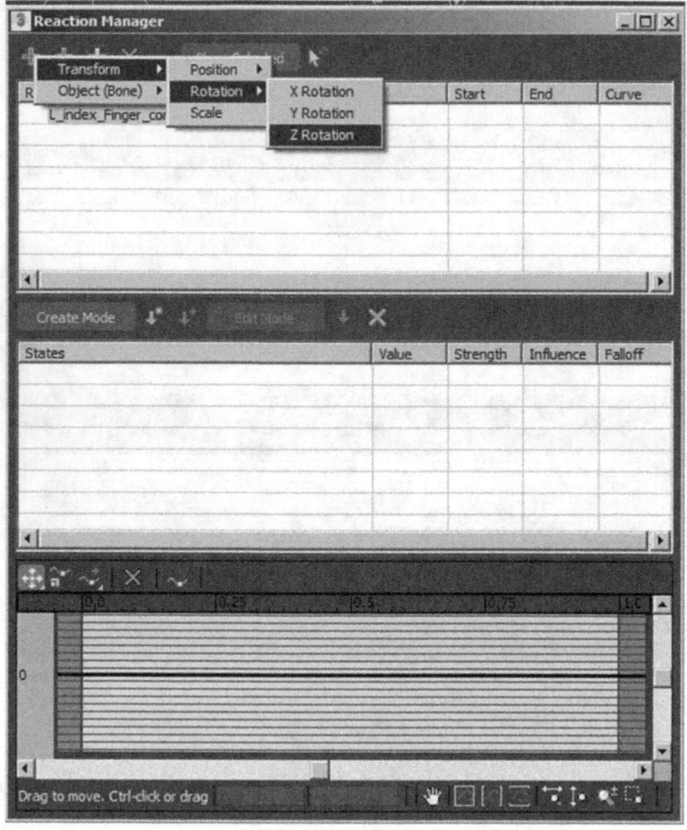

Figure 4-34a. *Assigning bones*

8. Once you click on the Z rotation, the list gets populated, as shown in Figure 4-34b.

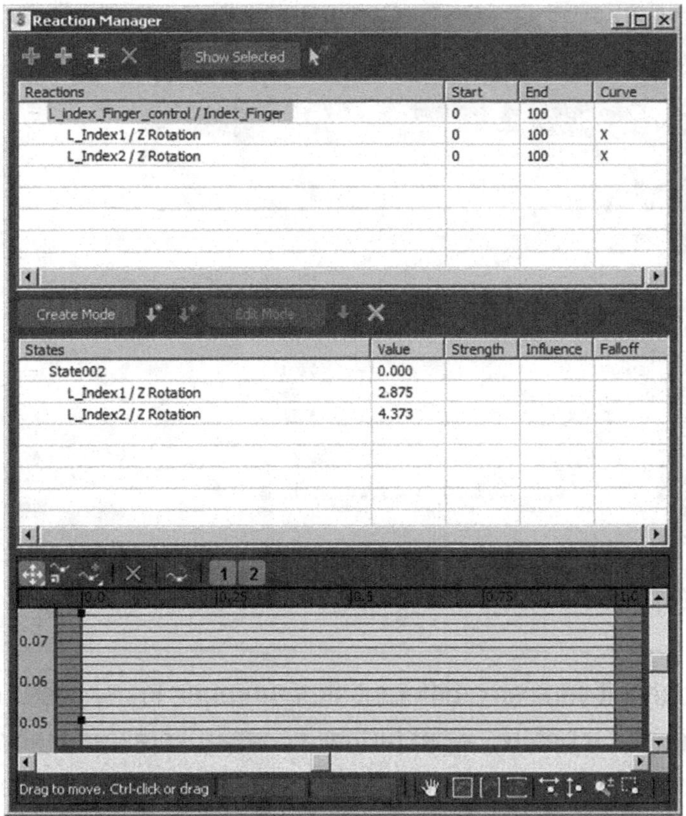

***Figure 4-34b.** Slave controls*

9. Click on Create a New State and set the values to 90 for the bones when the state is at 10. See Figure 4-35.

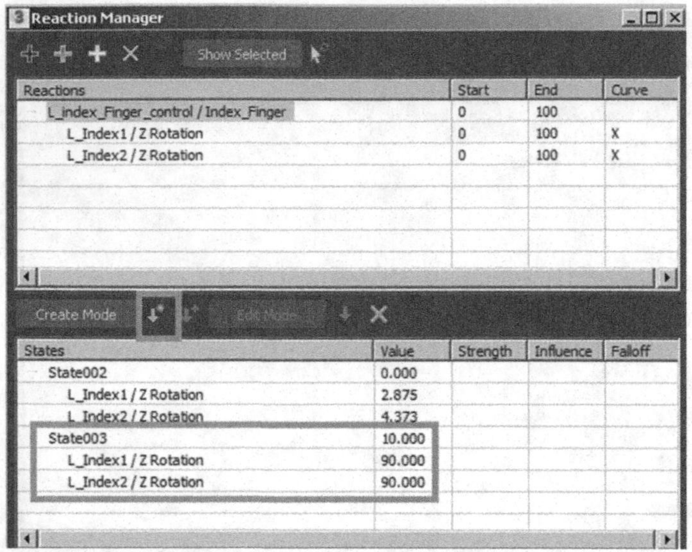

***Figure 4-35.** Reaction Manager states*

Note Do not panic if you see a different state number. In my case I created state001 and deleted it before I went further, so when I created a new state the numbers were state002 and state003. This is similar to any Windows application. Say you open a Word document called untitled 1 and open one more called untitled 2. When you close those documents and create another new document, it will be called untitled 3, because the software knows it's the third document you have opened in the same session.

---

10. Close Reaction Manager. Select the L_index_Finger_control and in the Modify panel, and then change the values of Index_Finger custom attribute from 0 to 10. Your fingers should curl. If you notice the fingers curling in the opposite direction, change the values in state to -90 to fix it.

11. Repeat this process for all the other fingers. The same technique can be applied to the toes.

IK Chain for the Spine

So far we have been using HI Solver from the IK Solvers menu to create IK chains for arms and legs. Let's begin by using a new solver type to demonstrate the new solver that 3ds Max provides for this purpose.

1. Open 3ds Max and create a spine set up with three bones—a neck bone, a head bone, and an end bone, as shown in Figure 4-36. Also create the line, as shown in Figure 4-37.

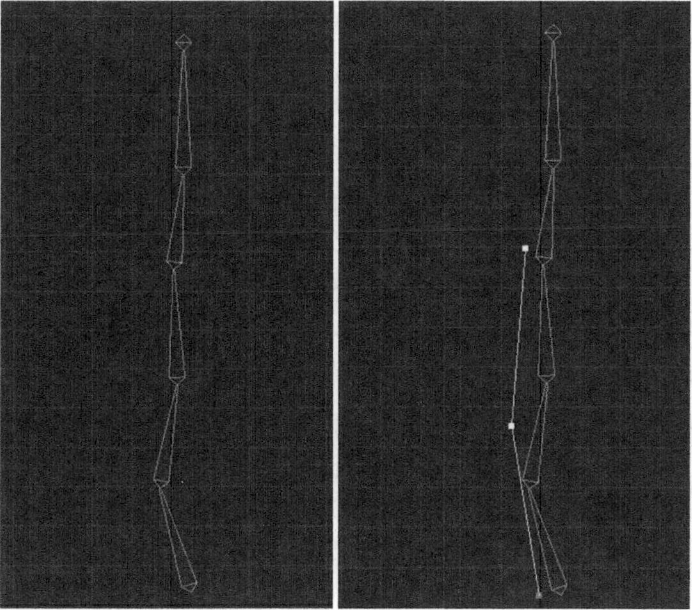

Figure 4-36. *Spine IK setup*

2. Rename the bones spine01, spine02, spine03, neck, head, and endbone.

3. Select spine01 and go to the Animation menu. Choose IK Solvers ➤ Spline IK Solver and then choose the neck. An IK handle will be created but the software expects you to click on the spline, so click on the spline that has been created. See Figure 4-37.

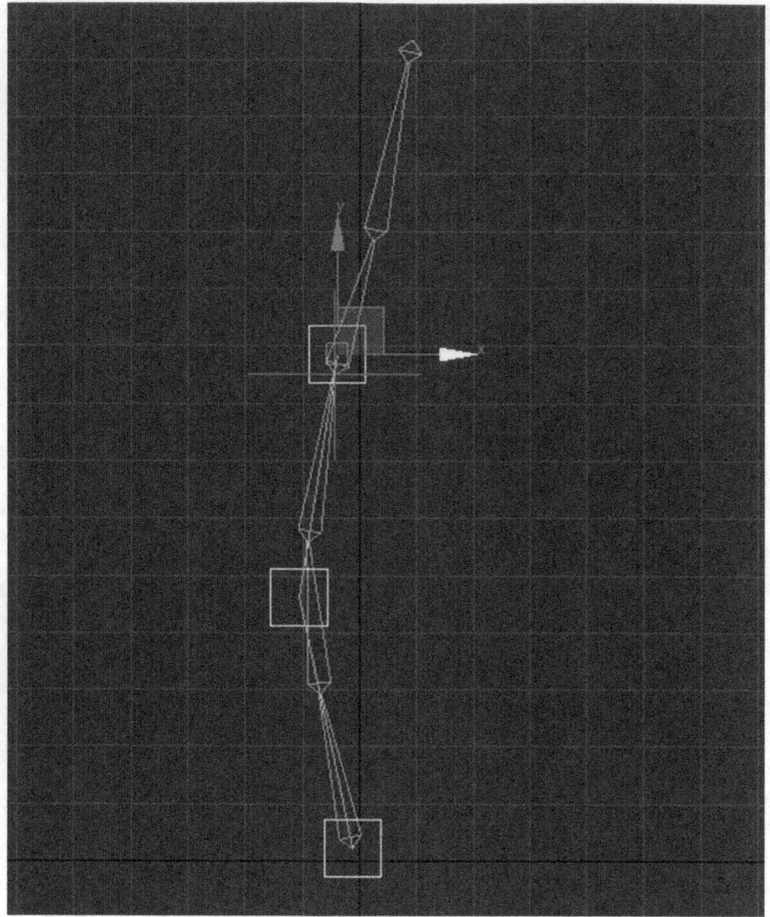

Figure 4-37. *Spine IK completed*

Note that control helpers are created for every vertex we had in the spline. Our initial path has three points so three control helpers have been created. The bottom-most is used to move everything as a whole; the middle one can be rotated to mimic the bend motion of a spine. The IK handle cannot be moved in this setup. The middle control helper can be moved or rotated.

You can re-parent and reorient as you see fit according to the need and motion derived. Try experimenting with more points in a path before applying the spline IK.

We have so far created a leg, arm, and spine IK chain. You can incorporate the same on a single file so it forms a complete rig. Once done, the root bone of each chain needs to be linked to the hip bone that was created and we would have a complete rig. A complete rig with facial morphs and facial bones will be provided for you at the end of Chapter 9.

HI Solver/HD Solver

One more section that we haven't covered is the types of solvers. So far, we have been using the HI Solver and not the HD Solver. Let's discuss this briefly. The solver's nature is to compute the rotations and positions of the bones based on their hierarchy and constraints attached if any. There are two types of IK solvers when creating an IK chain—the HI and HD Solvers. HI stands for history independent and HD stands for history dependent. Load `SolverHI_HD.max` to better understand this.

The file has two legs set up, with the left one using an HI Solver and the right side being an HD Solver. See Figure 4-38.

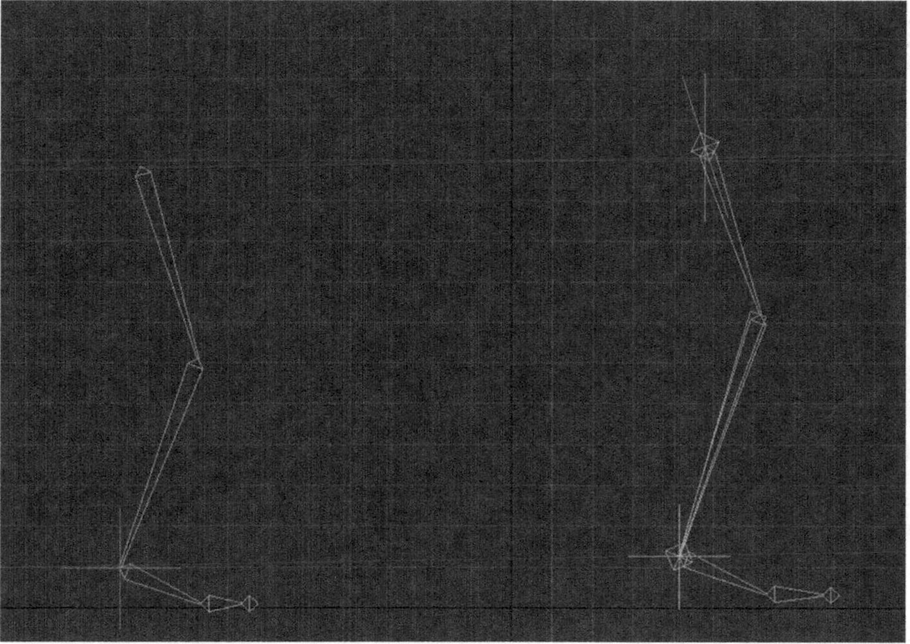

Figure 4-38. *HI and HD Solvers*

Select the left IK chain and move the leg up and down—it moves freely and quickly.

Now select the right IK chain and move it. Note that the bones jitter a lot. This chain is history dependent. Turn on Auto Key and set a keyframe for the right chain. Move a few frames ahead and try moving the IK chain. There is a keyframe created already in a previous frame, so the jitter will be nearly nil (still visible in some cases). In the HD Solver, the software is using the previous keyframe to compute a solution and get the positions and rotations of bones. In other words, the computing solution looks for previous keyframes and relies on them, which means it's HD (history dependent). In most cases, people use HI Solver, because it's a bit more advanced and you can fiddle around with the solving parameters in the IK tab in the Motion panel.

Summary

We will look at using bipeds and CAT tools as character rigs in the upcoming chapters and move on to skinning our bone_rig to our character in Chapter 7. I recommend you revisit this chapter and try the rigs over and over again to get practice. Also note that there is no one rig that fits all situations. We need to understand the animation that is required and place bones and set constraints as applicable. Keep practicing!

CHAPTER 5

Bipeds

In the previous chapter, we learned how to create a rig from scratch using bones. In this chapter, we look at creating/customizing bipeds and learn how to use them to drive character animation. A preset character model is provided, along in the contents folder and the reference filenames. Feel free to use any custom 3D model you have or download one and follow along. You can use the Autodesk character generator to generate a character or use any other software that generates human characters. We will be looking in-depth at the tools and options available for bipeds in 3ds Max, such as biped types, Figure modes, Footstep mode loading and saving motions, animation of a biped, and the Motion Flow Editor.

Getting Started with Bipeds

Bipeds is an animation utility that is provided with 3ds Max to create bone structures for characters and creatures that have two legs. It's mostly used to animate human figures, but animation of quadrupeds is possible too.

Creating Your First Biped

You can create a biped by going into the control panel and choosing the System tab. Click Create Biped. Then you drag on any viewport to create the biped. When you click and drag, you can adjust the height of the biped. Once you release the mouse, the biped is created. Right-click to exit Creation mode. See Figure 5-1.

P. Raju, *Character Rigging and Advanced Animation*, https://doi.org/10.1007/978-1-4842-5037-2_5

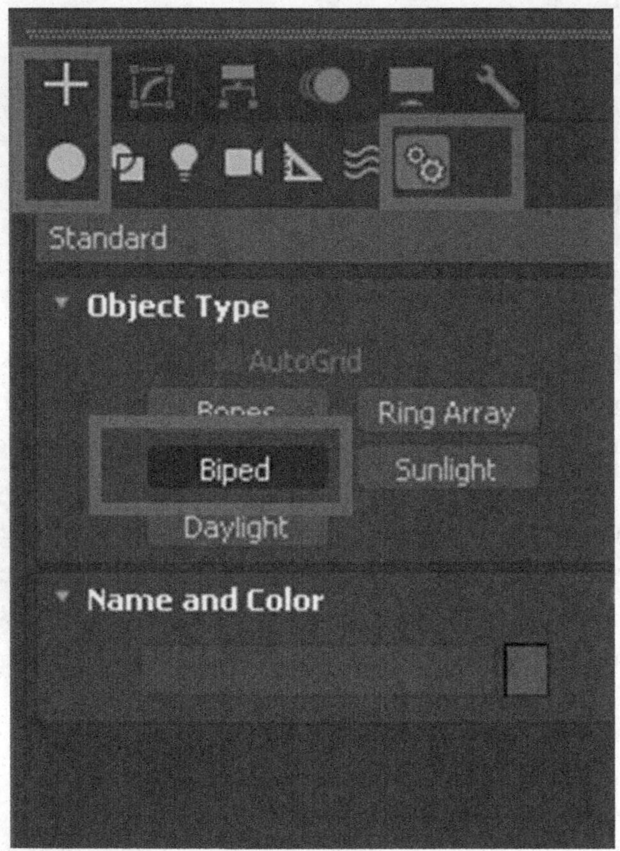

***Figure 5-1.** Command panel, biped creation*

A point to note here is that when you click on the biped, you have a lot of options to customize it.

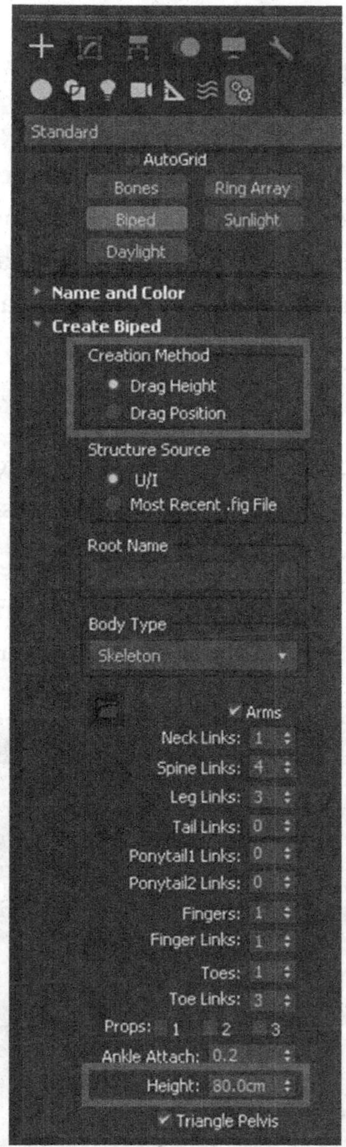

***Figure 5-2.** Biped's creation parameters*

There are two options for the Creation Method (see Figure 5-2):

- Drag Height: Allows you to click on any viewport and create a biped with a custom height.
- Drag Position: The biped is created at the point where the user clicks based on the height input of the biped rollout (as marked in the image).

Here are the Structure Source options:

- U/I: The software will create a biped with the default options that are shipped.
- Most Recent Fig File: This can be used if you have created, let's say a biped with six fingers and a tall neck and a lot other parameters tweaked. That biped can be saved as a .fig file and then can be loaded later. This saves you a lot of time in customizing a biped every now and then.

Here are the Root Name options:

- Root name allows you to specify a name system for your bipeds. Otherwise, they are named as bip01, bip02, and so on.

One more thing to note here is that the parts of the biped have a prefix of whatever name was set in the root name. In Figure 5-3, I use the Human01 root name. Note in the scene explorer how the various parts of the body have been named accordingly.

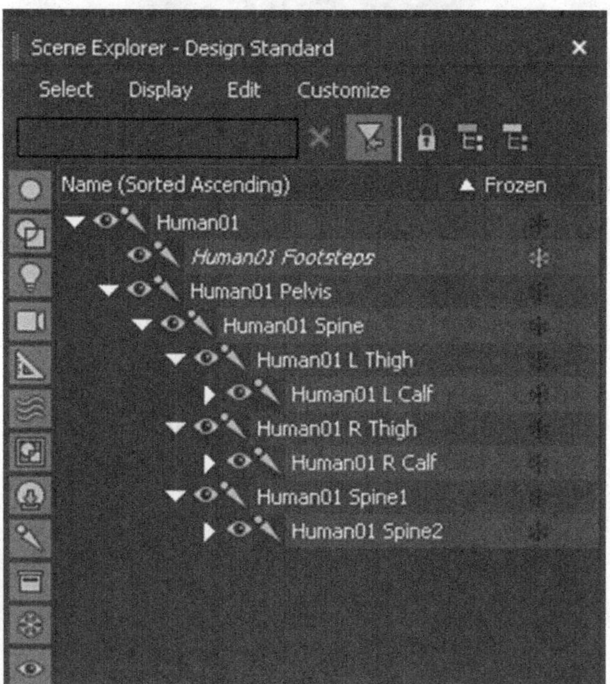

Figure 5-3. *Scene Explorer's biped hierarchy*

Biped: Body Types

In Figure 5-4, from left to right, the body types of the bipeds are Skeleton, Male, Female, and Classic. A reference file called `Biped_bodytypes.max` is available in the `content` directory of the Chapter 5 folder.

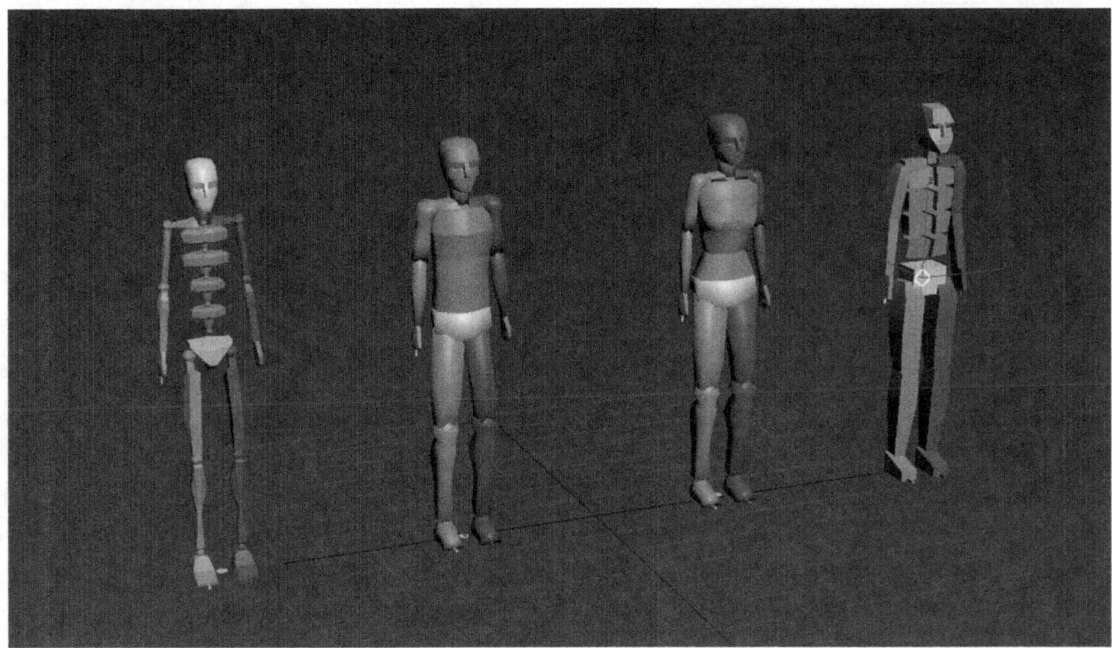

Figure 5-4. *Body types of the Bipeds*

Note that the type of biped is just an aesthetic and for visual differentiation only. It does not affect the animation or ease of use.

Here are descriptions of the other options seen in the biped rollout. (The following options can be tweaked while you are in the Creation mode of the biped.)

- Arms: When this checkbox is enabled, the biped will have arms. If not, the arms will be removed. Disabling arms will also disable fingers and knuckles.
- Neck links: This determines the length and segment of bones for the neck area. Increasing neck links will make the neck tall like a giraffe neck.

- Spine links: This allows us to create spine chain segment. The default is 4 and can be increased or decreased as per our requirements.
- Tail links: Allows us to add tails to the biped. Why would we need a tail on a human character? With the right tweaks in the biped, this can be converted into a dinosaur rig.
- Ponytail links 1 and 2: Allow us to add ponytails to characters, which is very useful if your character has long hair and you would like to animate the sway of the hair.
- Fingers: Allow us to tweak the number of fingers in the hands. Note that this is symmetrical, so we do not have feature to make one hand have more or less finger. However, there is a workaround for that that we will discuss as we go forward.
- Finger links: Allows for finger sections/finger bends.
- Toes and Toe links: Work the same way as fingers, but for legs.
- Props: These are useful when you are loading mocap data that has additional prop information; the prop that is added with the biped will receive the data and move accordingly. For example, a weapon in a character's hand. The process of capturing an object/prop's movement and rotation into 3D coordinates is called *motion capture.* A mocap file is nothing but a motion capture file that is captured using special cameras. The capture data contains the rotations and translation of the object and this data can be fed into 3D software to mimic the movement.
- Ankle attach: Allows us to move the feet below the ankle a bit forward or backward without affecting the leg.

These options should help us create a customized biped. There are advanced options that we will look at as we utilize the biped for animation.

Once you have completed the biped and dropped out of the Creation tool (meaning you have right-clicked or chosen another tool), the biped can still be tweaked by going into the Motion tab and choosing Figure mode. The structure rollout should have all the same details you had when creating it. See Figure 5-5.

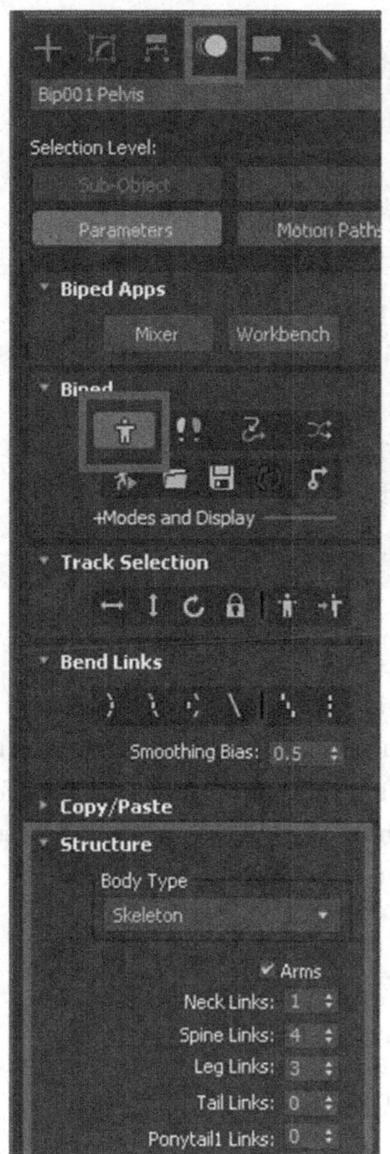

Figure 5-5. *Biped, Figure mode editing*

Biped: Figure Mode

Biped Figure mode is where you edit and customize your biped. This is done by going into the motion panel and enabling Figure mode in the biped rollout of the motion panel, as shown in Figure 5-6.

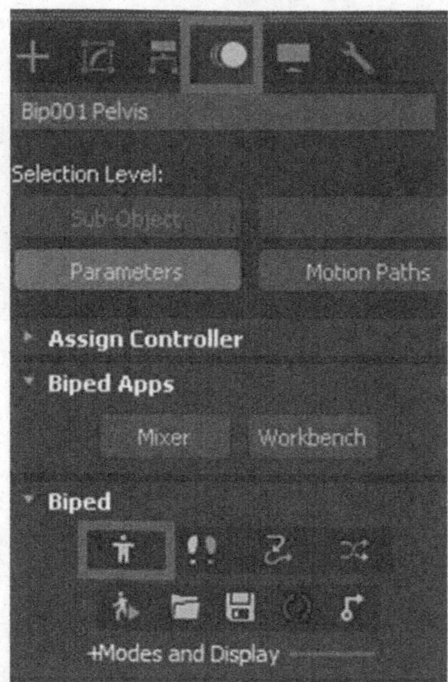

Figure 5-6. *Figure mode*

Figure mode is a toggle switch. You can switch in and out of Figure mode. Figure mode allows you to move, rotate, and scale the biped parts so that the rig is even more customized to your liking. Let's say we want to use this biped for a chimpanzee, so we need to elongate the hands. No problem. Enable Figure mode and scale them along the axis.

Load `Biped_Figuremode_edited` and see the reference.

Follow these steps:

1. Create a biped.
2. Get into the motion tab.
3. Enable Figure mode in the biped rollout.
4. Use the necessary transformation tools (in this case, use `Biped_Figremode_edited.max`).
    - I scaled the elbow section of the hand along the x axis alone using the Scale tool.
    - I rotated the spine section each so that the character leans and bends using the Rotate tool.
    - I scaled the right leg section below the knee and ankle again along the X axis.

5. Feel free to scale uniformly and see what happens. You can make one arm very huge or any part of body huge/small as per your 3D model.

Biped: Loading and Saving Figures

You have created a custom biped by tweaking the parameters in the structure rollout. You can now save the biped as a .fig file so that the same structure can be loaded in a different project. This saves the time of recreating the whole structure. Here are the steps to load/save a biped as a `.fig` for later use:

Note You need to be in Figure mode to save and load `.fig` files.

---

1. Create a biped from the systems rollout.
2. Customize it to your liking using the biped structure panel or any other tools.
3. Go to the motion panel in the control panel, under the Biped category.
4. The icons are marked in red in Figure 5-7. The folder icon allows you to load an already saved biped, while the Save icon allows you to save the bip for later use.

An example figure mode is available in the `content` directory of `chapter 05/Biped_Fig` named `Biped_Fig01.fig`. Load the figure file to understand how the load and save works.

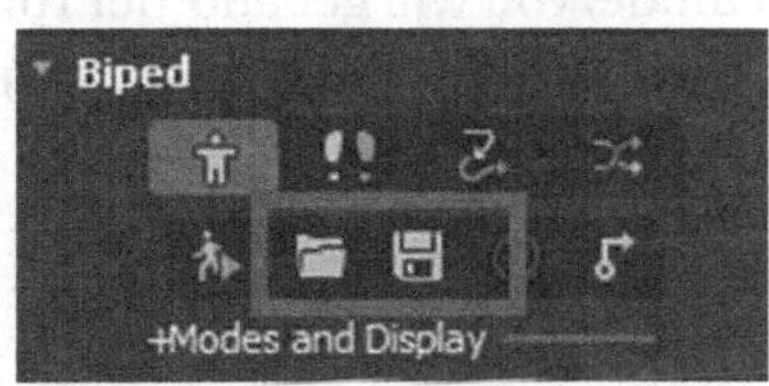

***Figure 5-7.** Load and Save icons*

Biped: Footstep Mode

Let's now create a walk animation of our biped using built-in animation tools.

1. Create a biped and tweak the structure to your liking or alternatively you can load `Biped_Walk_Start.max`.
2. Select any part of the biped and go into the motion panel.
3. Choose Footstep mode, as shown in Figure 5-8.

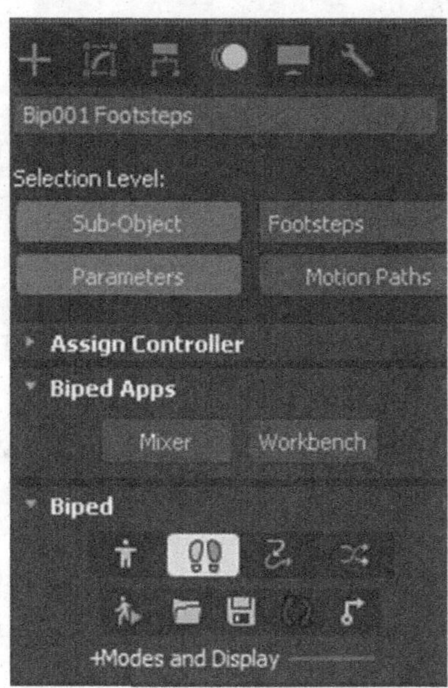

Figure 5-8. *Footstep mode*

4. Footstep has many modes, so let's look at each one at a time. Once you enable Footstep mode, you will get another rollout called Footstep Creation right below it (refer to Figure 5-9).

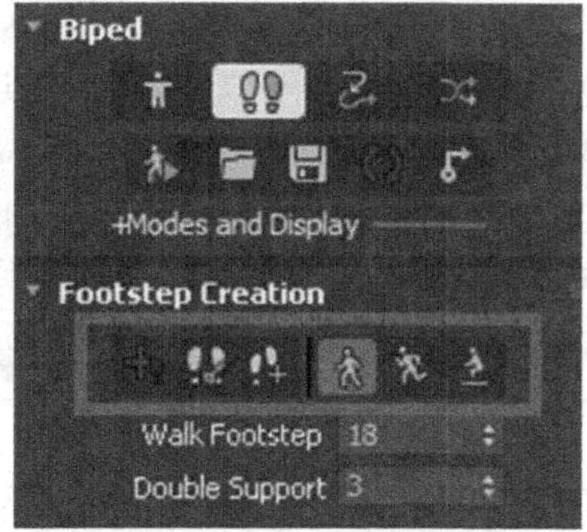

Figure 5-9. *Options in Footstep mode*

The options are as follows:

- Create footsteps append: This option enables us to add footsteps following with any existing footsteps. Do so will cause the character to seamlessly transition from the existing footsteps to the new ones. Currently our file does not have any footsteps, so the Append Footstep option is grayed out.
- Create footstep at current keyframe: Creates footsteps at the current frame your timeline is in.
- Create multiple footsteps: This option provides us with a dialog box that helps us create a determined number of footsteps with varied parameters. We will look into this option later in this chapter.
- Walk, Run, Jump: Whichever of these is selected will determine which animation is going to be created. If you wanted the character to do a jumping animation, you would choose Jump.

5. Now choose Create Footstep at the current frame:

   - The Walk Footstep option determines how many frames the biped takes in a single step.
   - Double Support is the number of frames in which both legs of the biped are on the ground.

6. In any viewport (preferably top or perspective), click on the World grid to create a footstep. You can create multiple footsteps by clicking on the grid in the viewport. As you click, it will create footstep icons, which is where the character is going to step and move forward. Think about where you want the character to plant her feet and move forward and create the footsteps in that position.
7. Note that the footsteps are numbered so that we can see which foot moves first. Note also that they are color coded. Green is the right foot and blue is the left foot.
8. Once you have created enough steps, right-click to exit Footstep Creation mode. You can confirm that none of the footstep modes are selected in the footstep creation box.
9. Individual footsteps can now be selected and moved to your liking, such as if you have placed them very far and want to tweak their position. Using the Move and Rotate tools. (See the reference file in the `asset` folder called `Biped_Walk_Start_FootstepC.max`.)
10. If you scrub the timeline, you will see no animation happening yet. In order for your biped to follow the animation, use the next steps.
11. In the Footstep Operation rollout (refer to Figure 5-10), click on Create Keys for Inactive Footsteps button (marked in Figure 5-10). Note that the moment you click it, the biped repositions itself so that its leg is aligned with your first footstep. Note that you can still tweak the footstep by selecting it and moving it to a new position; the biped will adjust accordingly.

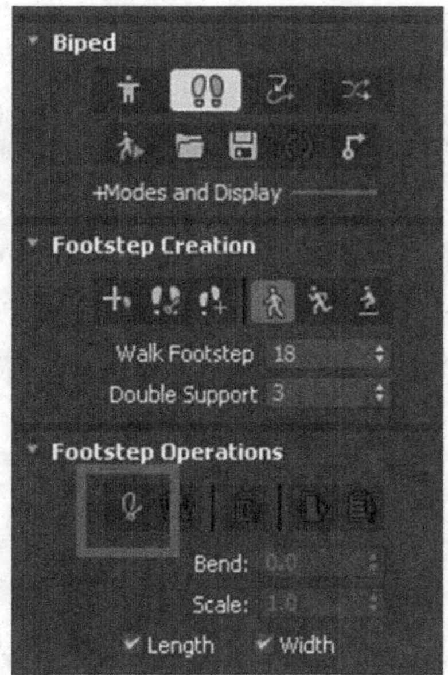

Figure 5-10. *Create inactive footsteps*

Biped: Footstep Mode, Climbing Stairs

Now let's create a biped animation of a character climbing up the stairs.

1. Load `Biped_Walkstairs.max` or create a setup of stairs with a biped in front of them.

2. Go into Footstep mode.

3. Choose Walk, Run, or Jump, based on how you want the character to climb the stairs.

4. Click Create Footstep at Current Frame in footstep creation. Your footsteps are not going to align with the stairs, but create them anyway. See Figure 5-11.

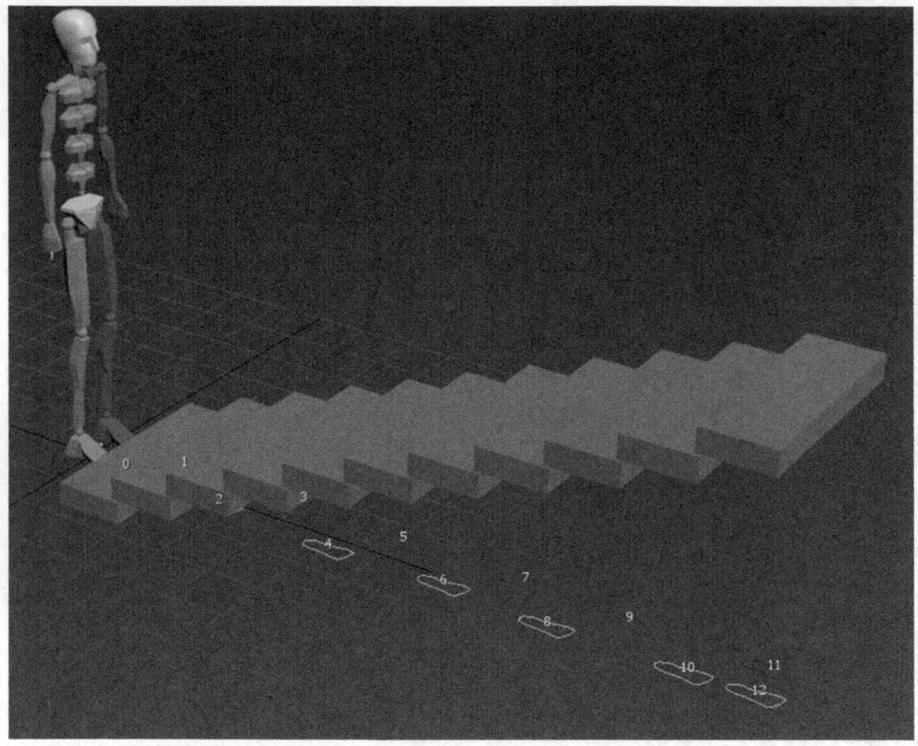

Figure 5-11. *Biped footsteps on the World grid*

5. Right-click to complete the Creation mode and use the Move tool to reposition the footsteps where they need to be. See Figure 5-12.

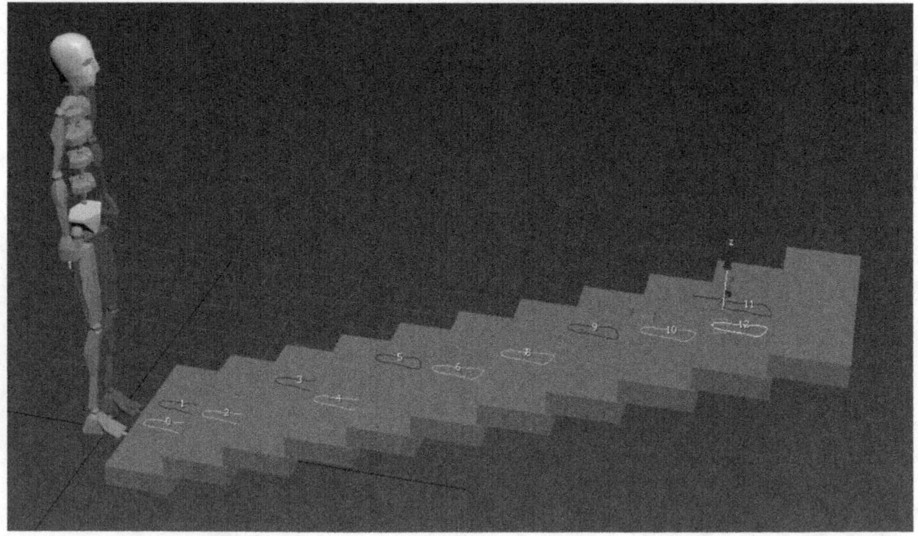

Figure 5-12. *Biped footsteps aligned with stairs*

6. Click on Create Keys for Inactive Footstep in footstep operation. Voila, you are done! Your character should be climbing the stairs as you scrub the timeline. The reference file called `Biped_WalkStairs_StartComplete.max` is provided so that you can see the complete file in action.

7. As practice, create an obstacle course and see if you can make the character move around it.

Biped: Create Multiple Footsteps

The Biped Create Multiple Footsteps option (see Figure 5-13) allows you to create multiple footsteps at once, be it for running, walking, or jumping. You can choose to create multiple footsteps when in Figure mode, as shown in Figure 5-13.

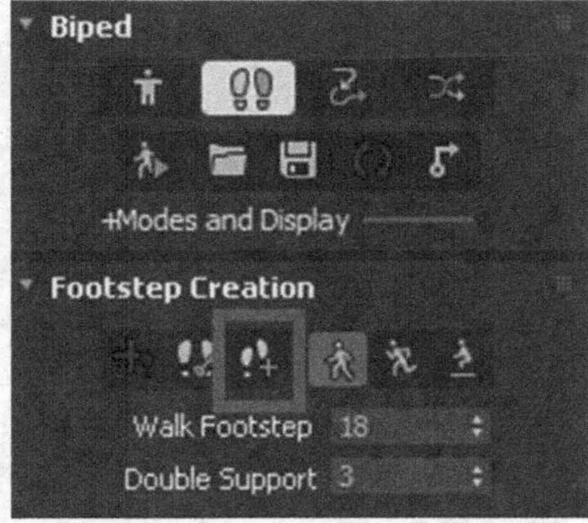

Figure 5-13. *Biped, Create Multiple Footsteps option*

Let's go step-by-step over the process of creating multiple footsteps for a biped.

1. Reset 3Ds Max from the File menu if you have another file open.

2. Create a biped from the Systems panel and tweak it to your liking.

3. Enable Footstep mode in the biped rollout.

4. Choose your preferred style—Walk, Run, or Jump—in Footstep Creation mode. I chose Walk so the following options are for walking. You can follow along with Run or Jump as well, except there will be two changes to the parameters, which are mentioned in the last part of this section.

5. Click on the Create Multiple Footsteps button, as shown in Figure 5-13.

6. A dialog box should pop up, as shown in Figure 5-14.

    - All the options here control how your character moves and gives varying options for varying values. We will discuss later what each value means.

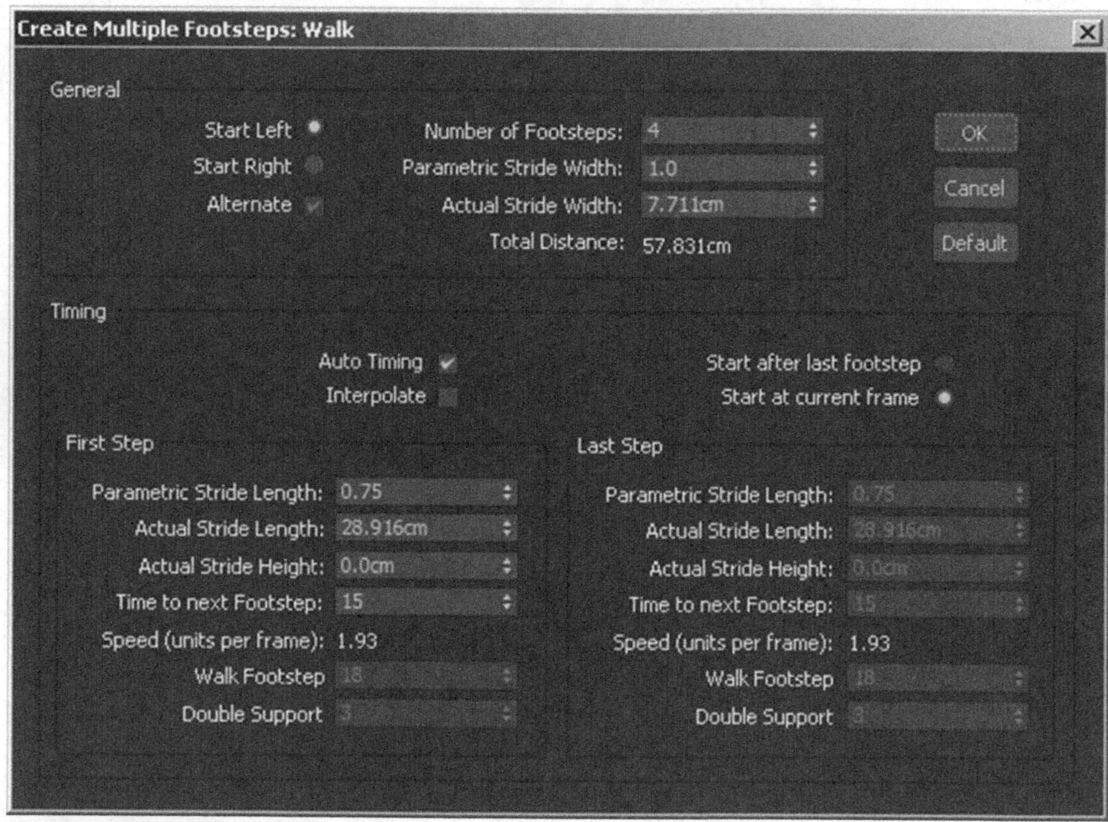

Figure 5-14. *The Create Multiple Footsteps dialog*

Let's look at each option in this dialog box:

- Start Left/Start Right: Only one can be enabled. This determines which foot begins. In Jump mode, this won't matter, as both legs go up at the same time. But the software needs to number the steps and whatever option is chosen gets the first numbering for the footstep.

- Alternate: This mode cannot be tweaked in Walk mode, but it can be disabled in Run and Jump mode. If you disable Alternate in Run or Jump mode, the character will hop with one leg only, and the leg that will hop is determined by the Start left/right option. Try it out!!
- Number of footsteps: This is the total number of footsteps that need to be created.
- Parametric stride width: This determines how spread apart the legs are during the animation.
    - In Figure 5-15, the left biped has a default stride width value, which is 1, whereas the right has a stride width value of 3. Notice the difference.

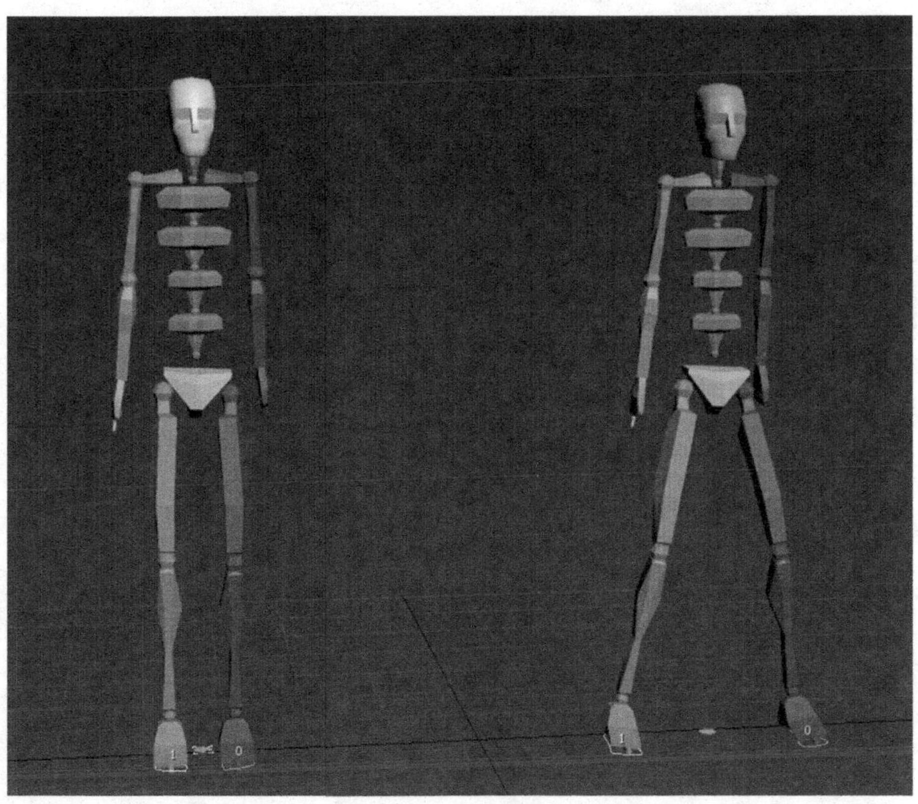

***Figure 5-15.** Parametric stride width of the left biped is 1 and the right value is 3*

- Actual stride width: Actual stride width and parametric stride width are connected. The actual stride width shows the distance between the two feet in the units as set in your file units and parametric always shows this in grid units.
- Total distance: This option will show you to overall distance the biped has to cover during the walk based on the number of steps you give. Increasing or decreasing the number of steps will show how much are the biped will cover.
- Auto timing: Enabling this affects a couple of parameters in the footsteps parameter—Walk Footstep and Double Support. Disable this and tweak the values if need be.
- Interpolate: By enabling Interpolate, you will be able to add a value for the last step for the following parameters—Parametric Stride Length, Actual Stride Length, Actual Stride Height, and Time to Next Footstep. When interpolate is disabled, the options are grayed out. Enabling this will give a varied motion where the character begins walking based on first step parameters and ends with the last step parameters in the Create Multiple Footstep dialog.
- Start after last footstep: Allows the multiple footstep dialog to use existing footsteps and append newly created ones to create a seamless transition.
- Start at current frame: Creates footsteps from the current frame and does not consider any existing footsteps while creating them.
- Actual stride height: Stride height should be 0 if you want the biped to walk in a straight line, using a positive number will make the biped take its next step that many units higher. A negative number can be used to simulate going down stairs. This is very easy to work with when you know the height of the stair.
- Speed: Determines the units the biped will cover per frame.
- Walk footstep: This determines the number of frames a footstep rests on the ground before going into the next step.

- Double footstep: This determines the number of frames during one walk cycle where both feet will be in contact with the ground.
- OK: Confirms the values and creates your footsteps.
- Cancel: Closes the dialog box.
- Defaults: Restores all the values to their defaults.

Play around with these values to experiment different Walk, Run, and Jump animations. The only parameter difference you see is in the bottom part of the dialog, where for Walk, it would be Walk Footstep and Double Support, which would be changed to Run Footstep and Airborne for a run cycle. The Jump dialog has the 2feetdown and Airborne parameters.

Biped: Animating a Biped

In earlier exercises, we created biped animations using Footstep mode. Now we will look at creating an animation from scratch by manually creating keys. For this exercise we are going to look at using the pose-to-pose method to animate a walk cycle. The walk cycle is going to be rough work and should give you an idea of the process.

Fire Up 3ds Max and proceed with these steps.

1. Create a biped and tweak it to your preferences.
2. If you look at walk poses for animation, there are several reference images with five or more steps for a walk cycle. Figure 5-16 shows a rough image to give you an idea. There are detailed drawings with lifelike pictures available on the Internet.

Figure 5-16. *Rough poses of a walk cycle*

- Note in Figure 5-16 that the first image and the last are the same. The second and fourth will be the opposite of each other but I provided variation in the sketch and the middle one is a unique pose. The first and last are called the contact pose. The second one, where the leg is firmly on the ground, is a down pose and the middle one is called a passing pose. The fourth one is called an up pose as the leg lifts up and the fifth is the same as the first.
- We keep the first and fifth images the same so that our animation can be looped.

3. Now let's create these poses in Biped and animate them.
4. Set the animation duration to 40 frames using the time configuration. We will animate each pose every 10 frames.
5. If you have completed these steps, you can move to the next step. If not, a file called `BipedAnimation_Start.max` is provided with all the steps.
6. Select one of your biped parts and go into the motion panel.
7. Expand the Copy Paste tab and close everything else. We need only this. See Figure 5-17.

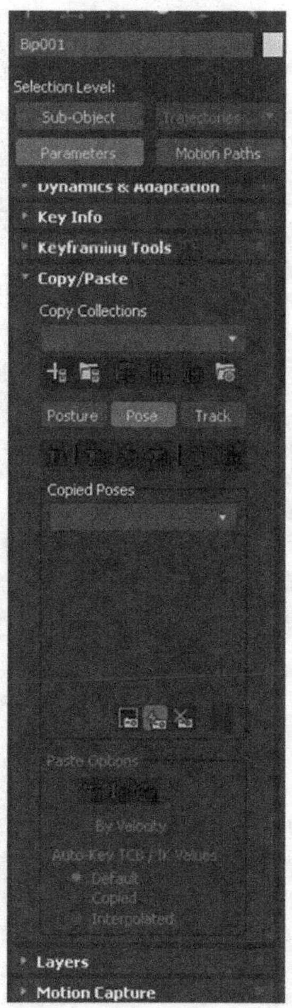

***Figure 5-17.** Biped motion panel, copy paste rollout*

8. In the Copy Paste rollout, click on Create a Collection. This collection is going to have all the poses. Multiple collections can be created. Once it's created, click on the col01 and type a name and press Enter. In the Copy Paste rollout, ensure that you are in Pose mode and not in Posture or Track mode. In my case, I am renaming the collection WalkCycle. See Figure 5-18.

Figure 5-18. *Motion panel, create collection*

9. Select the body parts and use the Move and Rotate tool to pose the character, as in the first person reference walk cycle.

10. Once you are happy with the pose (try to orient as many joints as possible to emulate the correct pose), click on the Copy Pose. A pose should be created. You can click on the name to rename it. Figure 5-19 shows a reference image of before and after creating the pose.

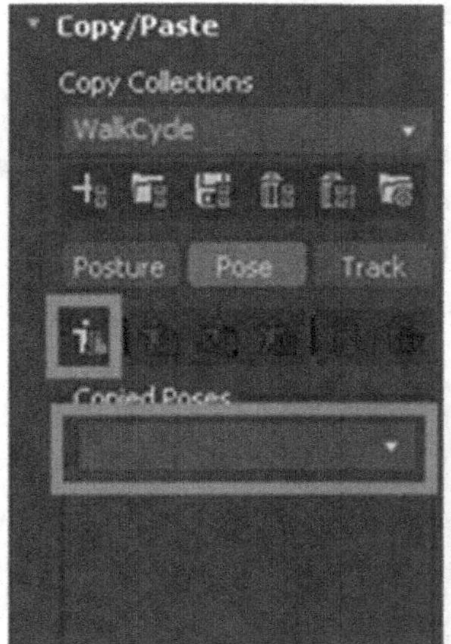

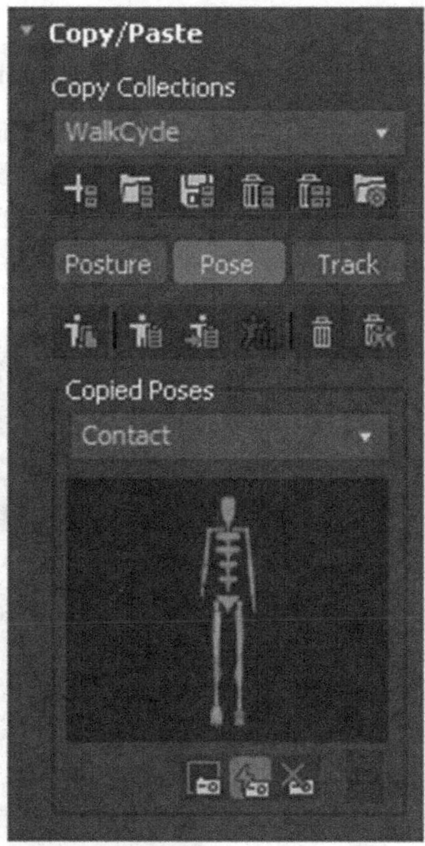

Figure 5-19. *Motion panel, create poses (left is before creating the pose, right is after creating the pose called Contact)*

11. When you create a pose, it is saved for future use in that file. Now let's create the second pose, which is the down pose. It's where the leg comes into contact with the ground.

12. Once you are happy, create a new pose using the Copy Pose button and rename it to downpose.

13. Now let's move to the third reference, the pass pose. Repose the character accordingly and create another pose called the passpose.

14. We are going to work with these three poses. So, why didn't we create the fourth one? It's the exact opposite of the second one and we are going to use 3ds Max's built-in feature to create one for us.

15. The `BipedAnimation_poses01.max` file shows all these poses.

16. Now turn on Auto Key and go to frame 0.

17. Choose the contact pose from the list and click Paste Pose. Now your biped is going to get into that pose. Since our end frame 40 is the same pose, go to frame 40 and click Paste Pose again with contact pose selected. See Figure 5-20.

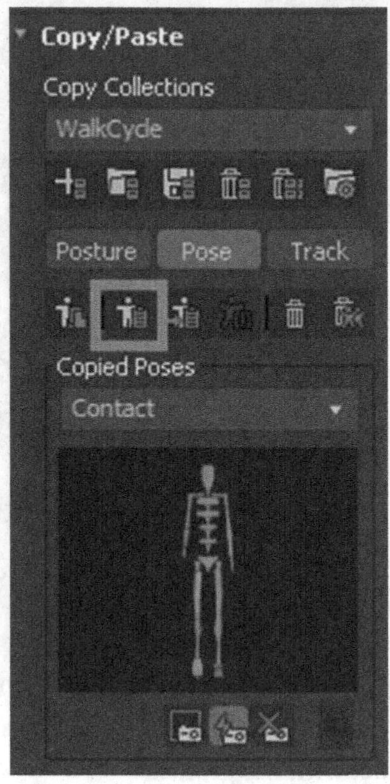

Figure 5-20. *Motion panel, Paste Pose*

18. Go to frame 10 and select the down pose. Choose Paste Pose.

19. Go to frame 20 and select the pass pose. Choose Paste Pose.

20. Go to frame 30 and select the down pose. Choose Paste Pose Opposite. See Figure 5-21.

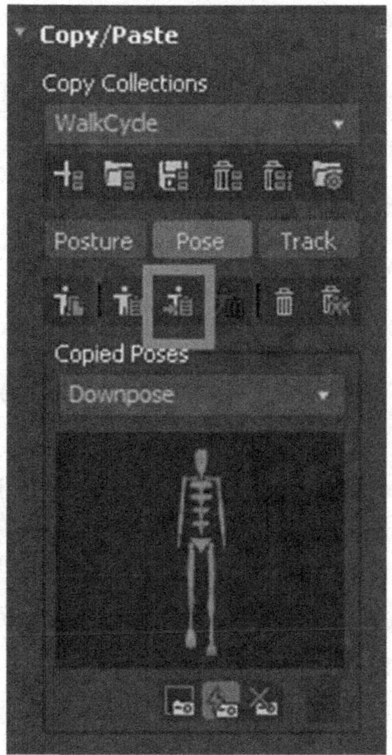

Figure 5-21. *Motion panel, Paste Pose Opposite*

So to summarize what we did:

- Frame 0 has a contact pose
- Frame 10 has a down pose
- Frame 20 has a pass pose
- Frame 30 has a pass pose (the pasted opposite)
- Frame 40 has a contact pose

Now play the animation to see the result. This is a rough block out animation. A completed file is in the `content` directory called `BipedAnimation_roughblock.max`.

So far we have learned to create and customize bipeds and use the character studio tools to make them walk, run, and jump. We also learned how to create an animation manually by creating keys. You might wonder if you use the biped animation from the Footstep mode to tweak the animation. Yes, you can, and that is what we are going to look at next.

Biped: Animation Layers

Let's use the power of layers to add more dynamic realism to a walking biped.

1. Create a new scene with a biped.
2. Get into Footstep mode.
3. Create a series of footsteps.
4. Apply the footsteps by creating keys for inactive footsteps.
5. Alternatively, you can load the `BipedAnimationLayers_Start.max` file.
6. Now let's say we want the biped to look around as it walks. Using the Set key, you can set the keyframes for the head; however, in most cases, this will result in weird, unpredictable movements. The right approach is to drop out of Footstep mode and then go into the Layers panel. See Figure 5-22.

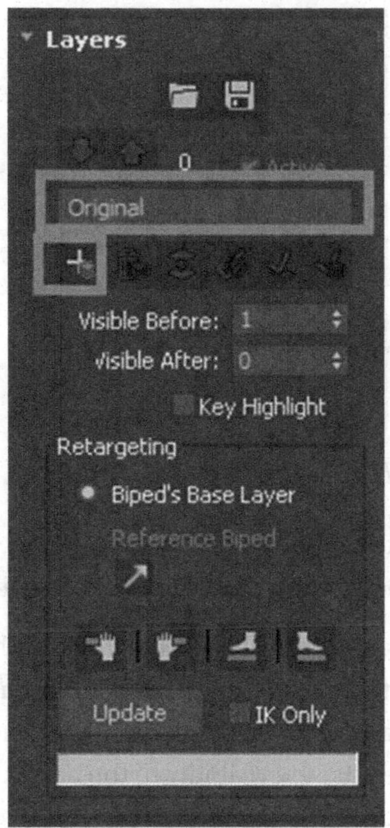

***Figure 5-22.** Motion panel, animation layers*

Note in Figure 5-22 that there is one layer by default, which is named original. This layer will have all the keys of the walk that we created.

7. Click on the Create layer and then click to rename it.

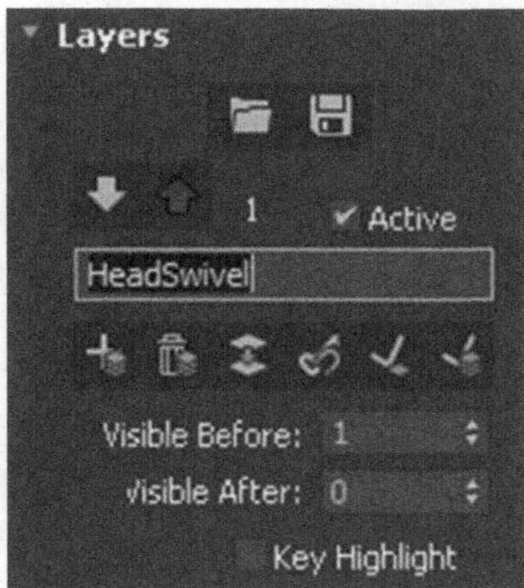

Figure 5-23. *Motion panel, Create Layer*

8. Now turn on auto key and tweak the parts as need. In this case, we will animate the head to turn around and look as it walks.

9. Now play the animation. You should see that the character looks around and walks, thereby merging two animations from two different layers. At any point if you do not want that layer, you can delete it. You can restrict the visibility of the animation from that layer by inputting keyframe numbers.

10. A reference file called `Biped_AnimationLayers_Complete.max` is available so that you can check the result.

Biped: Motion Flow

Motion flow is useful when you have multiple motion files saved and want to blend them so that the transition is smooth. In this exercise, I am going to use the bip files I saved using Footstep mode. There are a total of three bip files in the `content` directory; free to use any downloaded from the Internet to follow along.

1. Fire up 3ds Max.

2. Create a biped and tweak it your liking.

3. Click on Motion Flow mode, which is the icon next to Footstep mode. See Figure 5-24.

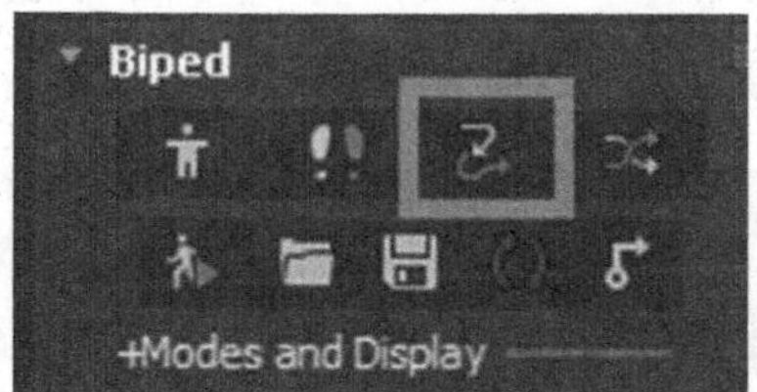

***Figure 5-24.** Biped, Motion Flow mode*

4. Now you should have only two rollouts—one is the biped and the other is the motion flow. Click on the Show graph in the motion flow rollout, as shown in Figure 5-25.

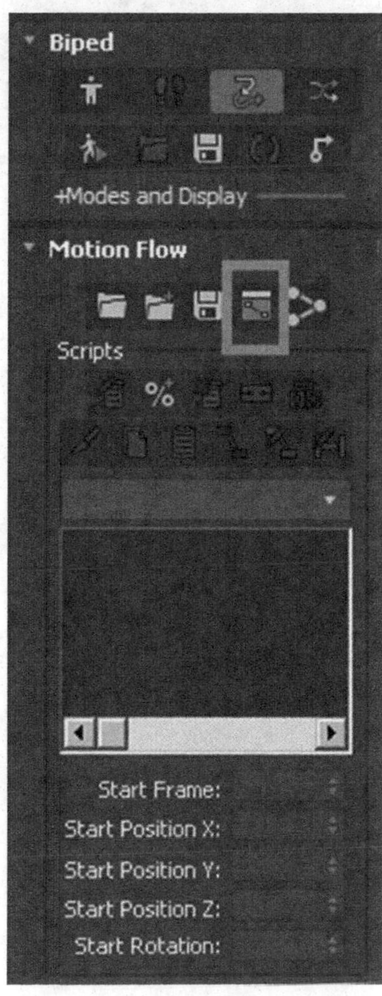

***Figure 5-25.** Motion Flow, Show Graph invoker*

5. The Motion Flow Graph will load, as shown in Figure 5-26.

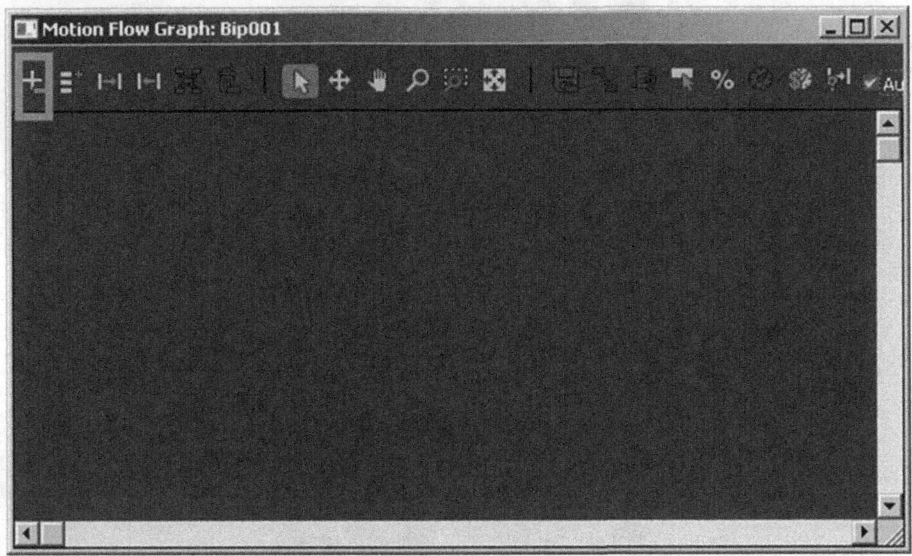

Figure 5-26. *An empty Motion Flow Graph*

6. In the Motion Flow Graph, click on the new clip. Click three times on the motion flow graph viewport to create three clips, as shown in Figure 5-27.

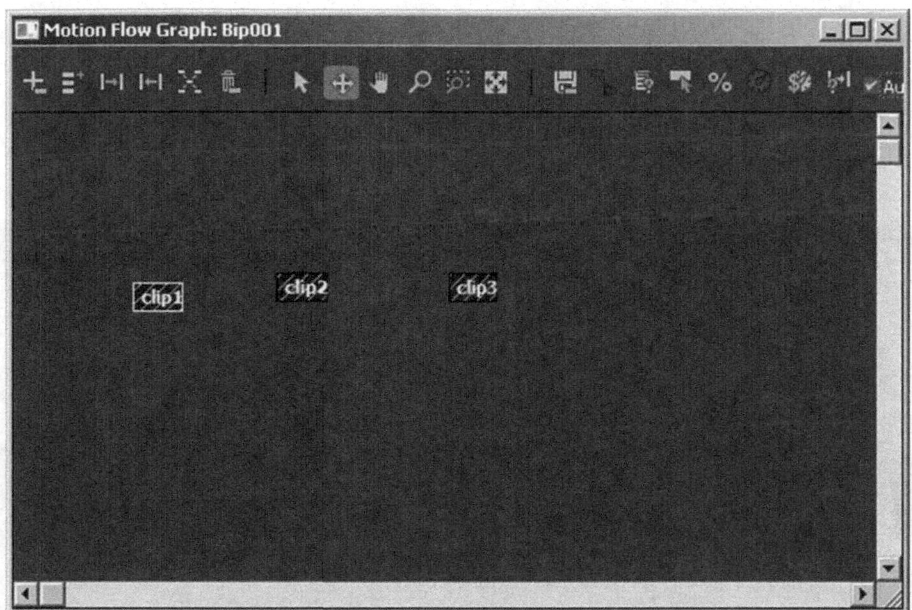

***Figure 5-27.** Motion Flow Graph with three clips*

7. Right-click on each clip and browse to the bip files provided in the `bip_motion` folder. Feel free to choose your own bip if you have any downloaded from the Internet. See Figure 5-28.

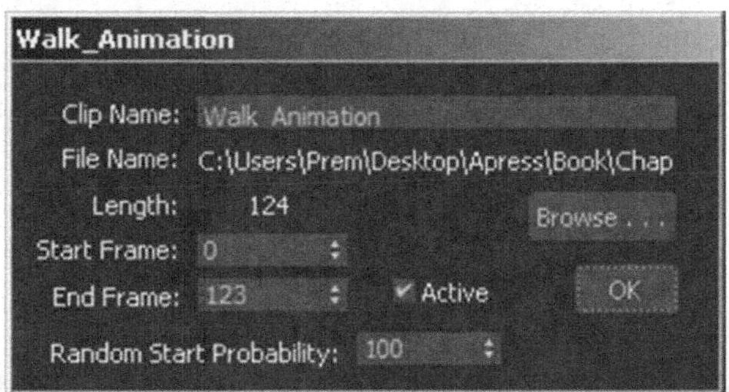

***Figure 5-28.** Clip loader*

Do the same thing until you have all three clips with the bip file loaded. The bip filename will replace the clip 1, 2, and 3 names.

8. Now click the Define Script button in the Scripts section of the Motion flow rollout. The Define Script is located below the show graph in the motion panel.

9. Feel free to rename it if you want to; I leave it at the default name.

10. Now, with the Motion Flow Graph Editor open, Click on the clips in the order you want them to animate. Your script interface should look similar to Figure 5-29.

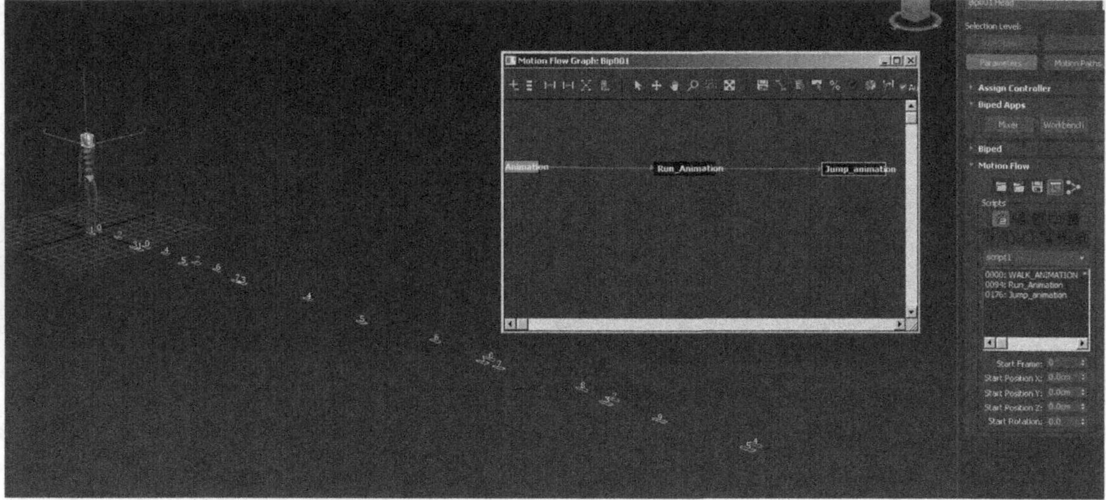

Figure 5-29. *Motion Flow 3ds Max UI*

11. Ensure that you have enough frames to play all the animations.

12. Note that transitions between the clips are seamless.

13. A completed file called `Biped_Motionflow.max` is provided in the `content` directory.

Summary

To summarize, we can create poses and convert poses to animation and save them to load them later and create transitions. The possibilities are limitless with these tools. Biped is far more powerful and capable than explained in this chapter, but this should get you started.

We haven't animated a character with the animation yet. We will look at attaching a character to the biped after we cover a few more tools. Practice and practice a lot until the animation "timing" and use of tools becomes second nature to you. This is the key to success! In the next chapter, we look at another tool, called the *character animation toolkit* or CAT, rigs (not the animal cat).

CHAPTER 6

CAT Rigging

In the previous chapters, we learned how to create a character rig using bones and bipeds. In this chapter, we look at using the improved animation toolkit known as CAT (the Character Animation Toolkit). We look at the tools and options available to aid in rigging a character. As in the chapter on bipeds, a preset character model will be provided along as 3ds Max scenes in the contents folder. Feel free to use any custom 3D model you have or download one and follow along. You can use Autodesk character generator to generate a character or use any other software that generates human characters. This chapter focuses on teaching you how to create and customize a CAT rig, and you will also learn to use the tools and options available for a CAT rig.

Understanding CAT Rig

The CAT toolkit allows you to create a comprehensive rigging system. The variations of rigs you can create are limited only by your creativity. You can have any number of heads, limbs, and tails for your characters. This is where it excels over the biped method. It is always good to understand how both function so you can choose the right tool for the job. Unlike with bipeds, you can create a CAT rig from scratch and build it as you need. However, let's first see how you can invoke the CAT rigging tool and look at the available presets.

Creating Your First CAT Rig

Fire up 3ds Max if you haven't already done so and go to the Create panel. Then go to the Helpers panel. In the Helpers menu, choose CAT Objects (see Figure 6-1).

P. Raju, *Character Rigging and Advanced Animation*, https://doi.org/10.1007/978-1-4842-5037-2_6

Figure 6-1. *Choose CAT Objects from the Helpers menu*

Once you choose CAT Objects, click on CATParent from the Object Type options (see Figure 6-2).

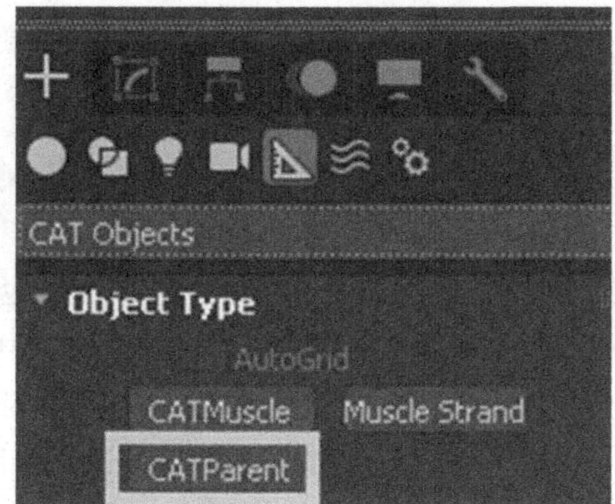

Figure 6-2. *CAT object types*

Once you choose CATParent, you will see a huge list of presets like alien, spider, angel, and so on (see Figure 6-3). For now, you can choose one to your liking and then click and drag it into the viewport.

The presets include a familiar looking biped named Bip01. Try these out to see what rig presets are available.

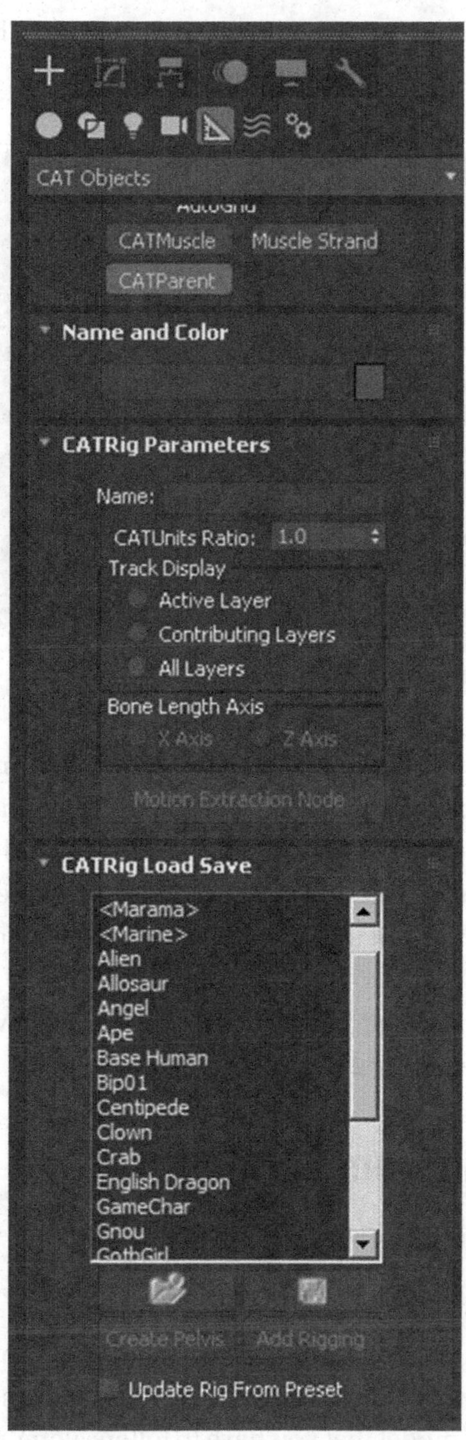

***Figure 6-3.** CAT rig presets*

Alternatively, you can load the CAT_Rig_presets.max file. This file has all the CAT rig presets created in a single file for reference (see Figure 6-4).

Figure 6-4. *CAT rig variations*

You can use these rigs as a starting point if it suits the anatomy of your model. Reset 3ds Max for a fresh file and create a CAT rig type of Base Human.

Now with the Base Human CAT rig created, go into the Modify rollout from the control panel on the right side and select the triangle that you see in the bottom of the rig. This triangle is a helper object that will allow you to reposition and reorient the rig as needed.

With the base triangle selected, in the modify options, you will be able to name your character and adjust its size using the CAT Unit Ratio.

Creating a CAT Rig from Scratch

In this section, we are going to create a custom rig.

1. Fire up 3ds Max.
2. Load Human_Start.max from the source folder. You should see a human character. I created this character using makehuman; you can use another model that you have to follow along.

3. We are going to create a rig for this character and not use the available presets.

4. Since the character is going to be a reference for us at this point, select the character model and press ALT+X to turn on Xray mode. Then right-click on the model and freeze it. This way you will be able to see the model but not select or move it. (See the `Human_Start_1.max` file.)

5. Go to the command panel and choose Create ➤ Helpers ➤ CAT Object.

6. Choose CATParent and ensure that None is selected in the preset. (We want to create a rig from scratch.)

7. Now click and drag in the viewport and you should notice that only the triangle helper is created. (Let's reference this part as rig_controller going forward instead of calling it a blue triangle.) When you are happy with the size, right-click to complete creation mode. (If you are using a custom model that you downloaded or created using other apps, ensure that the triangle and character are facing the same direction.) See Figure 6-5.

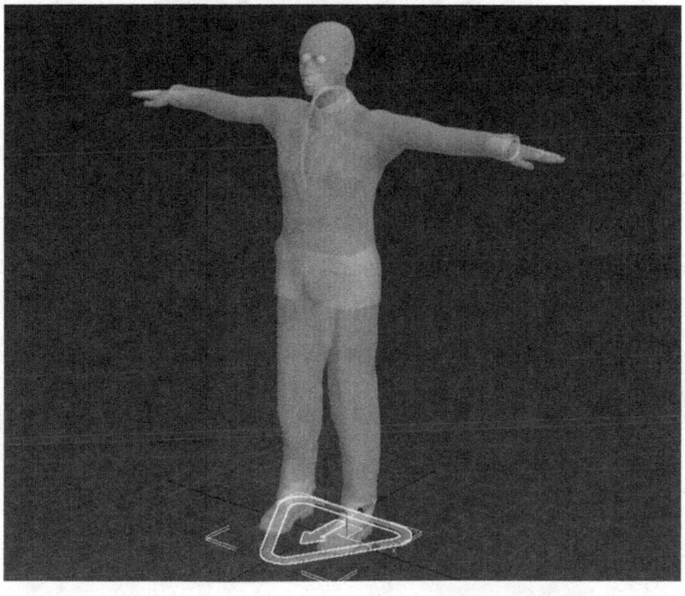

Figure 6-5. *Rig_Controller facing the direction of the model*

8. Go to Modify ➤ CATRig Parameters and give it a name. I call it `CustomRig`.

9. Reposition your `CustomRig` (the triangle helper) to 0, 0, and 0. You can select any object and, with the Move tool selected, press F12 to get the Move Transform dialog. In the Absolute world, type in 0, 0, 0. Alternatively, you can use the X Y Z input below the time slider to input the values.

10. Now with the CustomRig selected, click on Create Pelvis, as shown in Figure 6-6.

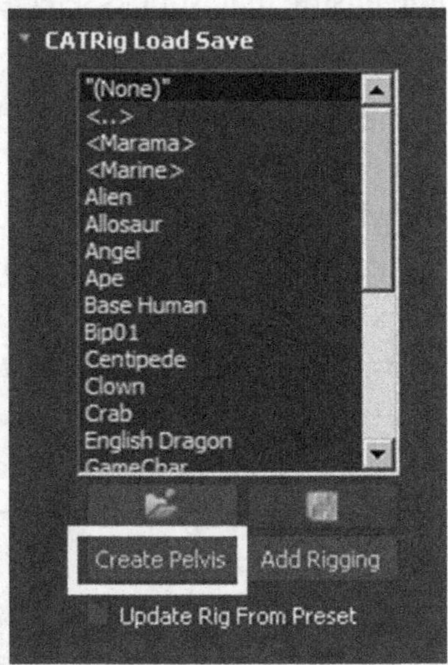

***Figure 6-6.** CAT rig, Create Pelvis option*

11. A new object called hub001 is created. Rename it `pelvis` by selecting it and going to the Modify tab to rename it. You can use the input parameters to tweak it or use the transform tools. See Figure 6-7.

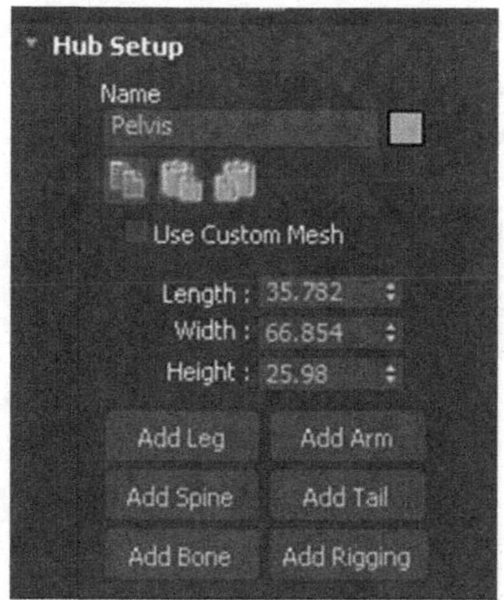

Figure 6-7. *CAT rig, Pelvis*

12. Now select the newly created pelvis and position it at the pelvis area of the 3D model. Feel free to reposition, reorient, and scale the pelvis mesh that was created to better suit the character's model.

13. Now with the pelvis selected, click on the Add Leg button, and you will have a leg created with ankle and feet. Again reorient the parts of the leg to match the geometry in all views. (In cases where your model is a dog, tiger, or any other quadruped, you can select the thigh bone and choose how many joints it has.) Refinement and absolute positioning is more important here, because the better the parts are aligned and oriented to the model, the easier the process of skinning will be. Also it is good practice to scale your bones to match the overlapping mesh for skinning purposes. This can be done later as well.

14. Select your character rig pelvis again and add a leg. It adds the leg with the transformations and rotations and scales on the other side automatically.

15. At any point, if you make a mistake, you can select a root bone and delete all its children bones.

16. If your foot bone requires toes, select the feet and change the number in Num Digits. For this exercise, we don't need toe bones, as our character is wearing shoes (see Figure 6-8).

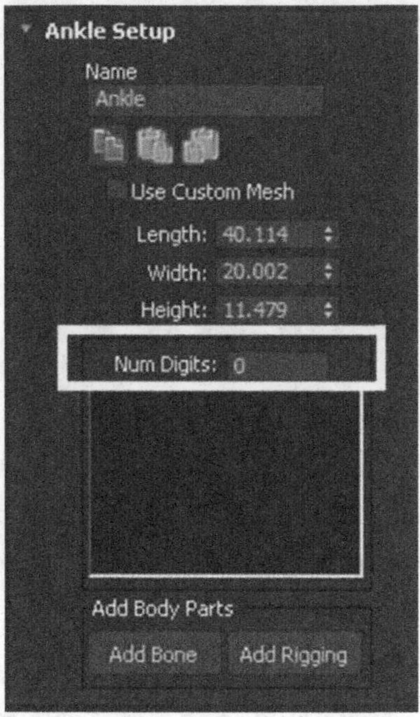

Figure 6-8. *CAT rig toe setup*

17. Let's move on to the spine area. Select the pelvis and add a spine.

18. Select the topmost part of the spine that is created and move and position it. The spines are not always straight up, so rotate and reposition them as needed. See Figure 6-9.

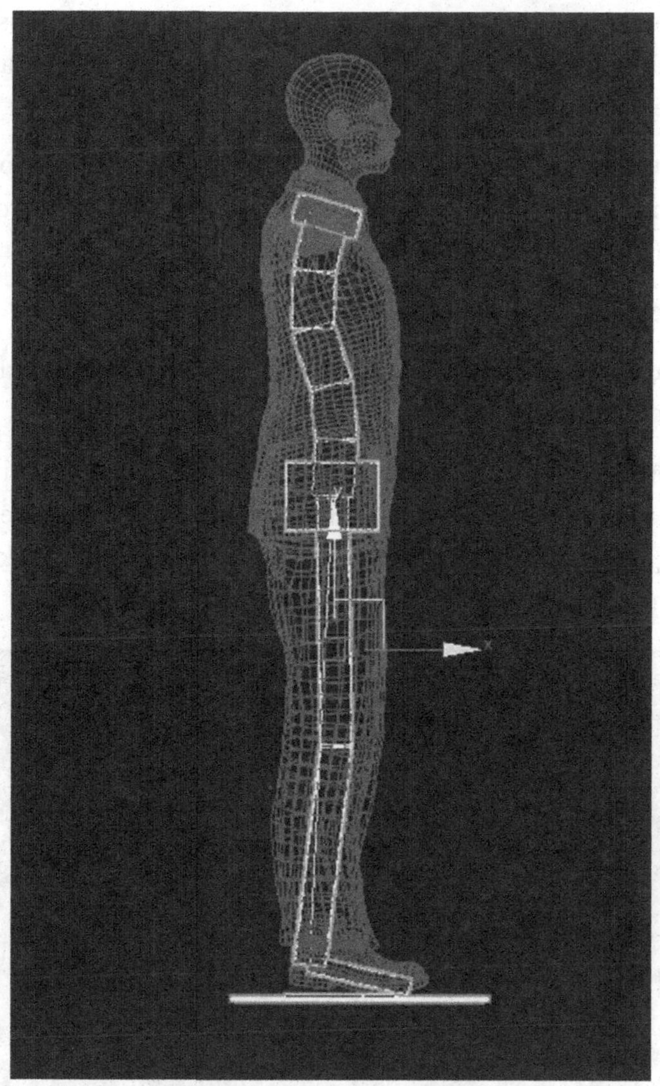

Figure 6-9. *CAT rig, spine setup*

19. With the top of the spine selected, go into Modify and click on Add Arm. Once the arm has been added, reposition, reorient, and scale it as needed, so that the arm fits inside the model perfectly.

Note If you double-click on any part of a rig, you can automatically select all the child rig parts associated with it.

---

20. If you need fingers, select the palm of the character and choose the number of digits (similar to leg toes). Ensure that you position the fingers in the right position.

21. Once you have positioned the parts of the arm correctly, choose the top part of the spine and click Add Arm. This should mirror it exactly. (See the `Human_Start_3.max` file.)

22. Now select the top part of the spine and rename it `Torso`.

23. Select the torso and choose Add Spine (this will serve as the rig's neck and head).

24. Select the start of the spine and choose the number of segments you want for the neck spine. Ideally, you should have one for the neck and one for head. In this exercise, I used three: two for the neck and one as the connector for the head and neck. See Figure 6-10.

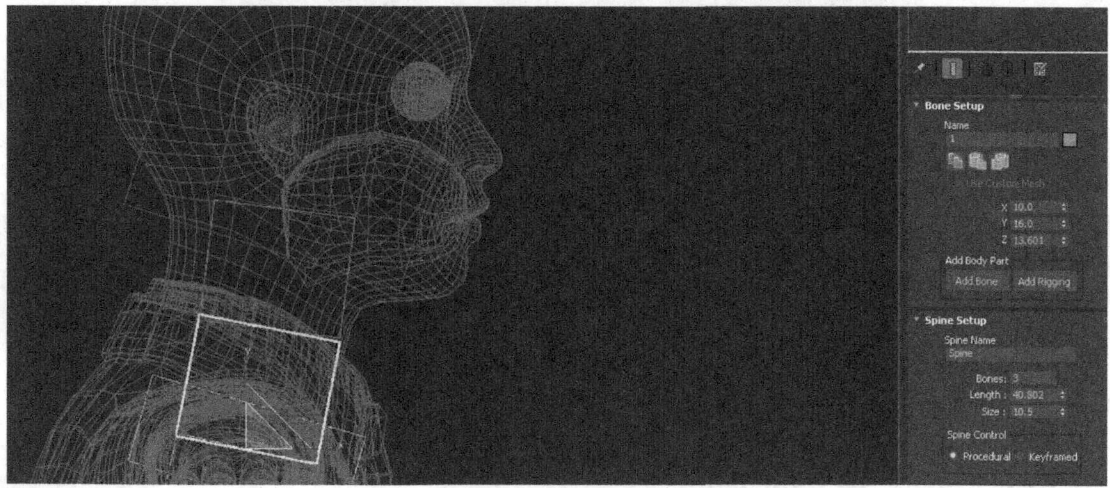

Figure 6-10. *CAT rig, neck and head setup*

25. Tweak the rig parts to cover the mesh as much as possible. This helps during the skinning process.

We have created a human rig entirely from scratch using rig parts. At this point, I recommend you reset 3ds Max and load the preset rigs and then analyze each part to understand how it's used to create an entirely different type of rig. There are cases where you need extra rig parts, so feel free to select a part and click Add Bone. (Reposition and reorient as needed.)

Saving and Loading a CAT Rig

Load 3ds Max and open the Human_Start_4.max file. In this section, let's look at saving the custom rig that we created for future use.

1. Open Human_Start_4.max.
2. Select the rig_controller (the triangle at the bottom).
3. Go into the modify options in the control panel and choose the Save icon. You can save the rig in .rg3 format. See Figure 6-11.

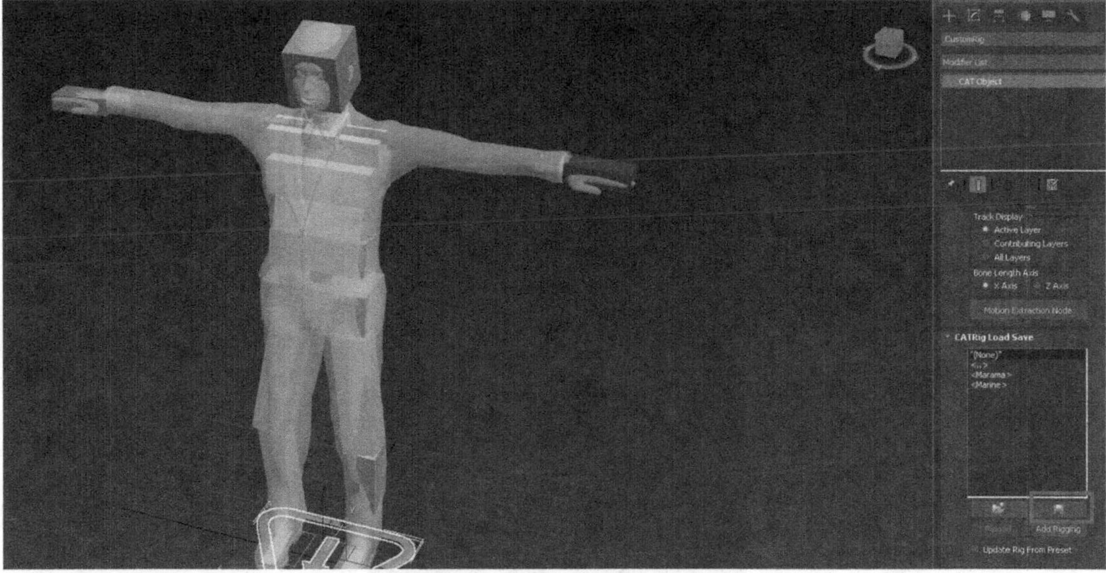

Figure 6-11. *Saving a CAT rig*

4. Your rig is saved for future use. You don't need to recreate it all over again.

Let's look at how we load a rig.

1. Reset 3ds Max.
2. Create a CAT parent with None as the type.
3. Select the triangle root of the rig.
4. In the modify options, click on Load and choose the rig. (The icon next to the Save Rig option.)
5. A rig named human_ch6.rg3 is provided in the rig folder.

CAT Rig Layers

Create a new scene in 3ds Max and create a Base Human rig. Customize it to your liking. Once you're done, go into the motion panel.

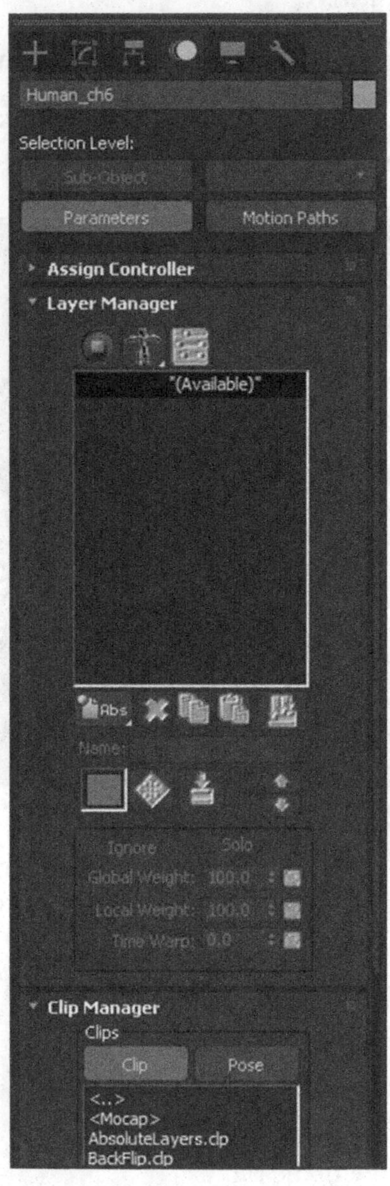

Figure 6-12. *CAT rig Layer Manager*

Note in Figure 6-12 the red icon in the Layer Manager. This is the default for all rigs, which means that you are in setup mode and the rig is being prepped. To begin animating this rig, we need an animation layer to be active.

Figure 6-13. *CAT rig layer types*

When you click on the fly-out of layers, as shown in Figure 6-13, you will see four layers types. They are discussed next.

Absolute Layer

The Absolute layer is the basic animation layer used for keyframe animation. Note that this layer will override any other layers below it.

1. Clicking on this option creates an absolute layer. Once the absolute layer is created, you can click on the red icon, the setup icon, and toggle it to animation mode. Animation mode is indicated by a green play icon. See Figure 6-14.

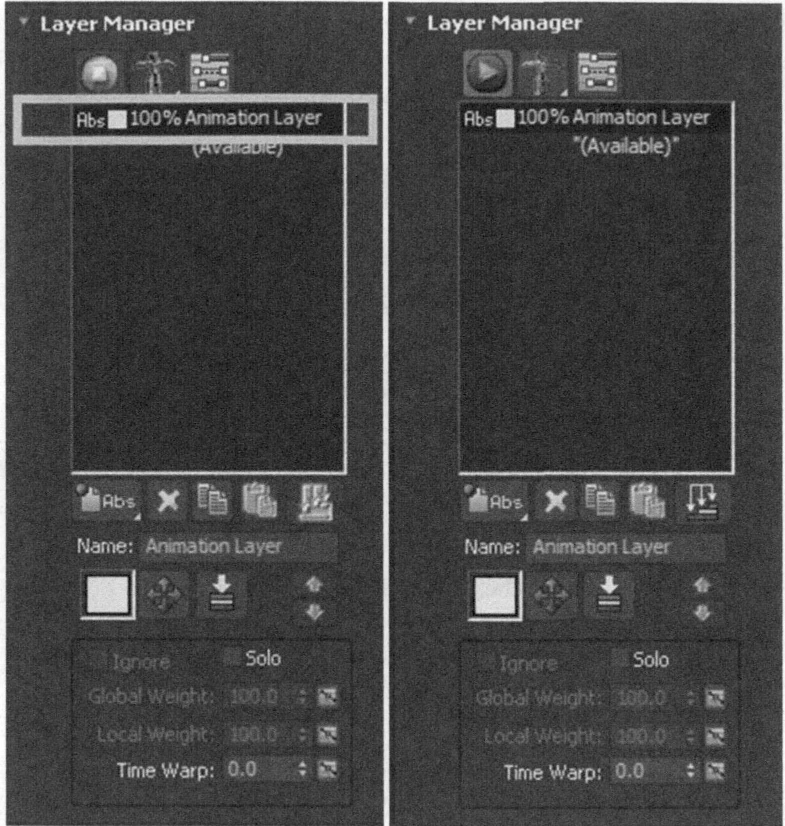

***Figure 6-14.** CAT rig, animation/setup mode*

2. Now select the pelvis and turn on auto key.
3. Move to frame 25 and bring the pelvis down in the Y axis. Move to frame 50 and move it up at 75, down again, and up at 100 (similar to a squat animation).
4. Now click on the Absolute layer once more and add another layer. To avoid confusion, let's name the layers SquatAnimation and HeadAnimation, respectively, in order of creation. See Figure 6-15.

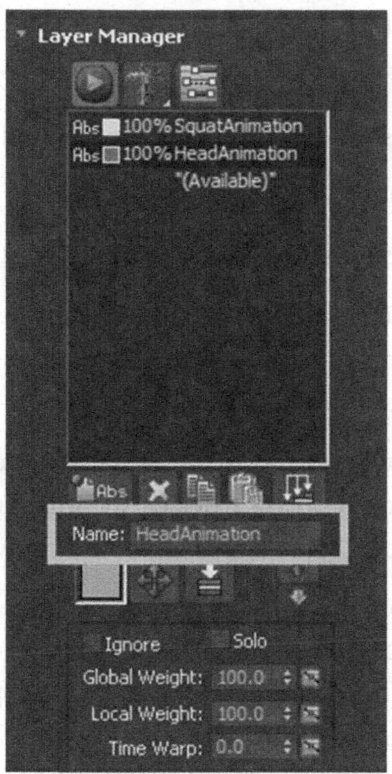

Figure 6-15. *CAT rig, layer rename*

5. Now choose the newly created layer called HeadAnimation and, with auto key on, make it look left and right or up and down, based on your preference.

6. If you play this back, you'll notice only one animation is playing. In the Global Weight, choose 50%. Now you should be able to see a blend of animation between the layers. Note that these values can be animated. You can animate the parts in individual layers or in one layer. By animating them as individual layers you have control over how one layer blends with the other.

7. A point to remember is that when there is more than one absolute layer, the top layer will play the animation and the other layers can be blended with the global and local weights.

Local and World Layers

The local layer is often known as the *adjustment layer.* Reset 3ds Max and create a new CAT rig. For this purpose, let's use the Human rig we created in an earlier section.

1. Alternatively, load `CAT_AdjustmentLayer.max`.
2. Select the triangle base and go into the motion options.
3. Go to the Clip Manager rollout and choose Browse for Motion Capture Files. We are going to use the bip motions that we created in the bipeds chapter. CAT rigs support them.
4. Go to the Tools menu and choose Measure Distance. You need to find the height of your CAT rig. Click on the top of the head and the bottom of the feet. Your status bar should show the distance.
5. Browse to the the bip motions in your source folder and load `Jump_Animation.bip` (If you can't see the file, ensure that the file type is set to bip in the Open dialog box.) I use `Jump_Animation.bip` for this exercise. See Figure 6-16.

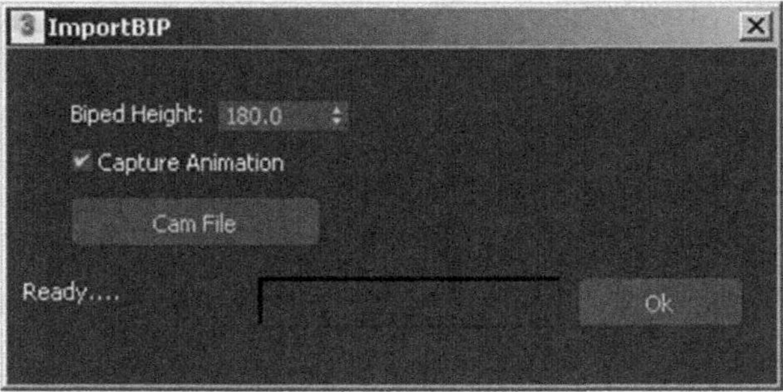

Figure 6-16. *CAT rig, import a bip*

6. Input your height. In my case, it was 180, so I input that value in the Biped Height and click OK.
7. Your biped will be imported and your CAT rig will follow the biped motion, as shown in Figure 6-17.

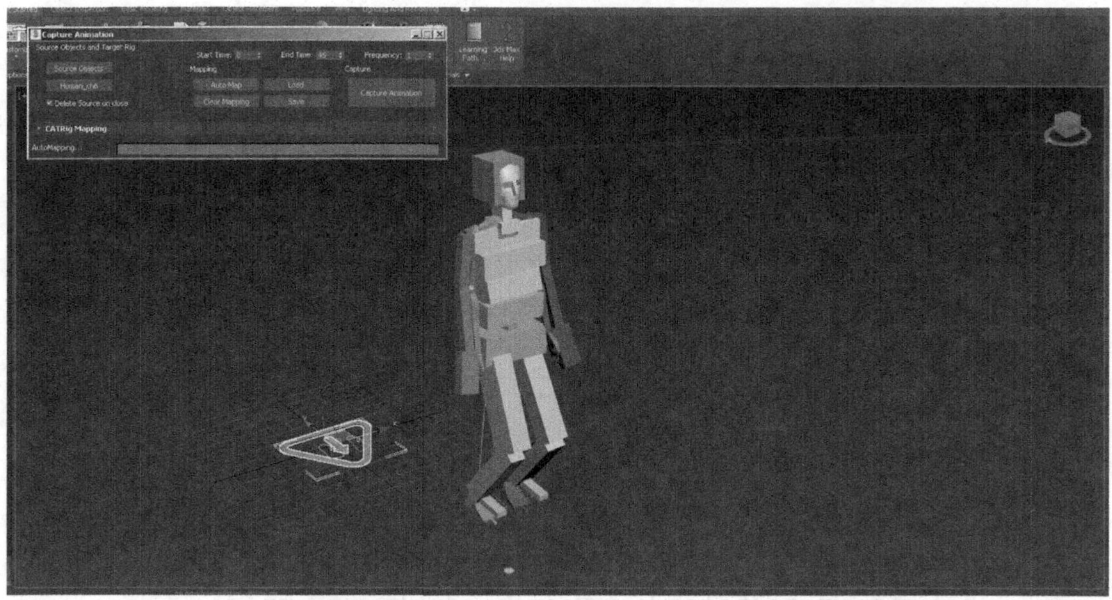

***Figure 6-17.** CAT rig imported animation*

8. Click on Capture Animation. This will bake the animation to the CAT rig. You might get a popup like the one shown in Figure 6-18.

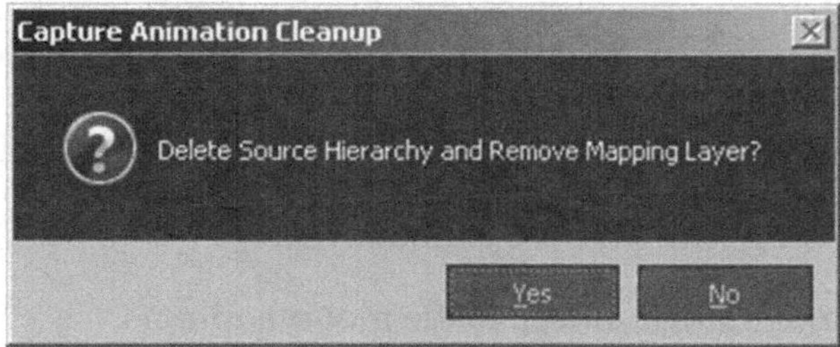

***Figure 6-18.** Capture Animation Cleanup dialog*

9. Click Yes. This is going to remove the bip and its supporting layers after baking the animation to the CAT rig.
10. Load the reference file called `CAT_AdjustmentLayer1.max`.
11. Scrub. You won't see the biped anymore, but your CAT rig still has the animation.

12. Select any part of the rig and go into the motion panel. Select the animation layer. You should see that many keyframes are created when you captured the animation from your biped.
13. In the motion panel, add a World adjustment layer. It has a layer icon of **[+W]** in the Layer Manager.

Note Adding a World adjustment layer does not affect the animation like with a Local adjustment layer.

---

14. With the adjustment layer selected, you can overlay tweaks to your motion that were already keyed and the rig will compensate too.

    In the reference file called `CAT Adjustmentlayer2.max`, I spread the legs apart and the hands rotate in the adjustment layer. See how it seamlessly fits along in the animation. Playing with the adjustment layer Global Weight is interesting as well. We can observe the adjustment of the weight in action.

CAT Motion Layer

Let's look at the last layer type—the CAT motion layer. Reset 3ds Max and create a CAT rig. Let's use Base Human for this exercise.

1. Create a CAT rig with the Base Human type.
2. Select the root triangle and go to the motion options.
3. In the layer type, create a CAT Motion layer (it's the last layer type in the layer manager and is denoted by a running icon). Enable Animation mode by clicking on the Setup/Animation mode toggle button.
4. If you play the animation, you will see the CAT rig is doing a walk animation.
5. In order to tweak the animation, click on the motion editor icon, as shown in Figure 6-19.

Figure 6-19. *CAT motion editor icon*

The CAT motion editor allows us to tweak the walk in an organized way. See Figure 6-20.

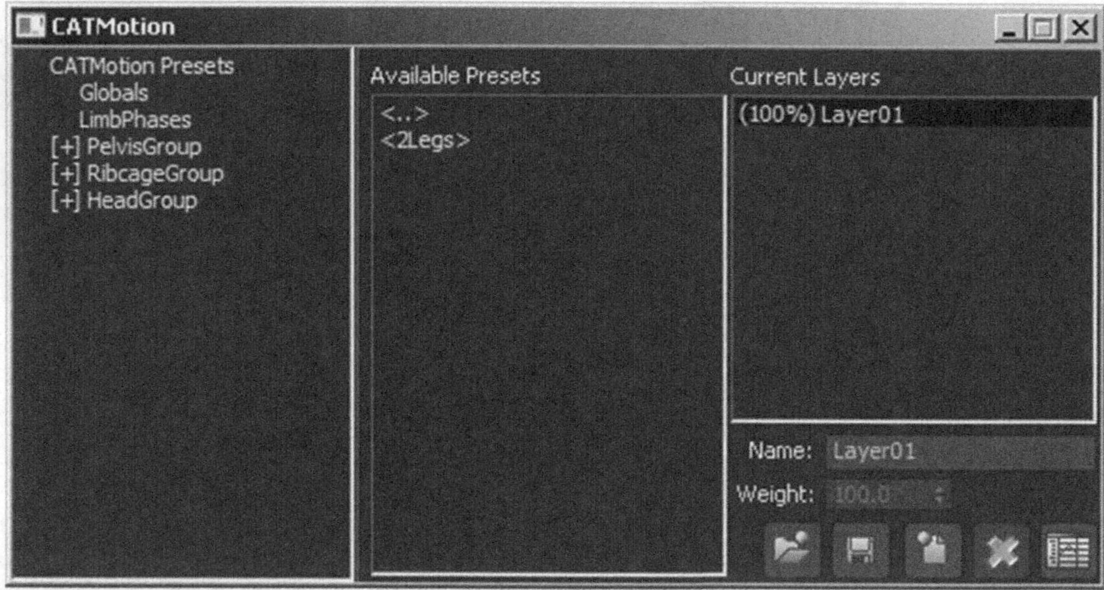

***Figure 6-20.** The CAT motion editor*

6. In the CAT motion popup window, the left panel lists the structure of your CAT rig.

7. Let's select the head and expand the HeadGroup, as shown in Figure 6-21. The head has all these animations.

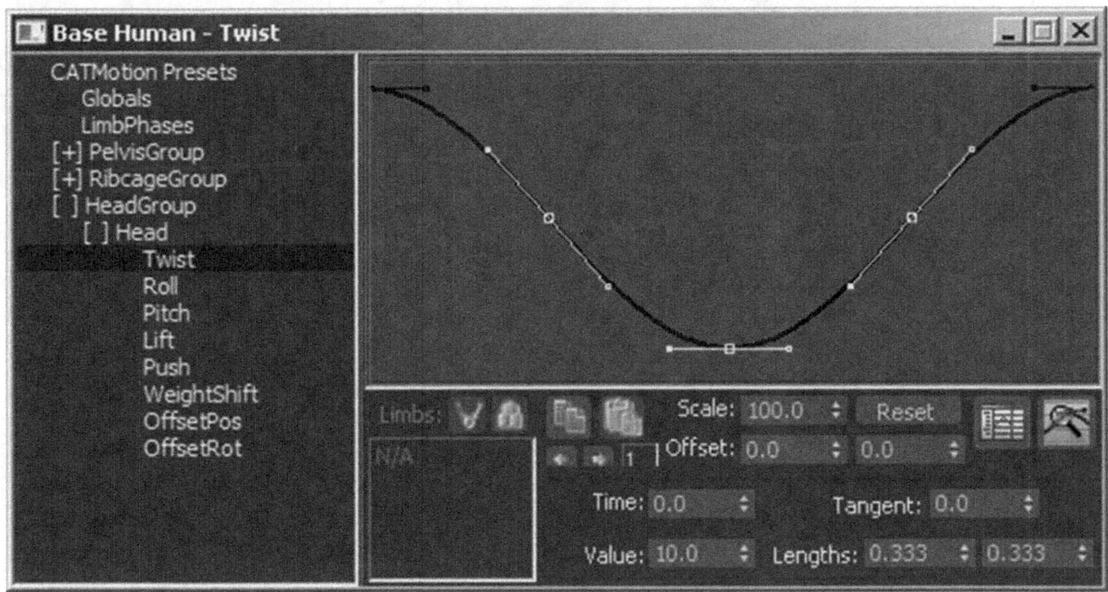

Figure 6-21. *CAT motion, head twist curve*

8. Select the twist and check out the graph on the right. CAT provides the functionality to edit during playback.
9. Play the animation and change the scale of head twist from 100 to 25, or increase it to extremes to see the preview.
10. This is a powerful tool and there are no precise values. It varies based on the rig and type of animation you want. Play around and tweak as needed until you are happy with the results.
11. Note that the CAT_Rig is walking in place; this is often called *in-place animation.*
12. In order to have the CAT rig move in the 3D space as it walks, you must go to Globals in the left pane of the CAT motion editor (see Figure 6-22).

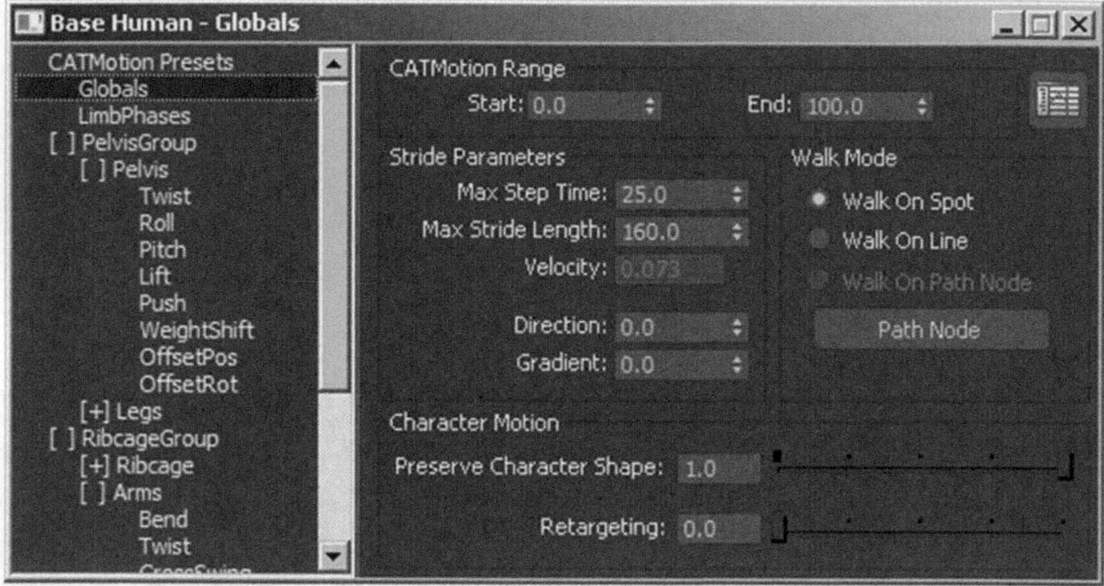

Figure 6-22. *CAT motion, Globals*

- Start and End determine when the walk begins and ends.
- The Max Step Time, when set to a lower value, makes the character move faster.
- Max Stride Length determines the distance between each step. The higher the number the longer the step.
- Walk In Line allows the character to move forward as it walks.
- Walk on Path enables the path node and allows you to select a path.
- The walk direction is determined by these settings:
  - 0 means the character moves forward
  - 90 means the character strafes to the left
  - -90 means the character strafes to the right (Think of it as a circle of 360 degrees, so 0 is forward and so on... If you input a 45, you will notice the character move diagonally.)
- A gradient of 0 means the character moves parallel to the ground. A positive value will make it climb up a hill and a negative value will make it climb down a slope.

This is a powerful tool and is very useful when used creatively. You can combine this animation with a World adjustment layer to get variations; the possibilities are limitless.

CAT Rig: Motion Path

In this section, we set up our CAT rig to follow a path.

1. Fire up 3ds Max and create a Base Human CAT rig.
2. From the Create panel, create a path using the Line tool in the top viewport.
3. Let's also create a helper to aid us. Create a standard dummy from the Helper section.
4. Position the newly created dummy at the beginning of path. With the dummy selected, go to Constraints and choose the Path constraint. Then choose the path.
5. Select the Rig_Controller of the CAT rig (the triangle at the base of the CAT rig) and go to the motion options.
6. Create a CAT motion layer and open the CAT motion editor. Ensure that you have animation mode in the Setup/Animation mode of the layer manager in order to see the preview of the animation as you tweak its values.
7. Enable Follow mode in the motion options panel of the dummy so that the dummy orients itself toward the path.
8. Now go to your CAT motion editor and, in the Globals, choose Walk On Path Node and choose the dummy helper.
9. You might notice that the character is in the wrong axis now, but it walks on the path. A simple fix would be to reorient the dummy in Local mode (Local mode can be chosen from the ribbon toolbar). The CAT rig will reorient itself. You might need to animate the dummy's orientation so that the CAT rig faces the direction it is walking.

10. Tweaking the path will force the CAT rig to follow the dummy, which is constrained to the path.

11. The reference file called `CAT_Motionpath_Complete.max` is available for your reference.

Summary

In this chapter, we learned about the different types of CAT rigs that are available. We also learned how to create a CAT rig entirely from scratch, as well as about the various animation layer types and how they can aid us in blending multiple animations. We took the CAT rigs a step further by looking at how at how we can load motion clips created from bipeds into CAT rigs and create procedural animation using the CAT motion editor. In the next chapter, we will look at binding our mesh to the rigs we created. This process is called *skinning*.

CHAPTER 7

Skinning for Animation

In Chapters 4, 5, and 6, we learned how to create character rigs using Bones, Bipeds, and CAT rigs. In the Bones chapter, we also looked at using wire parameters and reaction managers to create varied animations of human body. We also learned to drive the bones using IK and FK tools. In this chapter, we look at binding our rigs that we created in earlier chapters to the character model. This way, any animation done to the rig will deform the mesh accordingly. This technique is called *skinning*. In the following sections, you will not only learn how to skin your bones, bipeds, and CAT rigs, but also how to weigh them to get the right deformations.

Skinning

The process of binding the bones, bipeds, or CAT rigs to a mesh so that it deforms accordingly is called skinning. We will be looking at two modifiers that allow us bind our character mesh to the rigs we created in earlier chapters. The modifiers are Skin and Physique. Note that there are other third-party modifiers available as well and there are a lot of third-party plugins that ease the process of skinning.

Skinning Bones

In this section, we will use a modifier called Skin to bind our rig to a character mesh.

1. Load `Human_Rigged_Bones.max` from the scene files folder of Chapter 7. This rig was created from the techniques we learned in Chapter 4. At this point, I would like you to take some time and analyze the rig to see how it was created. I summarized a few points just to recap:

    - IK chain for arms and legs

P. Raju, *Character Rigging and Advanced Animation*, https://doi.org/10.1007/978-1-4842-5037-2_7

- Helpers for leg to get heel and tip toe animations: Orientation and position constraints and knee controller for knee orientation
- Helpers for arm to get wrist rotation and position: Orientation and position constraints.
- Fingers set with orientation constraint and wire parameters with reaction manager for curl animation.
- Spine to head: Orientation and position constraints.
- All the controllers have freeze transform applied so that they can be reset using transform to zero in the Alt+right-click menu. Experiment by moving the controls and see how the bones have been set up.

2. Open the Layer Explorer by going to Tools ➤ All Global Explorers ➤ Layer Explorer. Alternatively, you can load the Scene Explorer from Tools ➤ All Global Explorer ➤ Scene Explorer and the toggle Sort by Layers in the Scene Explorer.

    - We have three layers—the default, bones, and the meshes layers.
    - Enable the visibility flag and unfreeze the mesh so that it can be selected from the Scene Explorer or Layer Explorer.
    - Selecting the character model in viewport and pressing Alt+X will show textures, but for now let's work in see through mode. If you can see textures/color on the model, press Alt+X. You should see something like Figure 7-1.

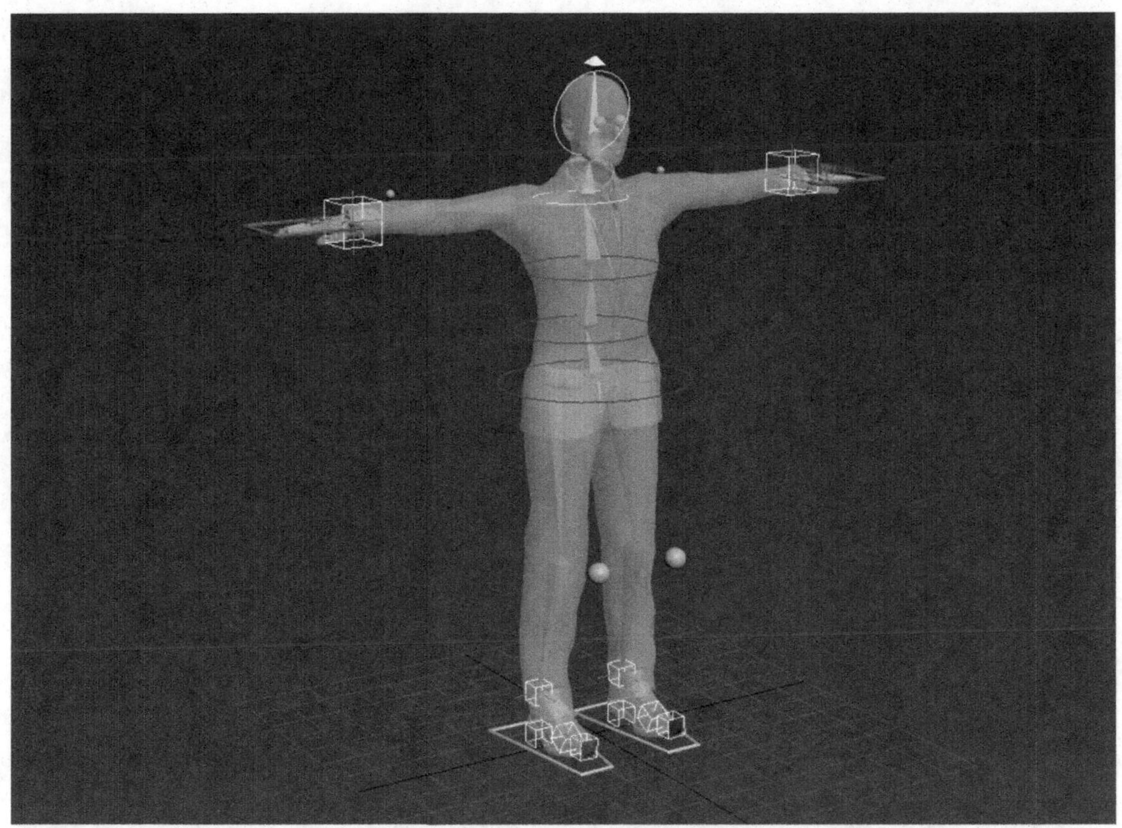

Figure 7-1. *Character in see through mode with the Bones rig*

3. Unfreeze the character from the Layer Explorer or Scene Explorer and add the Skin Modifier from the Modifier panel. Be sure to add the Skin Modifier to the character mesh and not the bones or controllers. See Figure 7-2.

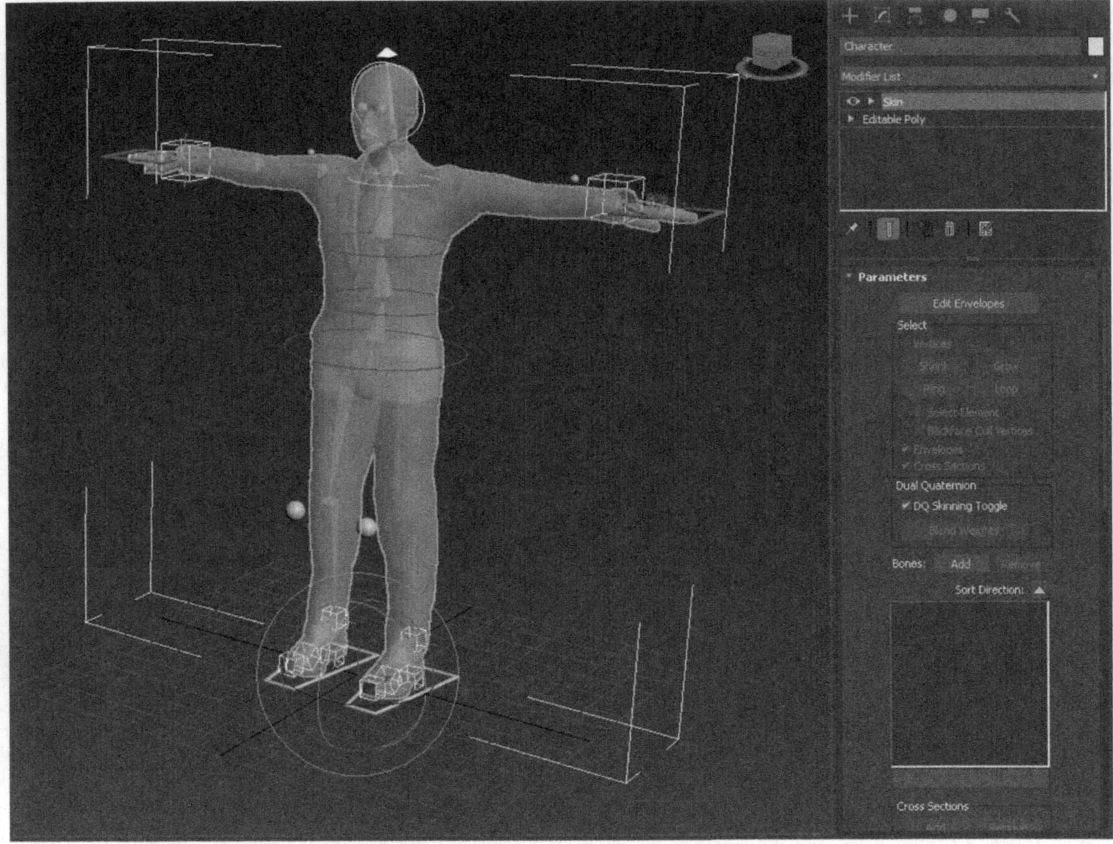

Figure 7-2. *Character with Skin Modifier applied*

4. Select the character's Skin Modifier. You should see that its parameters have a lot of options. We need to add our bones to the Skin Modifier.

5. If you look at the Skin Modifier, there is a Bones ➤ Add option.

6. Clicking on the Add option brings up a dialog box that shows all our controllers and bones. We need to select our bones alone from the list. It's not impossible but it's tedious to sort through the hierarchy and toggle the visibility flags to get the bones alone. Refer to Figure 7-3.

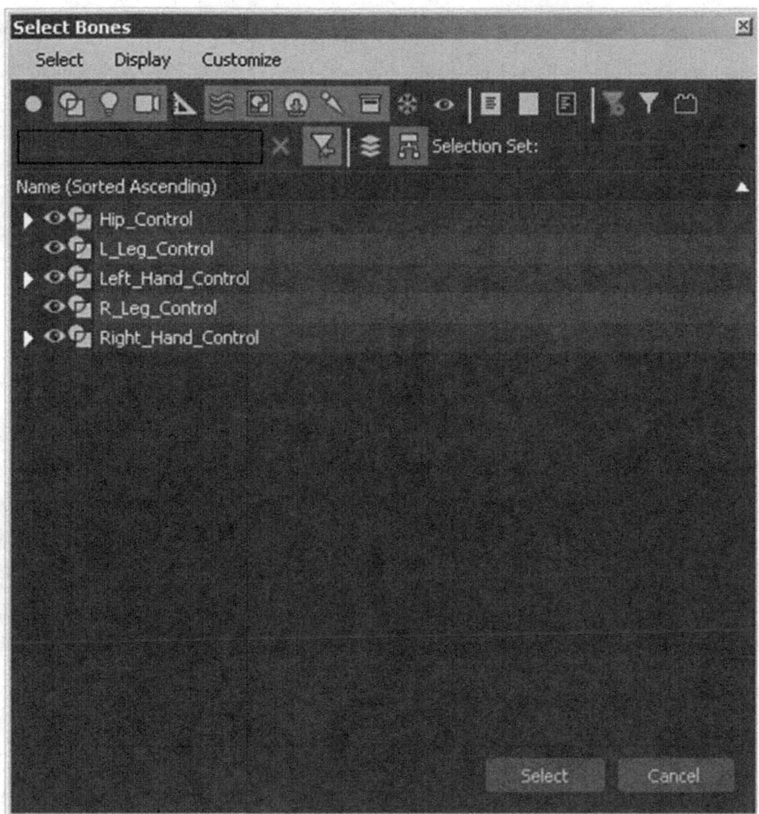

Figure 7-3. *Select Bones dialog*

7. You can choose bones this way, but I will show you an alternative way. Close the Select Bones dialog box.

8. Select the hip_bone and double-click on it. This will select all the bones. At this point, you should deselect the end bones of the arms, legs, and head, because we don't want the end bones to influence the mesh.

9. In the main toolbar you should see a Create Selection Set combo box (see Figure 7-3). Select it and give it a name. I named it Bones_Selection for this example.

10. Once you give a name and press Enter, you can deselect the bones by clicking anywhere in the viewport.

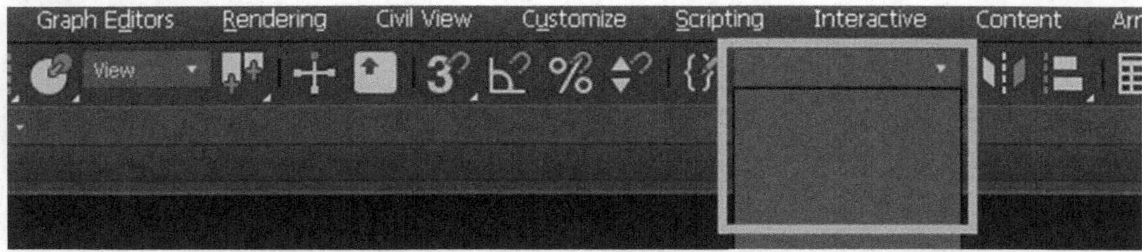

Figure 7-4. *Selection set, empty list*

Figure 7-4 shows no selection sets created and Figure 7-5 shows that the Bones_Selection has been created.

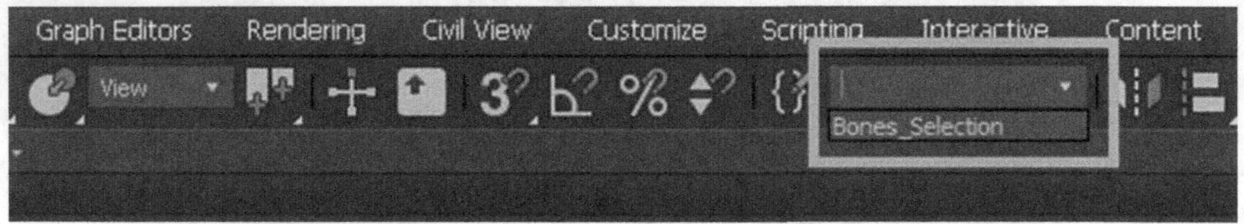

Figure 7-5. *Selection set with a selection list*

11. Now with the selection set created, let's select our character mesh and go to the Skin Modifier and click the Add button again. This time in the toolbar of the Select Bones dialog, you can choose Bones_Selection that we just created. Refer to Figure 7-6.

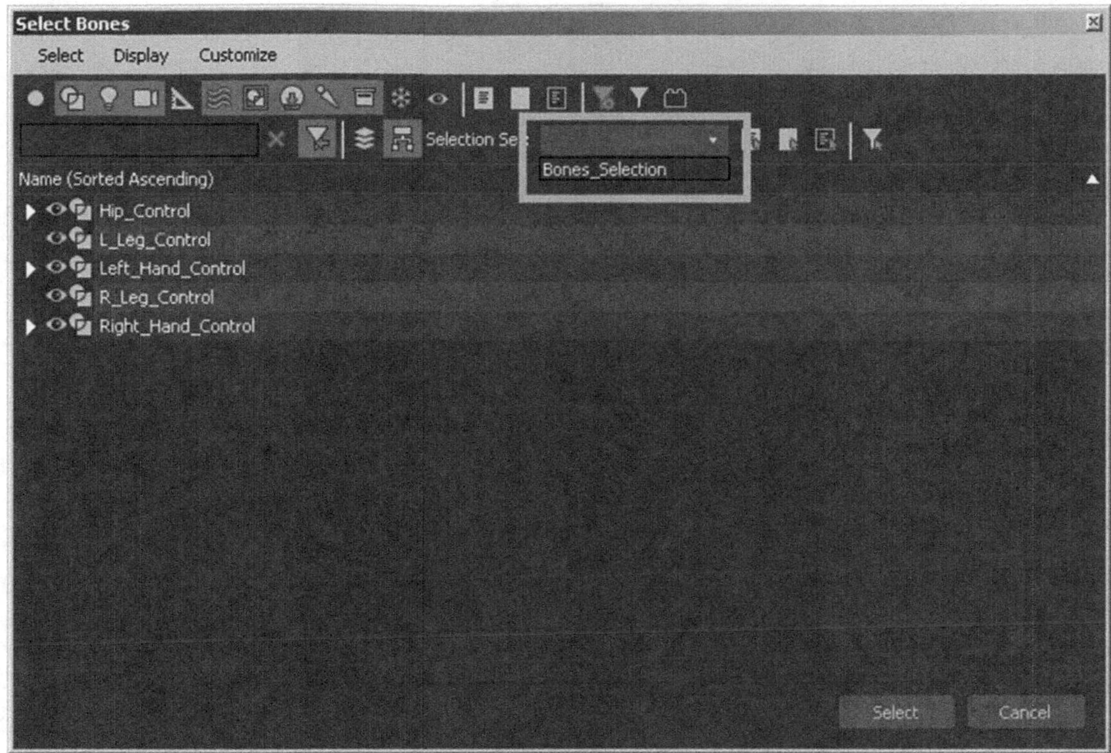

Figure 7-6. *Select Bones from the selection list*

12. Choosing Bones_Selection will cause all the bones in your selection set to be selected. Click on Select.

13. Note how the Skin Modifier lists all the bones and the Remove button is available now. If you want to remove an end bone you can select it from the list and click on Remove. Or if you missed any bone earlier, you can add it using the Add option. In this example, the end bones are still in the list, so we can select them and click the Remove button to remove them.

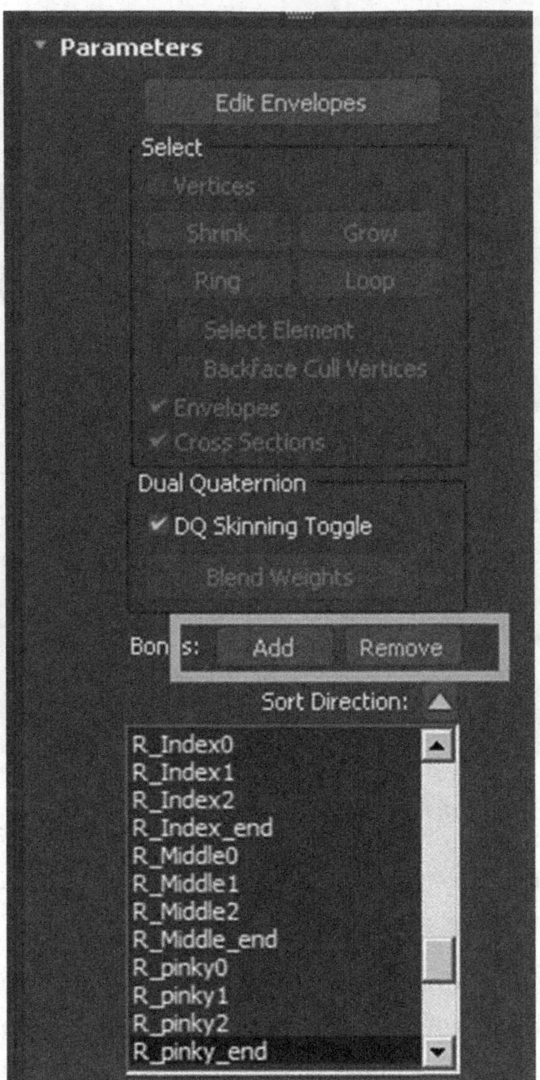

Figure 7-7. *Adding and removing bones*

14. With these steps done, the character mesh is bound to all our bones that we selected.

15. Play around by moving and rotating the hand and leg controllers to see how the character moves. You might notice that our mesh is not moving naturally in places like the pelvis area and shoulder joints. Also, the elbows do not match inside the mesh. It's important to be sure your bones are inside the mesh and perfectly aligned and then apply the Skin Modifier.

16. If you try to lift the left/right feet controller, you see an unwanted bulge near the hip area. Those are not the only mesh glitches; see the foot ankle area, shoulder clavicle, and neck areas as well. Figure 7-8 shows the potential problem areas.

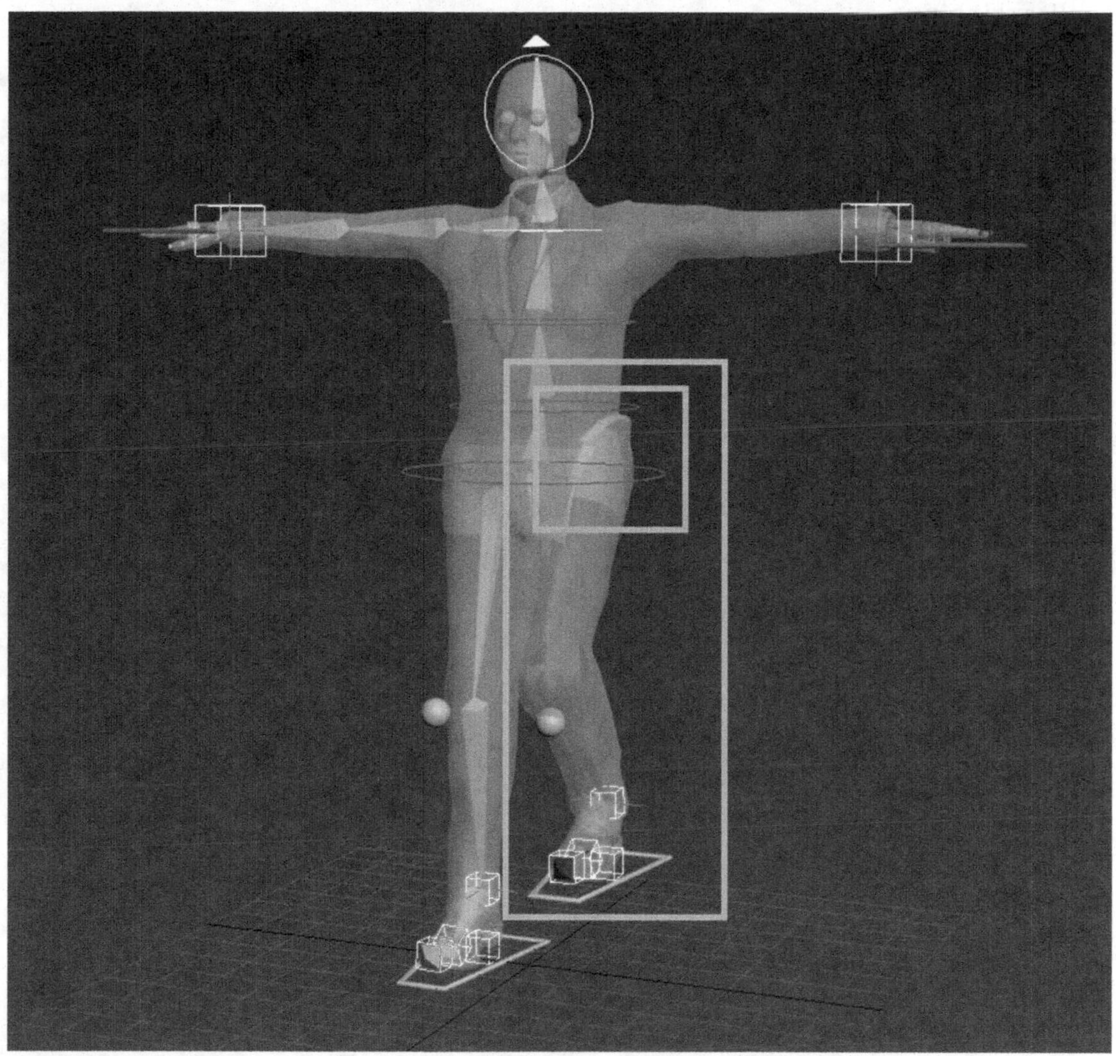

Figure 7-8. *A mesh error near the hip when lifting the left leg*

17. A checkpoint file has been created called `Human_Rigged_Bones01.max`.

Skin Envelopes

In the previous section, we noticed that our character mesh has weird deformations near the hip area when the leg lifts up. This is because the bone envelopes need to be set correctly. The position of the bone and bone fins greatly influence how the software applies skinning.

Let's look at editing the envelopes and tweaking the deformations.

1. Fire up 3ds Max and load `Human_Rigged_Bones02.max`.
2. Select the character model and right-click in any viewport. Choose Properties and disable see through in the Object Properties dialog.
3. Select L_Leg_Control and move it a bit up and forward until you see the mesh overlaps, as seen earlier.
4. With the character mesh still selected, go into the Skin Modifier and click on Edit Envelopes. Once Edit Envelopes is clicked, you should see something like Figure 7-9. In this mode, instead of bones, you see lines in place of bones.

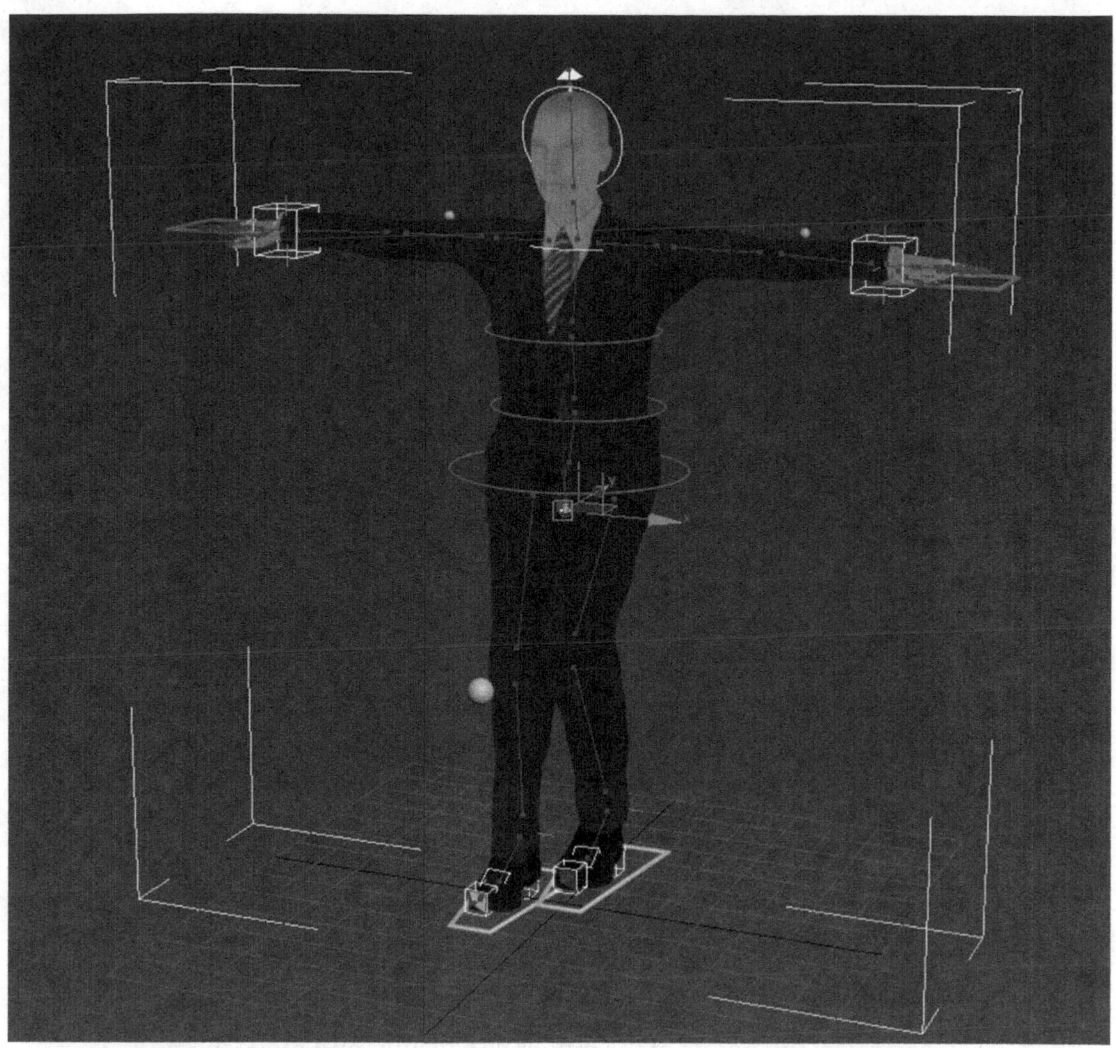

Figure 7-9. *Edit envelopes*

5. Now select the L_thighbone from the bones list in the Skin Modifier or click the corresponding line of the bone in the viewport.

6. Once the bone is selected, you should see the red influences, as shown in Figure 7-10.

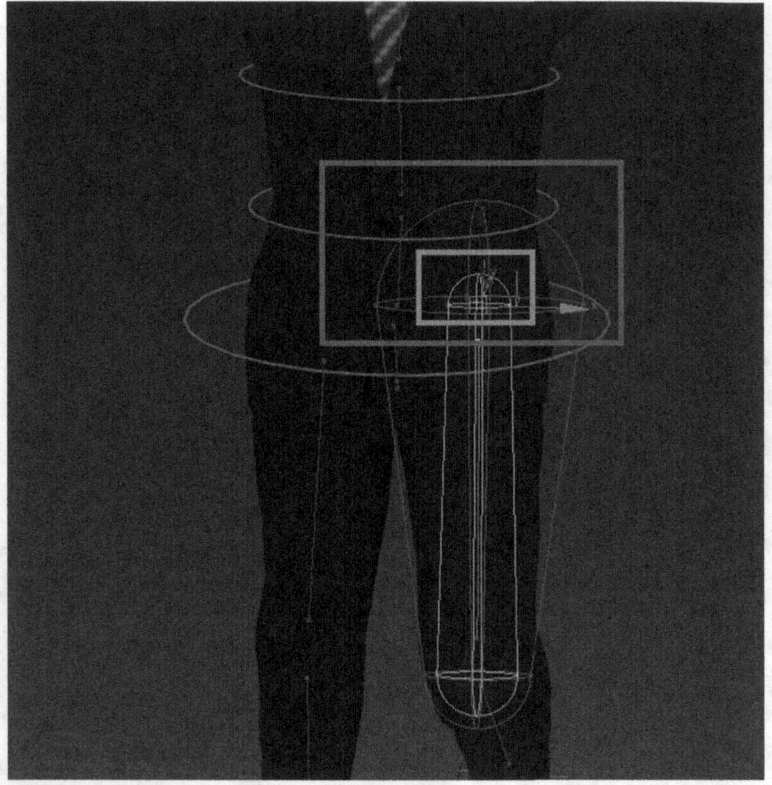

***Figure 7-10.** Edit Envelopes influence range*

7. The influence area includes a core influence (an inner capsule) and an outer capsule that's bigger and covers the inner one. It's used as a influence fall off.

8. You can select the points of the influence capsules and move them to increase or decrease the bone's influence area. Experiment by selecting the inner and outer points of both the top and bottom areas of the selected bone envelope. We can go the long way from here or the short way. Let's use the short way and speed up things by editing how 3ds Max creates these envelopes.

9. 3ds Max's default skin solution is called the *voxel solver solution*. We will tweak the solution to get better results.

10. Scroll in the Skin Modifier until you come to a section called Weight Properties. Currently it is set to Voxel. Click on the dotted button, as shown in Figure 7-11.

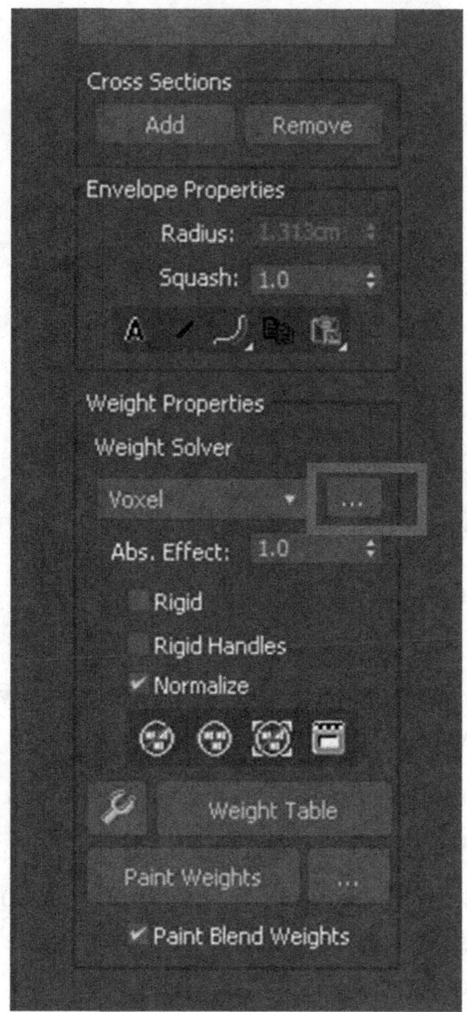

***Figure 7-11.** Envelope Weight Properties*

11. Once you click on the button, you should see the popup dialog shown in Figure 7-12.

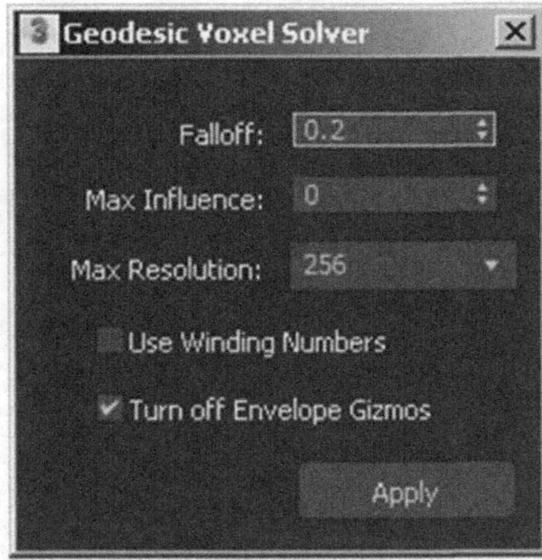

Figure 7-12. *Envelope Voxel Solver options*

Let's discuss the options:

- Falloff: This determines how smooth the falloff is. The bigger the number, the harsher the blend between the two bones. The default value of 0.2 should be enough.
- Max Influence: This determines how many bones the current envelope can influence.
- Max Resolution: The higher the resolution, the slower the calculation and the better the result. It's advisable to start with the lowest and gradually increase the number.
- Use Winding Numbers: If you check this box, a more accurate solution will be given but it will be slower. It's advisable to leave it off, unless you have a very powerful computer.
- Turn Off Envelope Gizmos: Once you enable this, the solution is baked and you lose the ability to edit envelopes.

12. Select the character and go to the Weight Properties. Choose the button to configure the solution, as shown in Figure 7-12.
13. Change the max resolution to 64 and leave the other data to the defaults. Press Apply.

14. Once you're done, choose Enable Envelope. You can see the solution in Figure 7-13. Notice how the envelopes eases in. The closer the color is to red, the more influence the selected bone has in that area. Blue denotes that it is not influenced by the selected bone.

Figure 7-13 has a falloff value of 1. Notice how the thigh bone has falloff influence to the adjacent bones. The glitch that we saw earlier is now nearly nil.

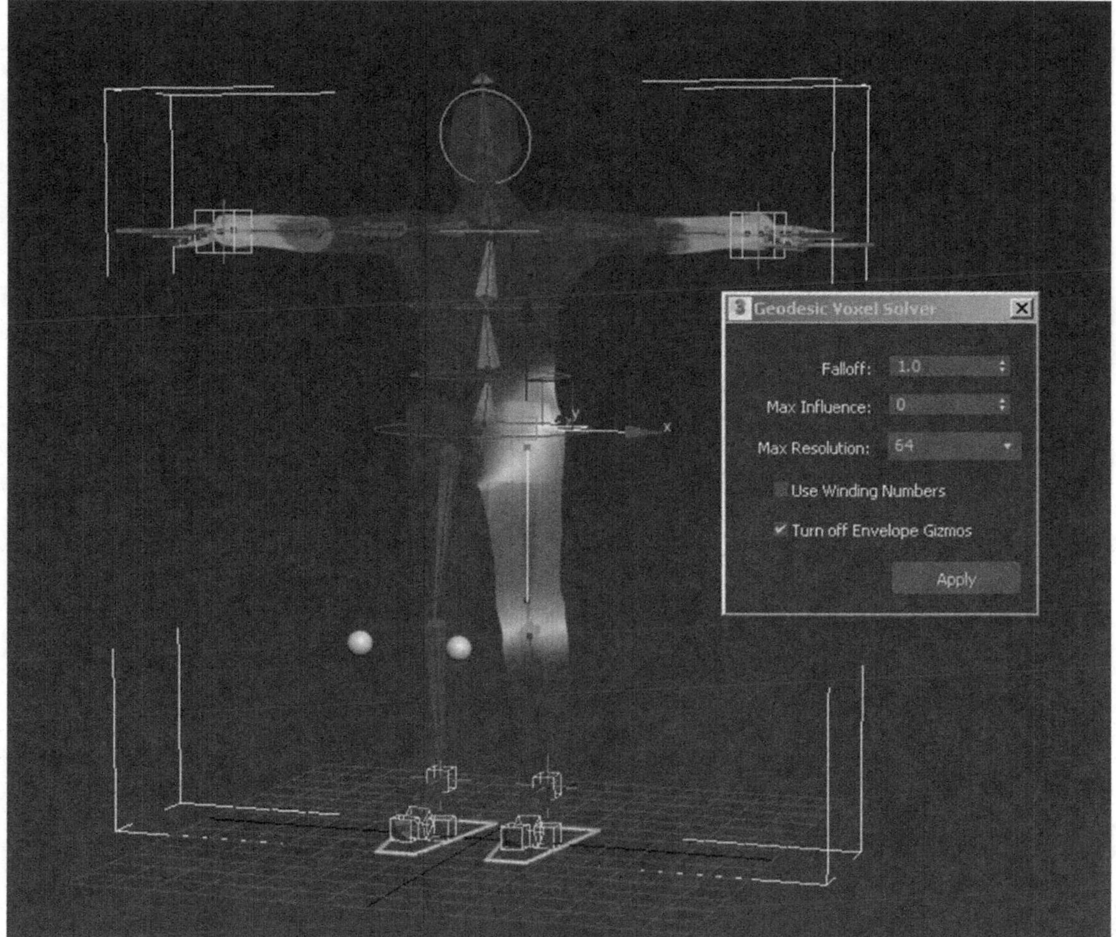

***Figure 7-13.** Envelope Voxel Solver with a value of 1*

Figure 7-14 has a falloff of 0.2. Note that the color influence of the mesh area near the thigh is not red, which means that the mesh is not fully influenced by that bone. Try lifting the leg with these values to see the results.

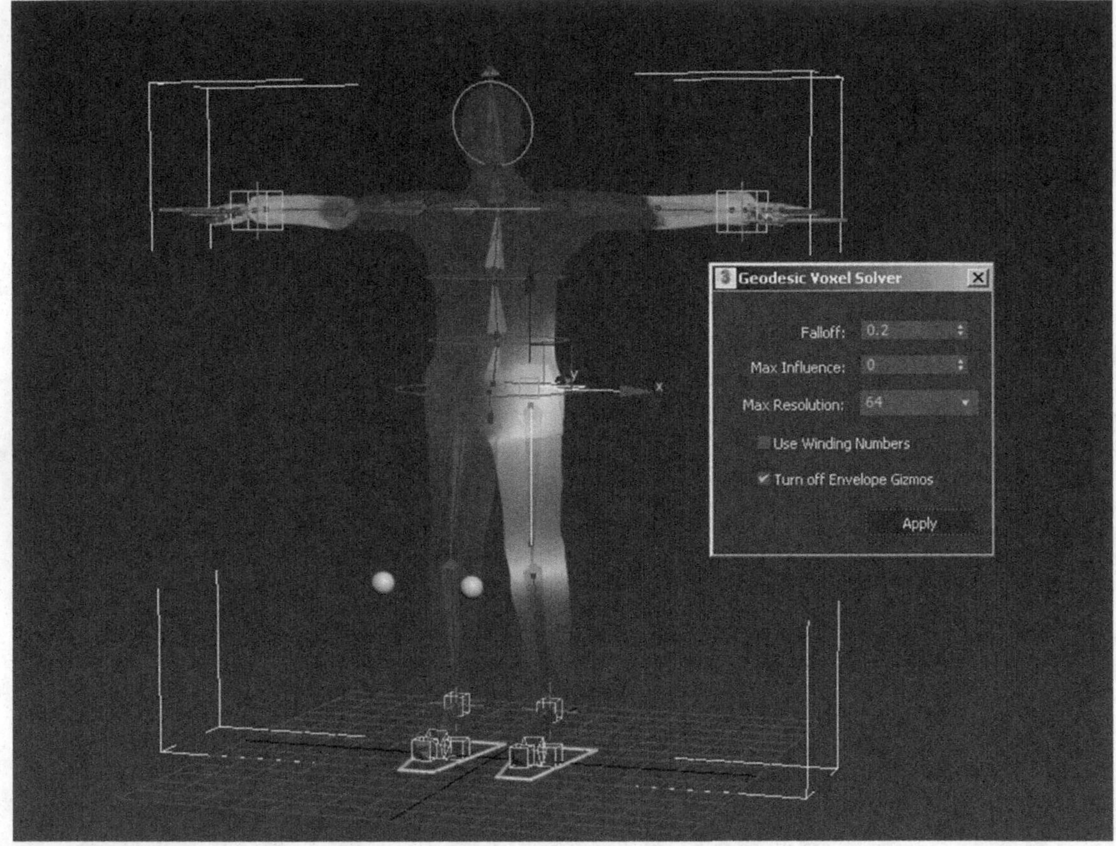

Figure 7-14. *Envelope Voxel Solver with a value of 0.2*

Try adjusting the Curl attributes of the finger controller that the rig has from the Modifier panel with a resolution of 64 and then 512 for the Voxel solution. You should notice the influence it has and the difference it makes.

Paint Weights

Now let's look at the longer procedure that we talked about and avoided in the previous steps. You might be wondering why we will now examine the longer route when the Voxel method worked. The answer is that sometimes you might need to paint weights for a particular set of edge loops or vertices in your model. This can be achieved by choosing a set of vertex and painting the weights manually.

Let's get into it.

1. Load Human_Rigged_Bones02.max.
2. Select your character mesh. Go into the Modifier and select the Skin Modifier. Then, click on Edit Envelopes and ensure that Select Vertices is checked below the Edit Envelopes button (this allows us to select vertices to paint weights).
3. To better demonstrate this, select the L_Ankle_Bone and choose the Weight tool from the weight properties. See Figure 7-15.

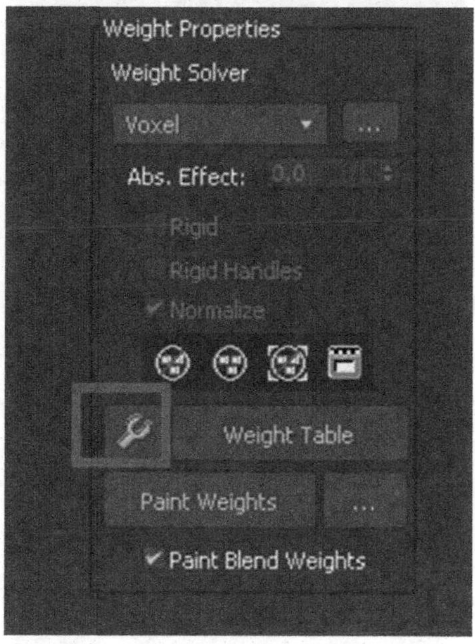

Figure 7-15. *Paint Weight tool in the Weight properties*

4. Clicking on the Weight tool opens the Weight Tool dialog, through which we will be painting weights. See Figure 7-16.

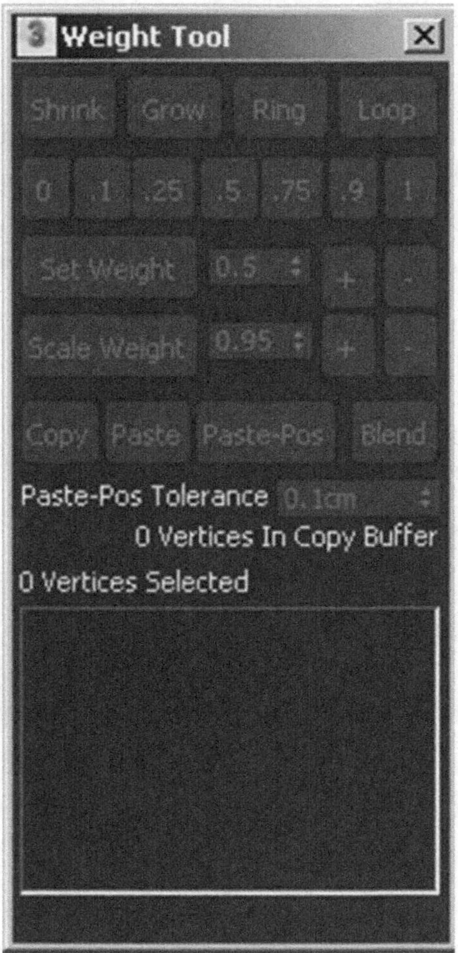

Figure 7-16. *Paint Weight tool options*

5. Note that all the options in the Weight tool are grayed out and no operation of any kind can be performed. This is because we have not selected any vertex or vertices.
6. Switch to a wireframe by pressing F3 or changing the viewport shading mode. It will be easier to select the vertices in wireframe mode.
7. In Figure 7-17, I have posed the character's legs in a running pose. Note the mess near the knee joints and ankle.

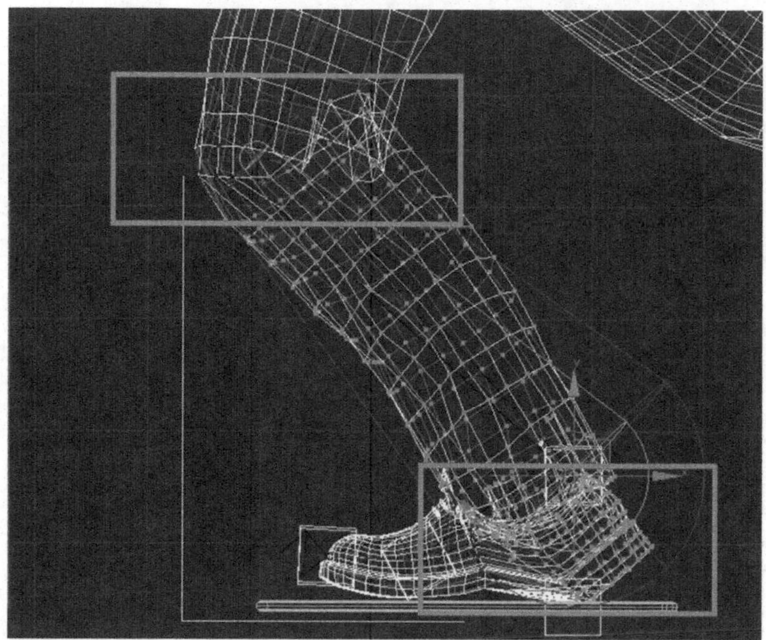

Figure 7-17. *Paint Weight: leg mess*

8. Do a lasso selection (using the selection modes in the ribbon toolbar) around the knee area, as depicted in Figure 7-18.

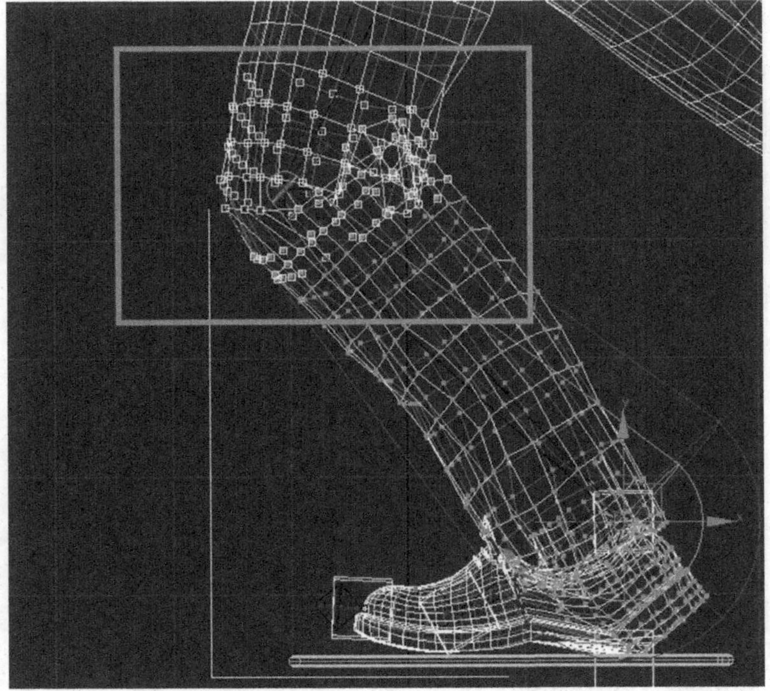

***Figure 7-18.** Paint Weight: vertex selection of the knee*

9. You don't need to be accurate in terms of selection. Just select vertices around that position.

10. With these points selected, now you should notice that the Weight tool has all the options available. Let's discuss a few options in the Paint Weight tools before we go any further:

    - Shrink: Contracts your current selection of vertices
    - Grow: Increases your selection area by adding adjacent loops
    - Ring: Selects all vertices parallel to the selected vertices
    - Loop: Selects the adjacent points that are in the continuous edge
    - These numbers will determine the weights for the selected vertices. If you select 1 for a set of vertices the bones will influence it 100%. Setting it to .5 will cause the bones influence to be 50%.

11. Now with the selection of the vertices mentioned in Figure 7-19, set the weight to .5 using the Weight tool.

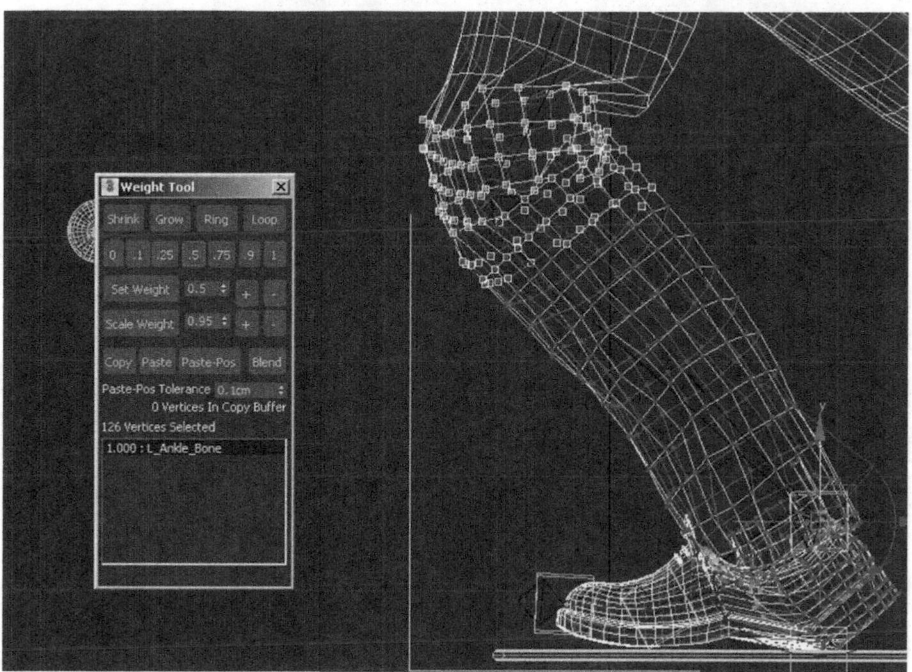

Figure 7-19. *Paint Weight: Vertex selection and weightage applied*

12. Don't panic if it looks like a mess, even more than before. We need to do one more tweak to fix it.

13. With the vertex still selected, click on Blend a couple of times to ease the weightage.

14. You might need to select adjacent vertices loops that are still not controlled. For example, the blue loop of vertices below the knee are not controlled, and the red loop of vertices above the knee are over influenced. We need to give a weight so that the influence is smoother (by increasing the weight value for blue and decreasing the weight value for red). See Figure 7-20.

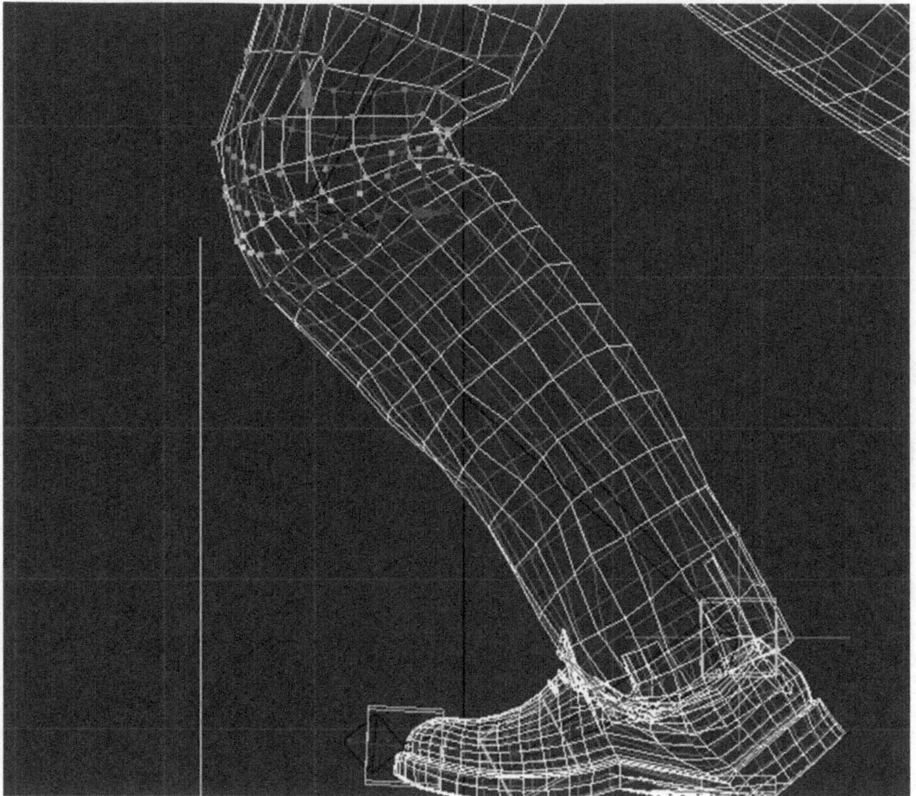

Figure 7-20. *Paint Weight: Vertex selection, knee fixed*

15. The yellowish-orange vertex areas need to be blended a little more with the red and blue loops. When you select the yellow loops and click on Blend, notice how the adjacent loops change color and the mesh eases in.

There are more techniques and plugins available for skinning, but a solid understanding of this should be enough to step into the world of 3D character animation.

Skinning Bipeds

In the previous sections, we learned how to skin our character rig using the Skin Modifier. The same Skin Modifier can be applied to bipeds as well. But the 3ds Max native skinning tool for bipeds is called *Physique*, so let's look at how to skin a biped rig with the Physique modifier. I recommend you try skinning with the Skin Modifier as well.

1. Load `Human_Rigged_Biped.max`.
2. In this file I aligned a biped to our character mesh in Figure mode. Take the time to align the biped parts to the corresponding positions according to your mesh. The better the alignment, the easier the skinning process is going to be.
3. Select the character mesh node in the Scene or Layer Explorer. Once the character mesh is selected in the modifiers, choose Physique from the list. See Figure 7-21.

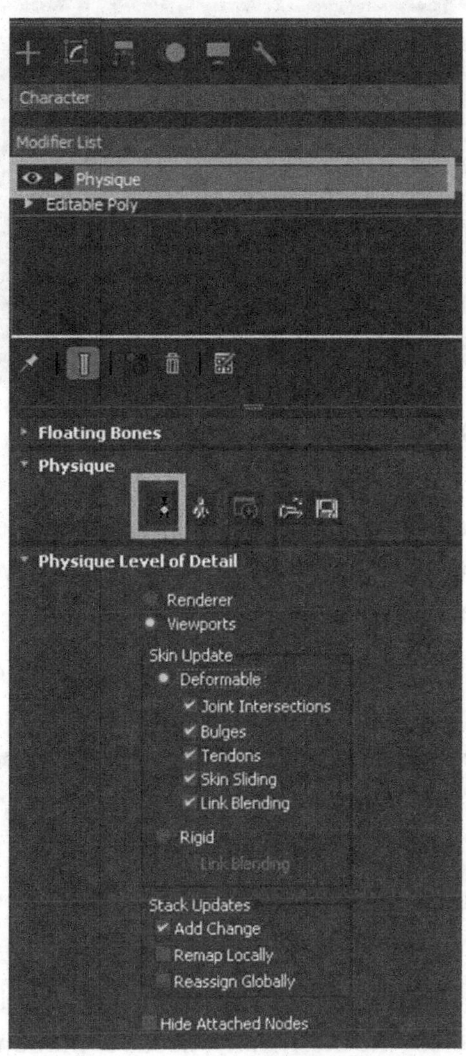

***Figure 7-21.** Physique modifier`*

4. In the Physique section of the Modifier tab, click on the Attach to Node, as shown in Figure 7-21.

5. When you click it, nothing will appear to happen. In reality, the software is expecting you to choose the biped, so press H and pick bip001, as shown in Figure 7-22.

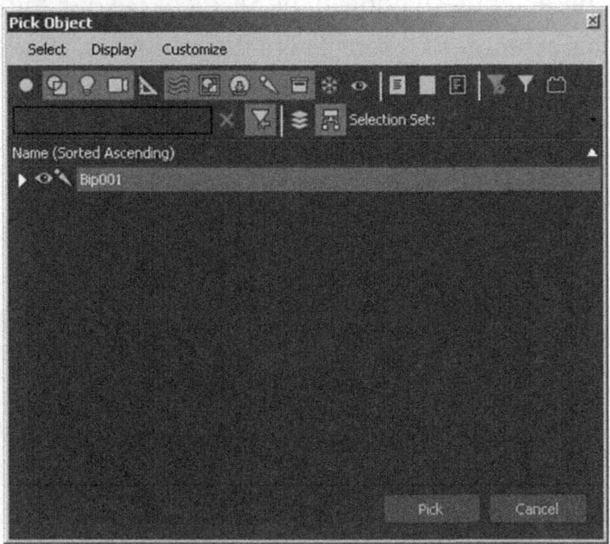

Figure 7-22. *The Pick Object dialog*

6. A Physique Initialization dialog box will pop up. Leave everything set to the defaults and click Initialize. Depending on your computer's speed, this may take a moment.

7. Once it has completed, you should see a faint yellow/orange line running across the biped structure. This denotes that the Physique Modifier has created the connection between your character mesh and the biped. If you want to see the line clearly, just select the parts of the biped and hide them.

8. At this point, you can turn off Figure mode and rotate and move the biped parts to see how the mesh moves.

9. In this case, there is a lot of work to be done. If we had scaled the biped part to enclose the mesh that it needs to influence, our work would be easier. I left it as such to show how to fix it.

10. Select all the biped parts in the Layer or Scene Manager and hide them.
11. With the character mesh selected, in the Physique Modifier tab, expand the modifier. You should see Envelope, Links, Bulge, Tendons, and Vertex. These are the submodes you can use to skin the biped to mesh. Let's look at Envelopes.
12. Click on the left thigh area to see the envelope. See Figure 7-23.

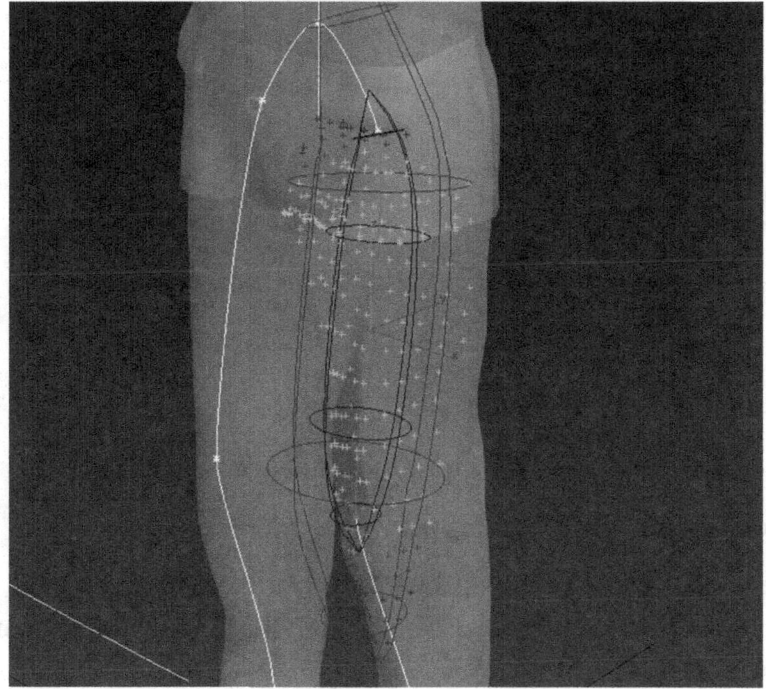

Figure 7-23. *Physique Envelope: left thigh*

13. The envelope works the same way here as in the Skin Modifier, except it lacks the interactive tweak control.
14. Be sure the envelope is selected in the Physique Modifier section. Set the options as shown in Figure 7-24.

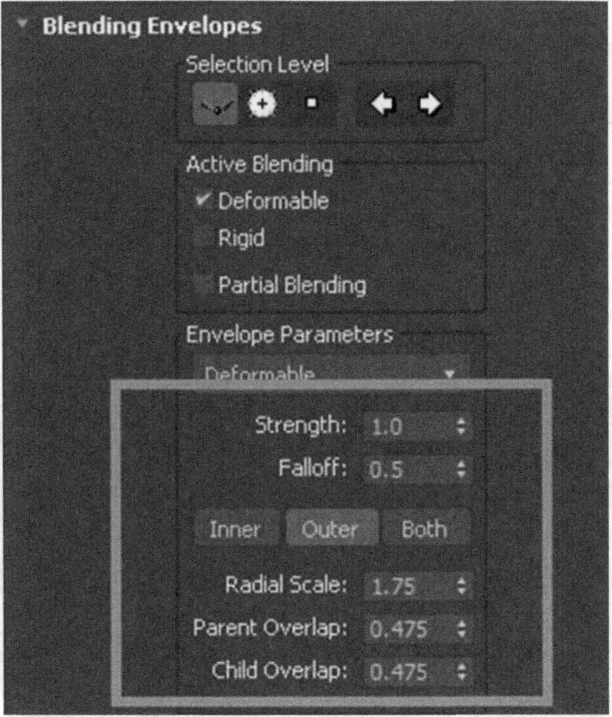

Figure 7-24. *Physique Blending Envelope*

- Strength: Determines how strong the influence is going to be.
- Falloff: Determines the strength decrease rate.
- Inner/Outer/Both: Choosing inner will only tweak the inner parameters. Choosing both will affect both the inner and outer parts of the envelope.
- Radial Scale: This increases the size of the influence area. Note we have to be cautious with this, as increasing this value too much will start pulling mesh from the other side or from unwanted parts.
- Parent Overlap: The influence area will be influenced by and pulled toward any parent bone structure (biped structure).
- Child Overlap: The influence area will be influenced by and pulled towards toward any child bone structure (biped structure).

By playing around with these values, you can make adjustments when the mesh is not conforming to the biped. We will not be covering bulges and tendons, as they are an add-on to the skinning process and not a prerequisite. Bulges are used to emulate muscle bulge, and tendons are used to create links between bones that deform and twist along.

Now let's get back to skinning a biped rig to our character mesh. This time we will be using the Vertex subobject mode of the Physique Modifier.

1. Once you select the Vertex mode for the Physique Modifier, you should see something like Figure 7-25.

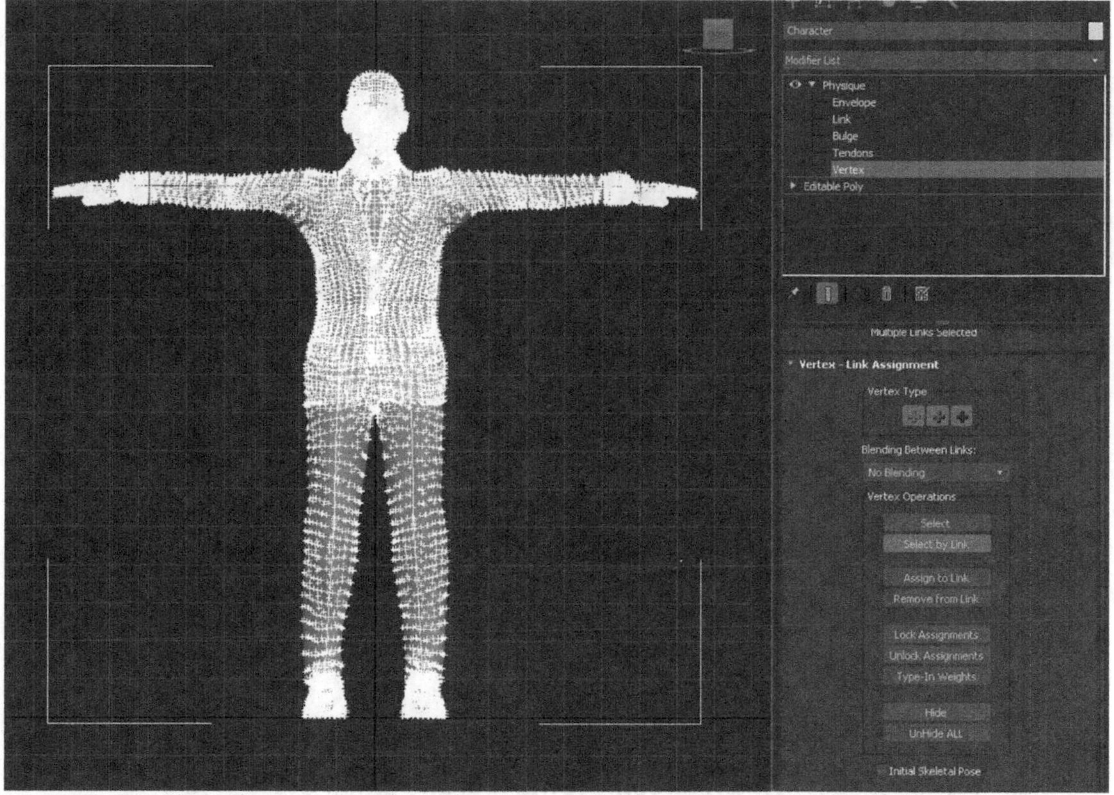

Figure 7-25. *Physique vertex mode*

2. To make sense of how this works, press Ctrl+A to select all the vertices. You should see something like Figure 7-26.

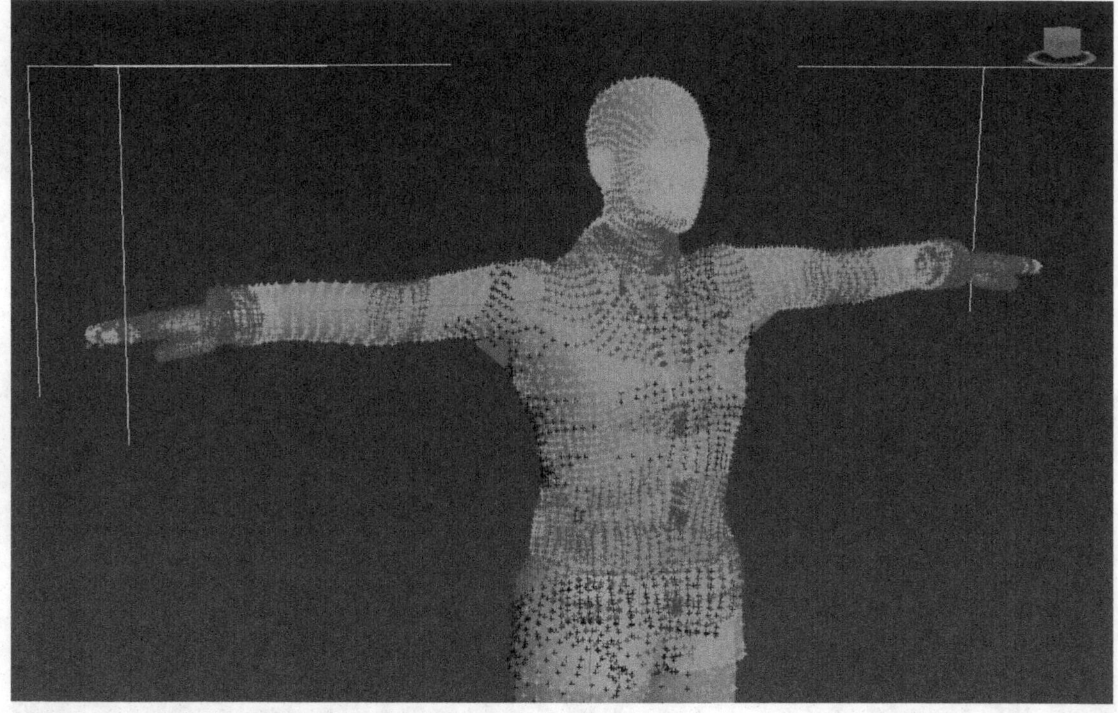

Figure 7-26. *Physique vertex mode: all selected*

3. Okay, let's discuss what is happening here. On the right in the Modifier panel, there are color codes for red, green, and blue. The icons in the modifier work as toggles. When the red cross is turned off, you can't select the red vertices.
   - Red: Deforming vertex
   - Green: Rigid vertex
   - Blue: Rooted vertex
4. We see shades of red (maroon/brown, red, and blue). Green won't be visible unless you set it to rigid.
5. You can select individual envelopes of biped sections only to see the vertex color for that section. In our case, choose Select from the modifier and select the blue vertex for the specific part of the biped rig. For example, let's focus on the Bip001 L Calf area. Select all the blue vertex using a lasso selection and choose Assign to Link.

6. Click on the yellow line area near the Bip001 L Calf to link the vertex. You need to work section by section on each biped part and link the vertices.

Let's now discuss the vertex operations of the physique modifier. See Figure 7-27.

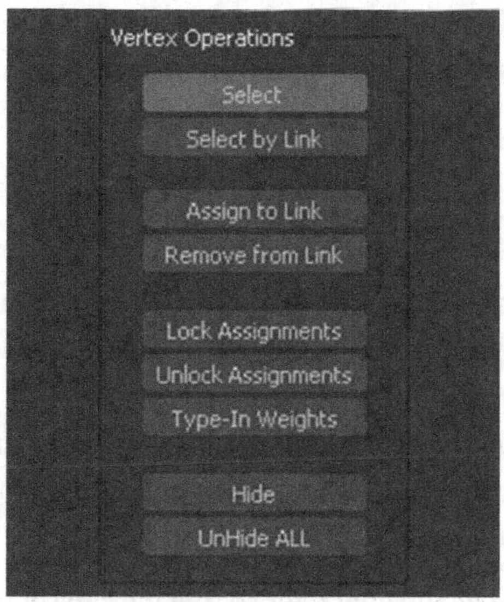

***Figure 7-27.** Physique Vertex Operations*

- Select: Allows you to lasso selected vertices.
- Select by Link: Choosing this and clicking on a link allows you to select all vertices influenced by it.
- Assign to Link: Select a group of vertices and choose Assign to Link. Click on a envelope link to assign the selection.
- Remove from Link: Select a group of vertices from a link and click on Remove from Link, then choose the link. This removes the selected vertices from that link.
- Lock Assignments: If you made an assignment and do not want it to be changed later when doing a selection, you can lock your assignment. Locked assignments are represented as bigger squares.
- Unlock Assignments: If you want to change an assignment, you can unlock the link.

- Type in Weights: Allows you to select the locked assignments and input weight values without unlocking them.
- Hide: Hides the current selection of vertices.
- Unhide All: Unhides all hidden vertices.

A word of note—the Physique Modifier is a legacy modifier. Even though it has changed a lot, it's rarely used and is used only for bipeds. Most of the riggers use and rely on CAT rigs or custom bone rigs for character animations.

Skinning: CAT Rig

Load `CAT_CharacterAnimation_Start.max` in the 3ds Max scene source folder. This is the same file that we used to create a custom CAT Rig. Now let's animate the rig and use it to animate our character.

Double-check to ensure that all the CAT rig parts are perfectly aligned and scaled accordingly. The more perfect the fit is here, the better the deformation is going to be on the model.

1. Remember we froze the character so that we can set up the bones in the previous section, so right-click on the viewport and a click on Unfreeze All, as shown in Figure 7-28. This makes the character model selectable.

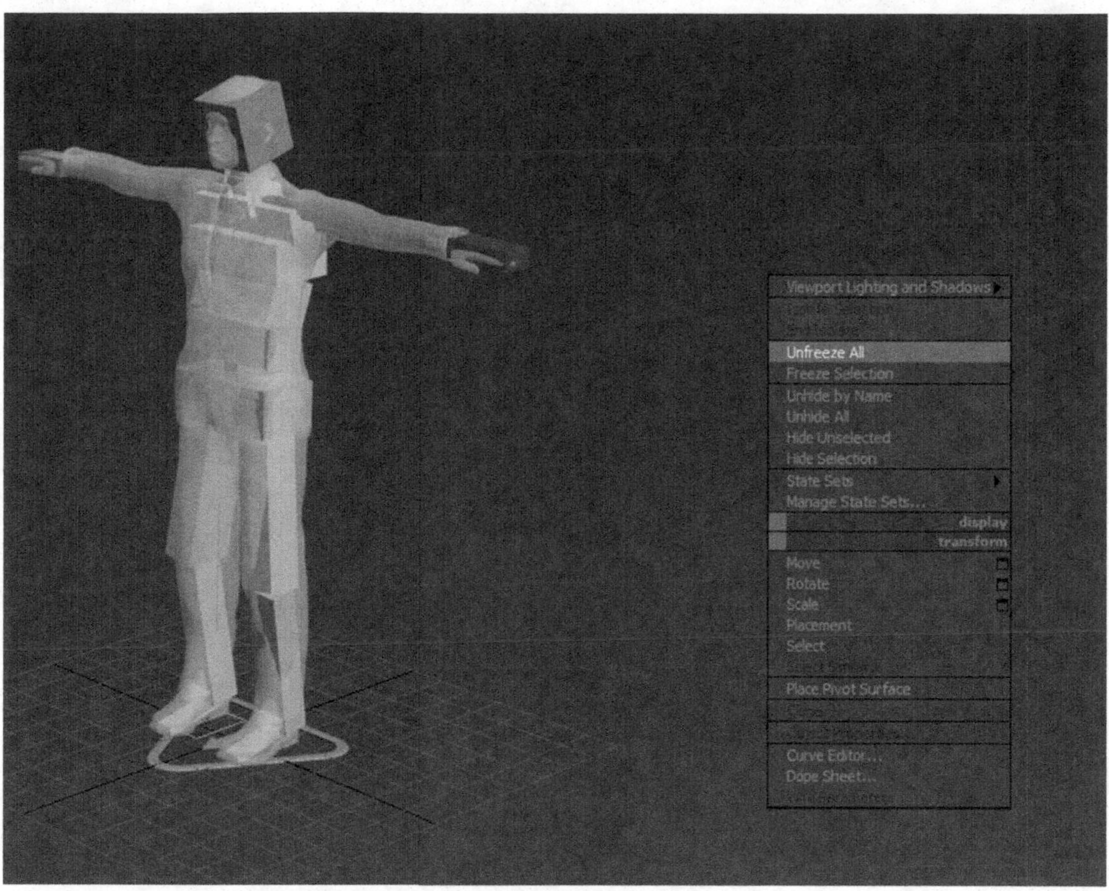

Figure 7-28. *CAT rig aligned to the character mesh*

2. Select your character model and go to the Modifier panel. In the Modifier list, choose Skin Modifier. Your modifier stack for the character mesh should look like Figure 7-29.

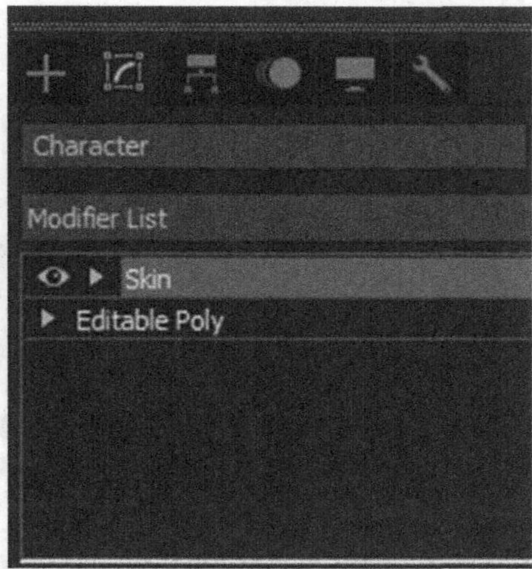

Figure 7-29. *Skin Modifier*

3. Select your Skin Modifier to populate the rollout and choose Add. See Figure 7-30.

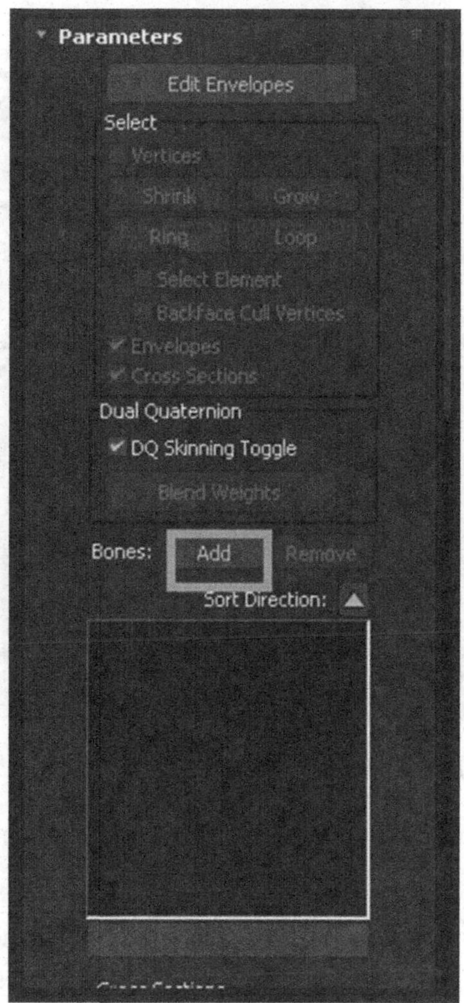

Figure 7-30. *Skin Modifier, adding bones*

4. In the Select bones popup box, choose CustomRigPelvis and press Ctrl+C to select all its children. Click on Select. See Figure 7-31.

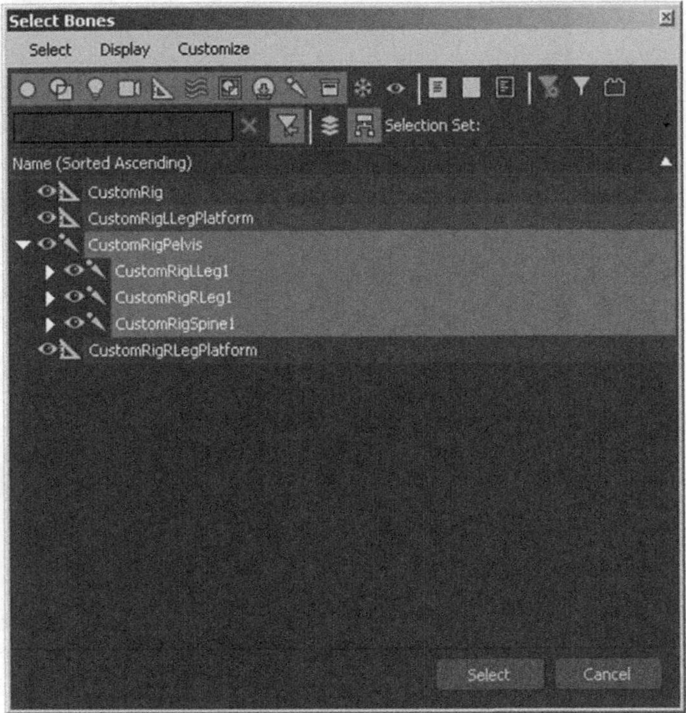

***Figure 7-31.** Skin Modifier, selecting bones*

5. A reference file has been created called `CAT_CharacterAnimation_Start1.max`.
6. At this point, try selecting parts of the character rig and move and rotate them to see the deformation. As you see results where deformations are not happening, scale the appropriate parts of the CAT rig.
7. Select your character model by selecting it in the viewport. Then go into the Modifier panel and choose Edit Envelopes. See Figure 7-32.

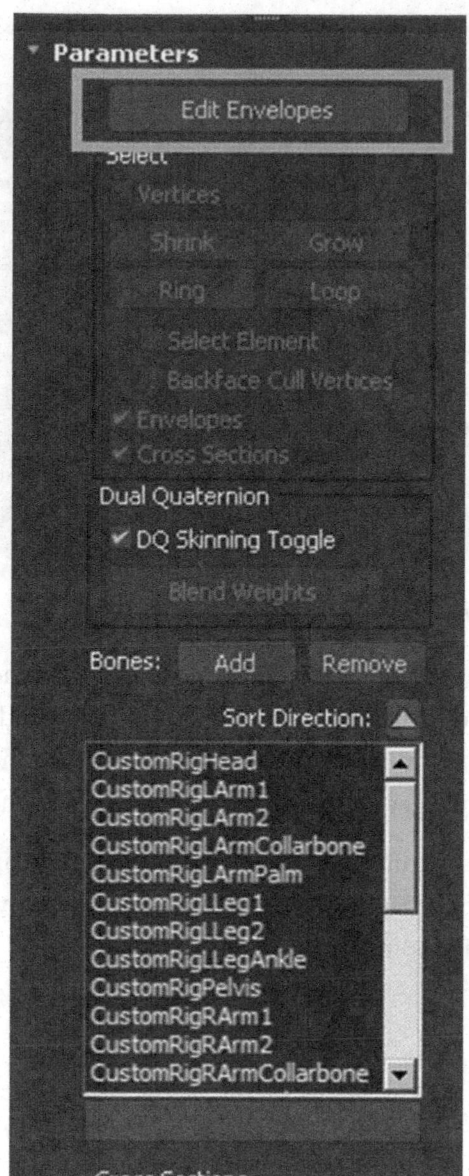

***Figure 7-32.** Skin Modifier, edit envelopes*

8. You can see the bones as lines. Note that there is a heat map around the mesh for the selected rig part. In this case, the head rig part is selected. See Figure 7-33.

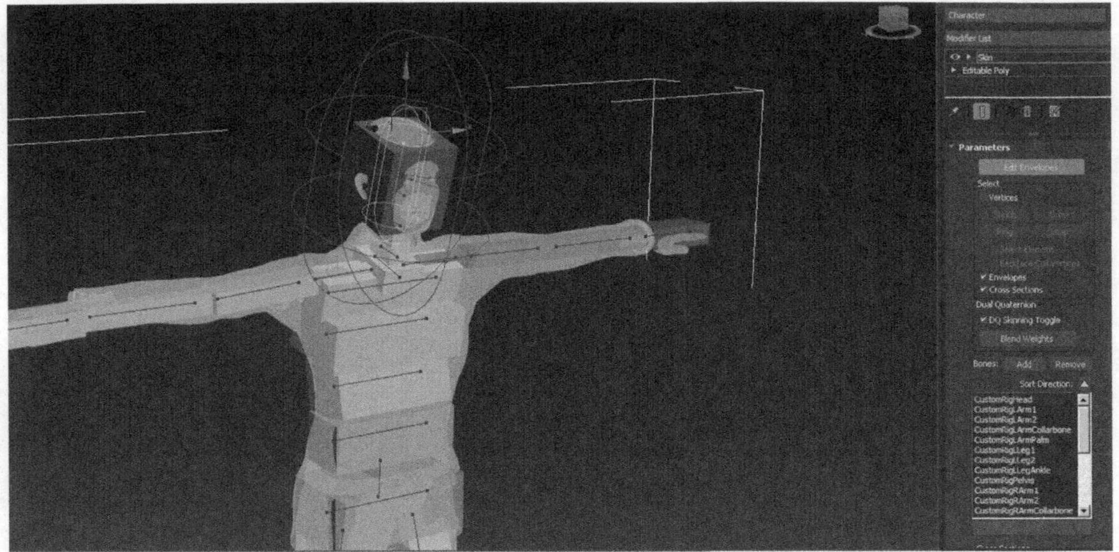

Figure 7-33. *Skin Modifier, envelope range*

9. The warmer the tone of a vertex, the more it is influenced by the selected part and the bluer it is, the less it's influenced. (Follow the steps from the beginning of this section in 3ds Max and look at the visual feedback we get of the influence based on the heat map.)

10. We can change the influence by selecting the outer capsule wireframe shown in Figure 7-34 and resizing it by moving the capsule points. Refer to Figures 7-34 and 7-35.

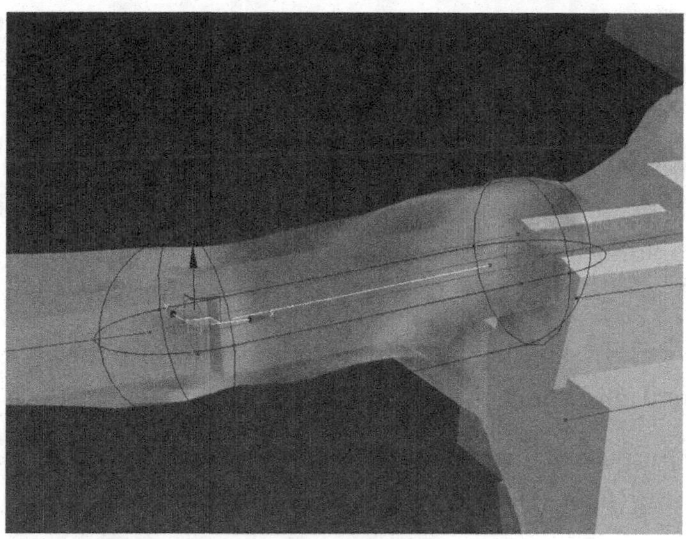

***Figure 7-34.** Skin Modifier, envelope original*

Note the influence in these two images. They show how the influence range is tweaked by increasing the capsule size. Also notice that the heat map is stronger near the elbow.

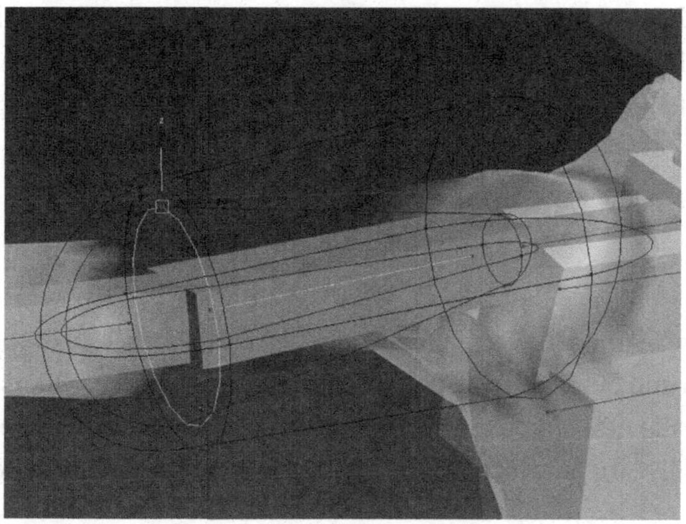

***Figure 7-35.** Skin Modifier, envelope altered*

11. The influence can be modified by tweaking the inner and outer radius of the influence envelope, as shown in Figure 7-35. The start and end tip can be repositioned too.

12. At this point, feel free to move and rotate biped parts and see how the deformation happens. Lift the legs up and see how the knee area is holding up and deforming and tweak the envelopes as needed.

    This process of skinning is time consuming but worth the effort for a polished animation.

13. For the purpose of this section, let's move on and select the CustomRig (Root Triangle base) and go to motion options.

14. Create a CAT Motion Layer and turn on animation mode.

15. You should see that the 3D model is deforming according to our CAT rig movement.

Skinning is an iterative process that requires you to set envelopes and test deformations. Think about how the bone parts in your body influence the flesh around it and set the envelopes accordingly. Refer back to the bones section for a detailed, step-by -step process of the envelope editing process and apply the same to CAT rigs. As a quick example: we could use the Voxel solver to handle the weight of biped parts as we did in the bones section.

Summary

In this chapter, we learned how to attach character rigs (bones, bipeds, and CAT rig) to a character mesh and bind them for proper deformation using modifiers such as Skin and Physique. In the next chapter, we look at creating walk and run cycles of the skinned characters. We will learn new techniques that will help us create a refined and polished animation.

CHAPTER 8

Animating: Walk and Run Cycle

In the earlier chapters, we learned how to create custom character rigs using bones, bipeds, and CAT tools. We also learned how to bind these rigs created to a character mesh. In this chapter, we look at and understand the various phases of the walk and run cycle and learn how to animate a walk and run cycle for bones, bipeds, and CAT rigs manually.

I use reference videos from `Endlessreference.com` as backdrops to animate the character in this chapter. You will not see these files in the chapter folder, since they are third-party copyrighted content and I cannot share the videos with you. I recommend their YouTube channel (`https://www.youtube.com/user/endlessreference`) for similar videos and their official website (`https://endlessreference.com/`), which has more than 500+ reference videos of various actions of humans. This is a must-have reference for anyone who is looking to advance in the field as an animator. To follow along, you can download any of the available content on the Internet or shoot a video as a reference, as seen on the YouTube channel provided here.

In order to animate realistically, we need to understand how our body parts translate over time. In the coming section we will analyze a walk cycle and split it into key phases. The techniques learned here can be applied to character animation as a whole in any 2D or 3D animation program.

Analyzing: Walk Cycle

Okay, first let's ask this—why is a walk animation called a *walk cycle*? I want you to take a few walk steps and analyze your footing as you move. Now observe the picture in Figure 8-1.

P. Raju, *Character Rigging and Advanced Animation*, https://doi.org/10.1007/978-1-4842-5037-2_8

One Stride/Half a Cycle

The picture shown in Figure 8-1 is of half a cycle. Note that the character starts with its left step first and ends with the right leg in front.

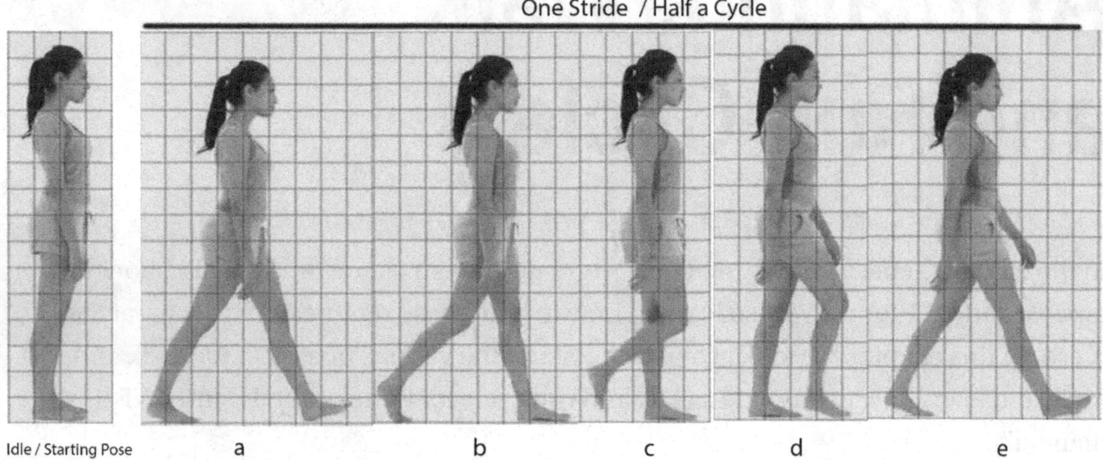

Figure 8-1. *Walk cycle poses (image courtesy* `https://endlessreference.com/`*)*

If you notice in this image, the character is at a standstill initially. Consider each pose:

- **Pose** a: This is called the *Contact pose*. This is where the character has neither of its feet completely planted on the floor, as in Figure 8-1. The character's left foot is about to rest entirely on the ground and the right foot is about to lift off to transition to the next pose.
- **Pose** b: This position is called the *Down pose* or weight down pose. In this position, the character's leg in front will take on the weight of the whole body, as the other leg transitions to the next pose.
- **Pose** c: This is called the *Passing pose*. From this point the character takes on the whole weight of the body while the other leg comes to the front.
- **Pose** d: This step is called the *Up pose* or weight up pose. In this position the character's back leg will take on the weight of the body. At this position, the character will also be at its peak height.
- Pose e: This is the Contact pose again and at this stage we are at half a cycle.

Now I would like to bring your attention to a couple of things happening here.

- Poses a and e are opposites.
    - In a, we have the left leg forward and the right leg in the back.
    - In e, we have the exact opposite of a, wherein the right leg is forward and the left leg is back.
- Poses b and d are the same in a way. In b, the character begins to take on the weight of the body so that the other leg can transition. In e, it's the opposite because it takes on the whole weight on one leg and pushes itself up so that the other leg can transition.

Two Strides/Complete Cycle

Now let's look at a complete cycle, which is two strides. See Figure 8-2.

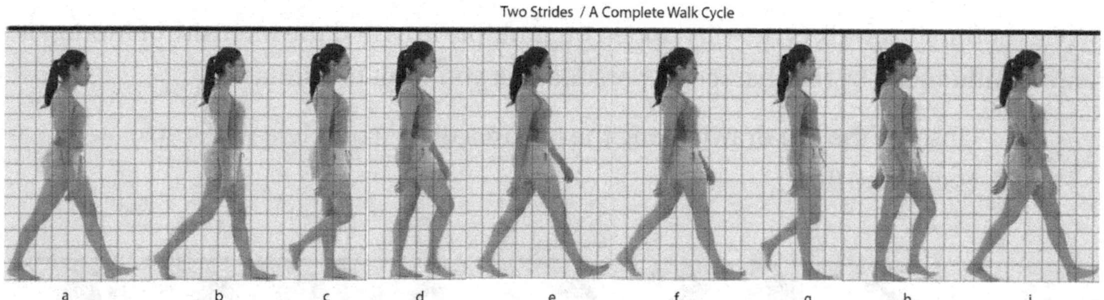

***Figure 8-2.** Complete walk cycle poses (Image courtesy: `https://endlessreference.com/`)*

Here again, I would like you to observe the image. If you have followed along so far, you should be able to catch the repetitiveness.

- a and i are the same in terms of leg footing, which makes this a loop.
- b and f are the same with the exception of alternating footing, wherein e changes our footing for the second stride.
- c and g again are the same with alternating footing. Both are a passing pose.
- d and h are the same with alternating footing.

I would also like you to keep in mind so far we looked at only the leg footing, now let's look at the arms motion on a complete walk cycle.

Arm Locomotion

Generally if you notice when you walk, your arms alternate movement based on your legs. For example, if your left foot is in front, the right arm swings forward. If the right foot is in front, the left arm is swinging in front. One important factor to becoming a good animator is to observe and analyze motion around you. When the left leg is in front, the right hand swings forward. The amount and intensity of the swing varies from person to person. We discuss later about creating varying persona, which affect the way one walks, by altering the timing and spacing of keys. Note how the arms come into a neutral position (close to straight down) during passing poses.

Upper Body Locomotion

Pelvic motion in a walk cycle will happen on multiple axes and the intensity of motion is heavily influenced by the character's persona that you want to animate.

- Observe the line drawn along the hip area of the complete walk cycle. See Figure 8-3.

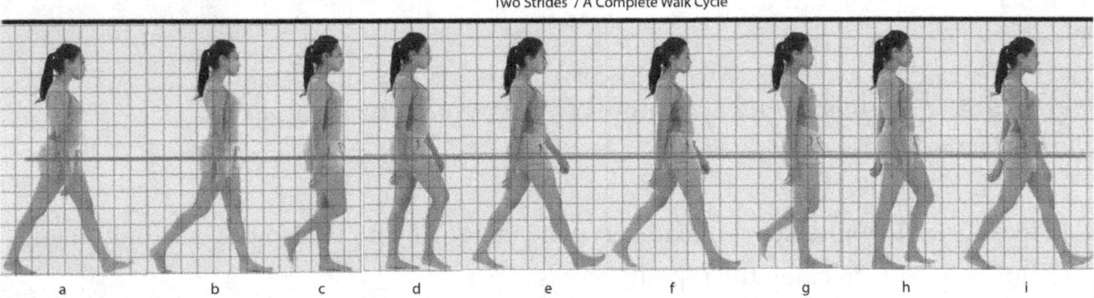

Figure 8-3. *Pelvic motion: up/down reference (Image courtesy:* `https://endlessreference.com/`*)*

Notice how the pelvic area goes above and below the line. You can see the character is at peak height at d and h.

- The motion of the pelvic area is not limited to this. The pelvis moves to the left when the left foot is forward and moves to the right when the right foot is in front. This motion will create a hip sway motion.
- The pelvic area will also rotate favored by the foot in front. This rotation will be on two axes, the Z and Y. This combination of rotation and translation can make a walk seem masculine or feminine. Refer to Figure 8-4. The axis of rotation is the green and blue, which are Y and Z, respectively.

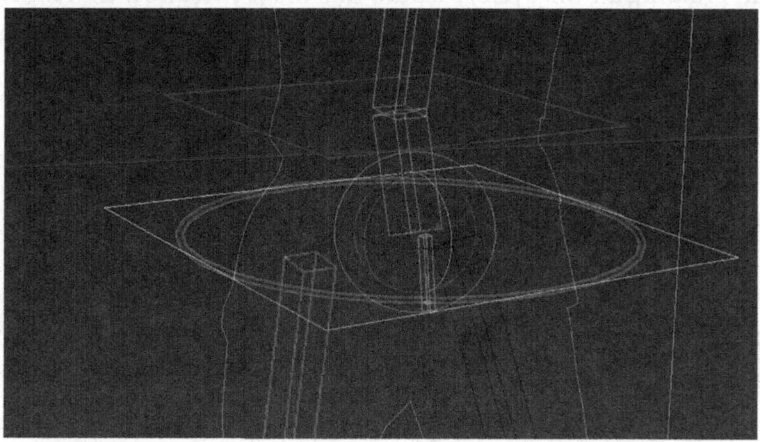

***Figure 8-4.** Pelvic rotation*

- Another advantage when animating the pelvic controller is that when you move or rotate the pelvis, the IK chains that we have set on the rig allow for natural human motions. When you bring the pelvic controller down, the knees will start to bend. The leg will straighten up when you move the pelvic controller up in your rig.
- The upper chest area also sways a bit to the left and right and inherits an acute translation and rotation from the hips.

Head Locomotion

The head motion for a walk cycle animation is very limited. In most cases, the character is looking head on straight and swaying a few degrees from its neck towards the left and right and a bit of up and down motion. Again, much of this depends on the animation we are creating. For example, if the character is taking a stroll in a park, we would want our character to look around and admire the surroundings.

Enough with the theoretical lessons—let's go ahead and animate a walk cycle.

Animating: Walk Cycle

Before we begin creating a walk cycle, I would like to let you know that there are two ways in which a walk cycle can be created. One is where the character walks in place (most widely used in games) and the other is known as walk away, where the character moves forward in the 3D world.

Animating the Walk in Place

Let's begin by creating an in-place walk cycle. In this walk cycle, the character is not moving forward at all. Instead it is kept in the initial position of the animation but can execute all the animations (an example would be walking on a treadmill, whereby you are walking but going nowhere). In-place animations are mostly done for games. The characters are translated as per need by the game engine.

1. Load 3ds Max.

2. From the command panel on the right, choose the Create tab ➤ Helper section ➤ Dropdown and choose CAT Objects. Click on CAT Parent and choose Base Human.

3. With the base of the CAT rig selected, align it to 0, 0, 0.

4. Let's set up our timeline to be 60 frames and be running at 30fps so the overall animation will be two seconds. This should be sufficient for to fit a two-stride walk cycle.

5. Let's look at the two-stride walk cycle and space out the keyframes. Refer to Figure 8-5, which shows a two-stride walk cycle. We will be creating the animation using this as reference.

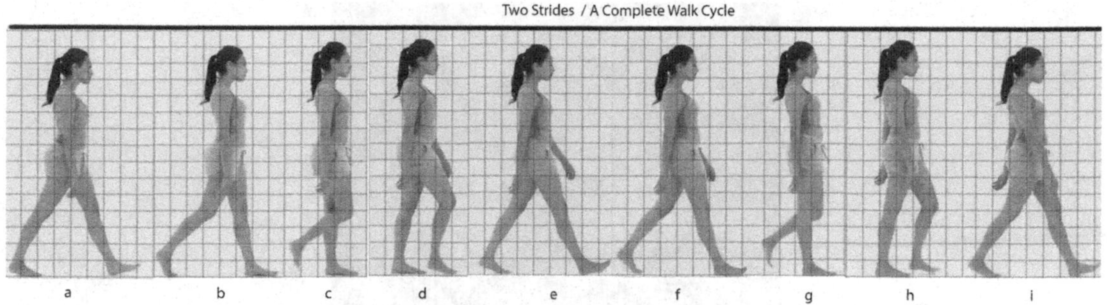

Figure 8-5. *Complete walk cycle poses (image courtesy: `https://endlessreference.com/`)*

6. We want this walk cycle to fit in a 60-frame animation. So:
   - Pose a at frame 0
   - Pose b at frame 7
   - Pose c at frame 15
   - Pose d at frame 22
   - Pose e at frame 30
   - Pose f at frame38
   - Pose g at frame 45
   - Pose h at frame 52
   - Pose i at frame 60

In order to animate a CAT rig, we need to set up an animation layer, which was covered in Chapter 6.

7. Select any part of the CAT rig and, in the command panel, switch to the Motion tab (Command Panel ➤ Motion).
8. In the motion panel, layer manager rollout, click on the Abs button. From the flyout, choose Create an Abs Layer.
9. Select the newly created layer in the layer manager and change its name in the Name section to Walk_Cycle_Feet. See Figure 8-6.

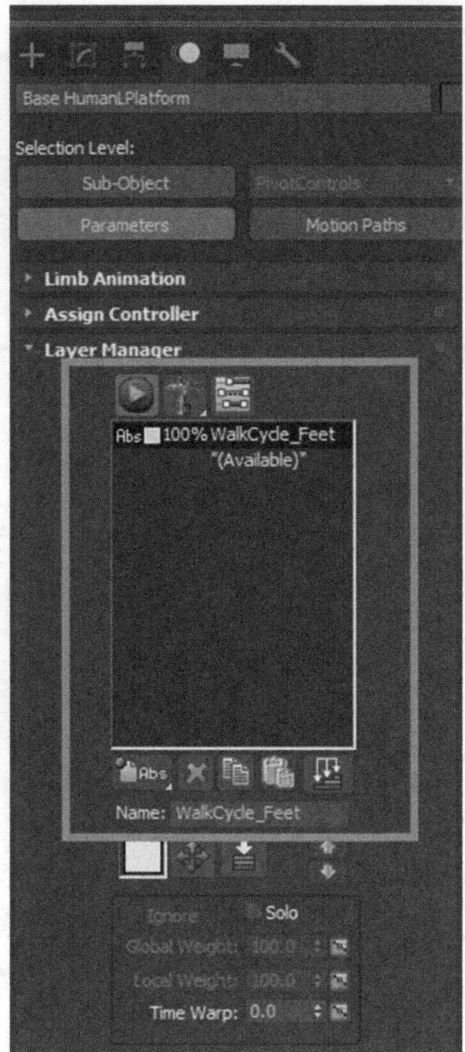

***Figure 8-6.** CAT rig animation layer*

10. When you see a red stop button below the layer manager rollout, click on it. It should turn into a green playhead. In this state, you can begin setting keyframes.

11. Once it's set, turn on AutoKey and begin posing the characters. For the legs, I use the Base HumanLPlatform and Base HumanRPlatform.

A checkpoint file has been created called `Walkcycle_Inplace.max`. At this point, you can create the arms movement in the same layer, but I suggest you create a new local adjustment layer with the icon **[+L]** and do the arm swing motion in it.

12. Now let's begin working on the arm swing. Create a local adjustment layer in the layer manager and, with Figure 8-5 as a reference, position the arms accordingly. The person in this reference doesn't swing her arm much. We can mimic her motion in three keyframes for a rough draft. I will be animating only Base HumanRPalm and Base HumanLPalm for the arm animation.

    - Pose a at frame 0
    - Pose e at frame 30
    - Pose a at frame 60

    I am using pose a again at frame 60, because at frame 60, the arm is in a different place and at frame 0, it's in an entirely different place. In order to loop animation, we want the beginning and end frame to be the same. I have gone ahead and tweaked the hand motion.

    A checkpoint file, with the feet and arm animation, is provided for your reference: `Walkcycle_Inplace01.max`.

13. Now let's begin animating the character's hips. Create one more local adjustment layer and rename it Hips_Adjustment.

    If you look at the reference image (Figure 8-7), note that I drew a line near the pelvic area. Notice the up and down position of the hips in various poses. Note that the hip is at its peak height at poses d and g.

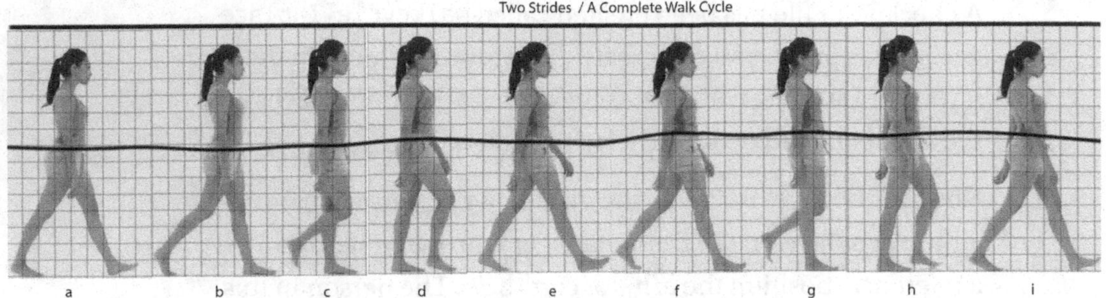

***Figure 8-7.** Hip motion: up/down reference (image courtesy: `https://endlessreference.com/`)*

14. Let's animate the hips. Select the Hip_adjustment layer in the layer manager.

15. Try to mimic the hip motion by moving it up and down a few units. Play back and preview the animation and tweak the keys as needed.

16. Add one more local adjustment layer and name it Hip_Sway. In this layer, animate the sway of the hips based on the footing. I recommend that you analyze body postures as you walk.

    A checkpoint file has been created for reference: `Walkcycle_Inplace02.max`

17. Let's add one more local adjustment layer and name it UpperBody.

18. In this adjustment layer, we are going to animate the base HumanHead movements and base HumanRibcage movements.

    In the reference image (Figure 8-7), the person walking is looking straight at the camera so there is very little to no movement.

19. I have tilted the head and rib cage up and down and sideways a bit, based on the footing of the character. Play back and preview the animation.

A checkpoint file is saved as `Walkcycle_Inplace03.max`. We have completed one walk cycle. Now we'll see how the character walks multiple steps.

I exaggerated the head animation a lot. If we had created an animation adjustment layer for head movement, we would be able to delete that alone and recreate it.

Animating the Walk Away

Note that we covered the CAT automated walk cycle in Chapter 6, where you created a CAT motion and tweaked it to your liking. In this section, we learn how to create a walk cycle where the character moves ahead in world space. The steps are more or less the same as when creating in-place movement, but the approach to creating the keyframe differs.

1. Load 3ds Max.
2. From the command panel on the right, choose the Create tab ➤ Helper section ➤ Dropdown and then choose CAT Objects. Click on CAT Parent and choose Base Human.
3. With the base of the CAT rig selected, align it to 0, 0, 0.
4. The frame rates are the same as earlier. Let's make our timeline 60 frames and the playback speed set to 30 frames per second in the Time Configuration window.
5. We will be spacing the keyframe the same as for the walk in-place, but we will be posing the character for all the body parts (see Figure 8-8):
    - Pose a at frame 0
    - Pose b at frame 7
    - Pose c at frame 15
    - Pose d at frame 22
    - Pose e at frame 30
    - Pose f at frame38
    - Pose g at frame 45
    - Pose h at frame 52
    - Pose i at frame 60

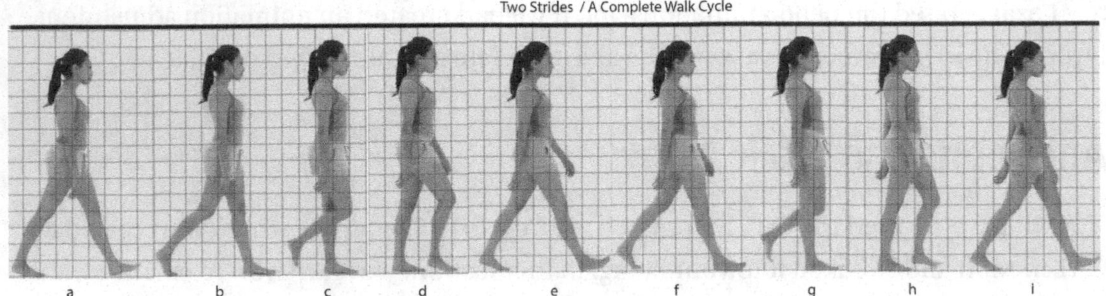

***Figure 8-8.** Complete walk cycle poses (image courtesy: `https://endlessreference.com/`)*

6. With any part of the CAT rig selected, go into the motion panel and, in the layer manager, create an absolute layer. Name it Walk_Away_Cycle. This is the only layer we are going to use.

7. Ensure that the setup animation is turned on in the layer manager of the CAT rig motion.

8. Turn on Set Key.

9. Set pose a at frame 0. Tweak the legs, arms, head, and any other parts at this frame.

10. Move to frame 7 and animate the parts. This time I want you to select the hips and move forward. Move the forward leg until it is no longer bending at the knee. Notice how the other parts of the body compensate.

11. Make any manual changes in frame 7, such as the leg rotations.

12. Let's move ahead to frame 15. Select the hip and move it forward until the leg that is forward is perpendicular to the ground. Now make adjustments to the other feet and arms.

13. Keep progressing with poses over time, as indicated in Step 5. The only thing you need to do is move the hip position forward.

A checkpoint file has been created called `WalkCycle_WalkAway01.max`. Note that I animated only the hips forward motion and the legs. If you play back the animation, the character will be moving forward in 3D space.

Animating: Walk Cycle Loop

We created an animation of one walk cycle in 60 frames, so now let's look at making the walk cycle loop as long as we need it.

1. Load `Walkcycle_Inplace03.max`.
2. Open the time configuration and set the end frame to 600. The Time Configuration dialog can be accessed by clicking on the stopwatch icon below the play controls. Once the end frame is set to 600 frames, play the animation to see how the character walks for 60 frames.
3. Open the mini Curve Editor and select Base Human from the viewport.
4. In the Curve Editor, expand the rollouts until you can see layers, as shown in Figure 8-9.

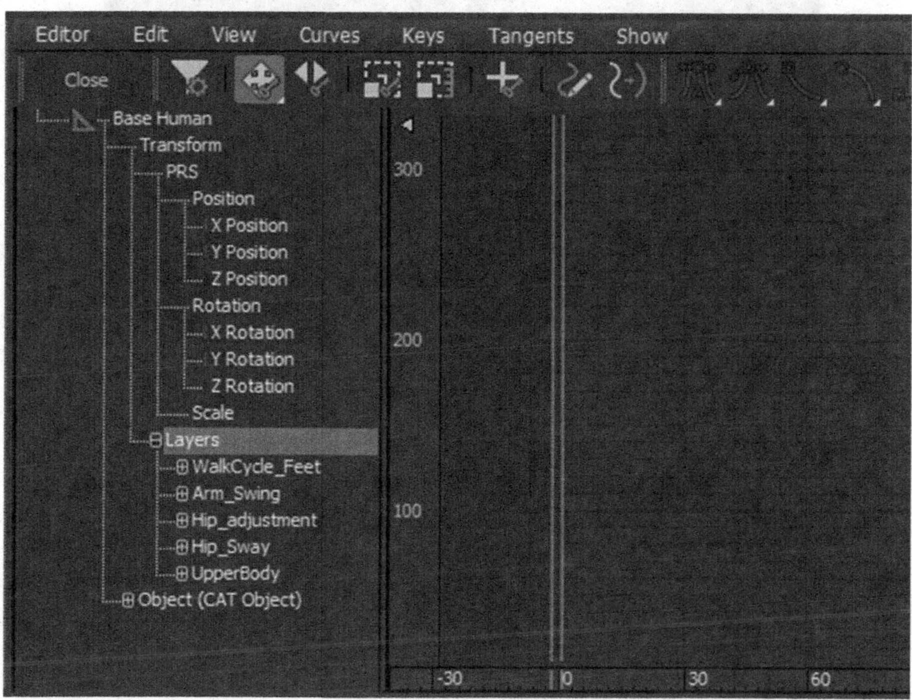

Figure 8-9. *Mini Curve Editor*

5. Note that these are the animation layers we created. Now select all the layer names that we animated. You can select the first name and hold Shift and then click on the last one to select all the animation layers. See Figure 8-10.

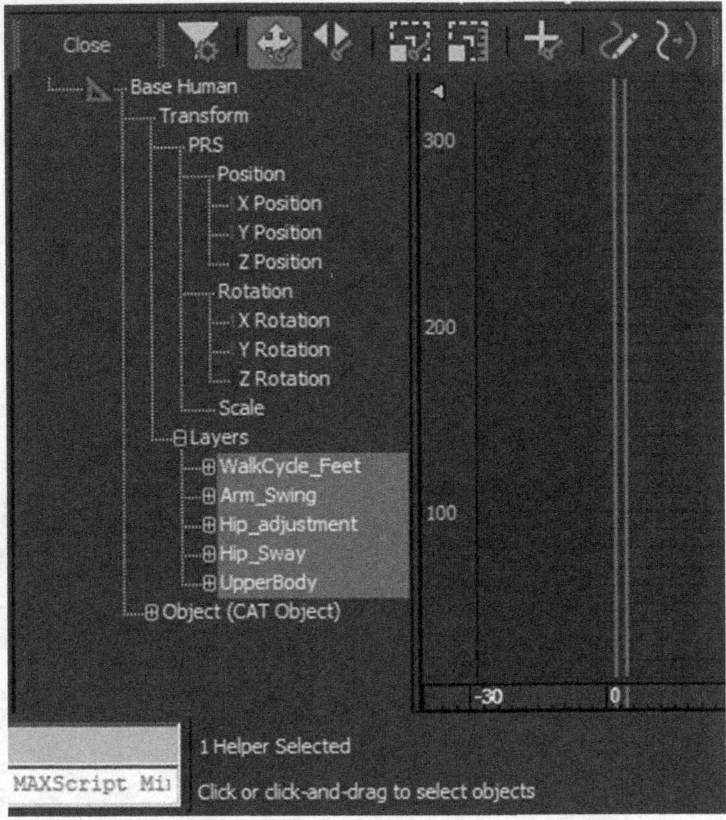

***Figure 8-10.** Mini Curve Editor: all animation layers selected*

6. Once all the animation layers are selected, in the mini Curve Editor, choose Edit ➤ Controller ➤ Out of Range Types. See Figure 8-11.

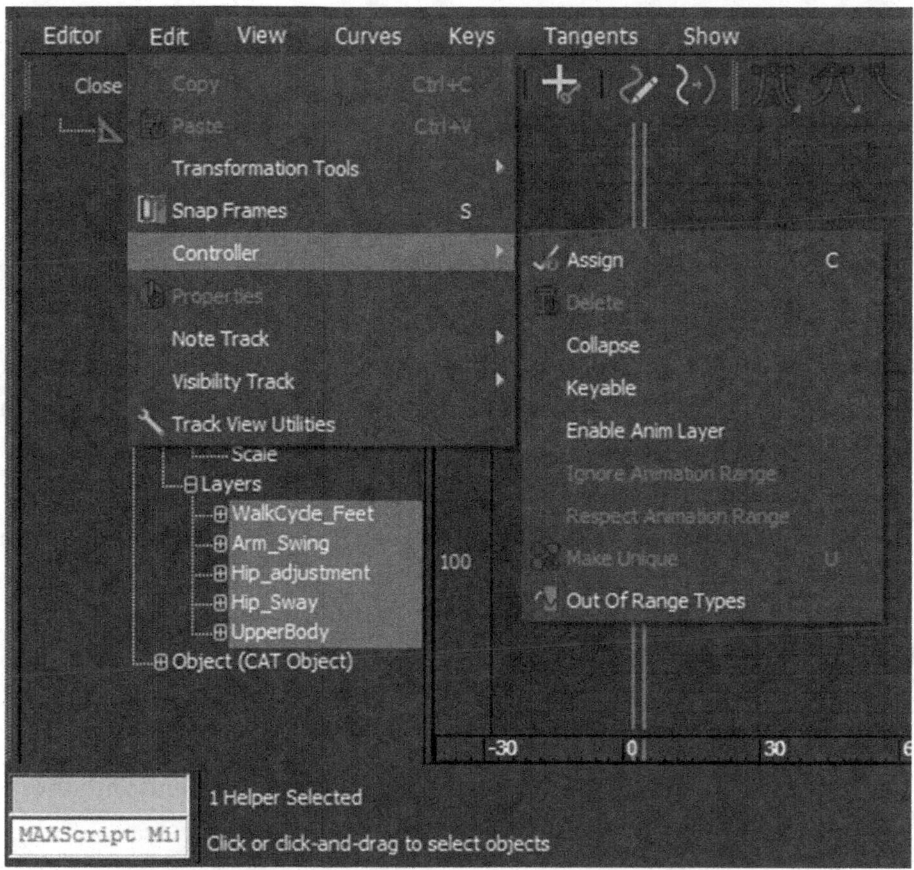

Figure 8-11. Mini Curve Editor: Out of Range Types option

7. Once you click on the Out of Range Types option, you will be presented with a dialog box, as shown in Figure 8-12.

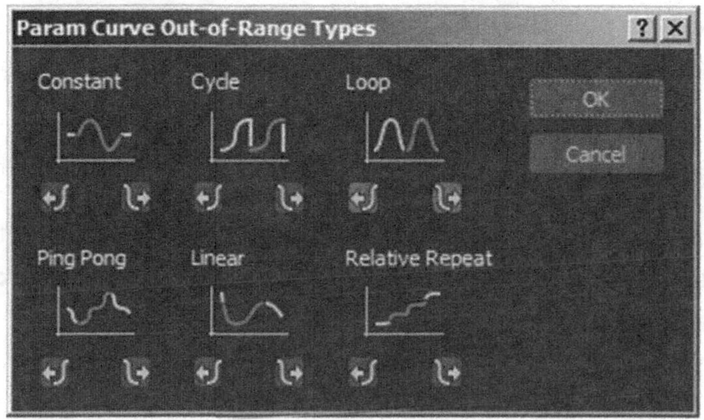

Figure 8-12. The Out of Range Types dialog box

8. Click on the Loop thumbnail. Note that the in and out points turn blue, which indicates that the current selection is loop.

9. Click OK and then wait. It might take a moment for the software to apply the loop. Do not panic; the software is not frozen.

10. Once the dialog box vanishes, play and preview the animation. Voila, you have created a looping animation!

A checkpoint file has been created called `Walkcycle_InplaceLoop.max`.

This technique can be applied to any animation that has beginning and ending keyframes with the same values for position, rotation, and scale. Unfortunately, this cannot be applied to the Walk Away cycle because the position of the rig parts are at different coordinates in the first and last frame of the animation.

You can still attempt to loop it, but the results will be very erratic and undesired.

Analyzing the Run Cycle

The key poses for the run cycle (one stride) are as follows:

- Contact pose a: This is the key pose where we begin and end with the same pose for a loopable run cycle, as seen in the walk cycle.
- Pass through pose b: The running pose. This is similar to our pass pose in walking. This is where the legs change lead to front.
- Up pose 1/Kick off pose c: This is where the character begins to gain momentum to lift up.
- Up pose 2/Air pose d: This is where the character gets air time. In this pose the character has both its legs up in the air.
- Contact pose e: This is the same as the contact pose, but with alternating legs.

In the running pose, notice that both legs are on the ground. The footing needs to go through a contact pose a, pass through pose b, up pose 1 c, up pose 2 d, and then the contact pose e. See Figure 8-13.

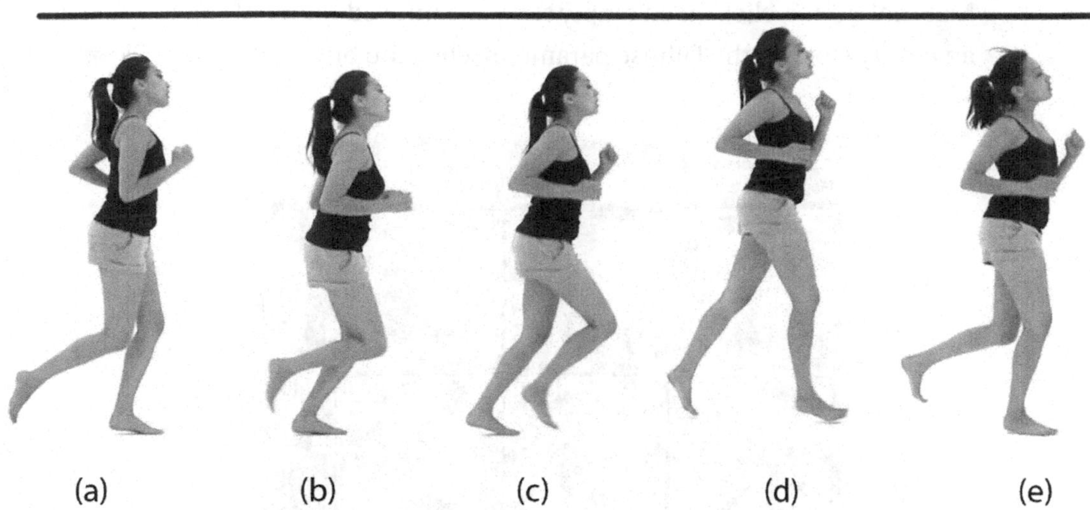

Figure 8-13. *Run cycle poses, half a cycle*

Rotomation

Another technique used by animators to animate lifelike motion is called *rotomation*. Rotomation is like tracing artwork on paper. We sketch frames over time and create an animation. Let's dive into an example of how to set one up. Again for this purpose we need a video reference. As I mentioned earlier, I recommend the YouTube channel (`https://www.youtube.com/user/endlessreference`) for reference videos. Their official website (`https://endlessreference.com/`) is good for high-quality videos of varied animations. The kind of video required is something similar to `https://www.youtube.com/watch?v=G8Veye-NOA4`. The grid overlays are optional but helpful.

Once you have the video, you need to convert it to image sequences. Note the frame rate and aspect ratio of the video. You will need it.

1. Fire up 3ds Max.

2. In the left or right viewport, create a box. The dimension of the box should match the video dimensions. For example, the dimension of the video I used is 1280x720. I do not want to create a box that is 1280 units big, so instead I can simplify it by dividing it by 100. So my box will be 12.80x7.20.

3. Once the box is created, press M to create a material. In the Material Editor, click on an empty slot (any unused material slot is an empty slot). In the Diffuse parameter, click the button next to it.

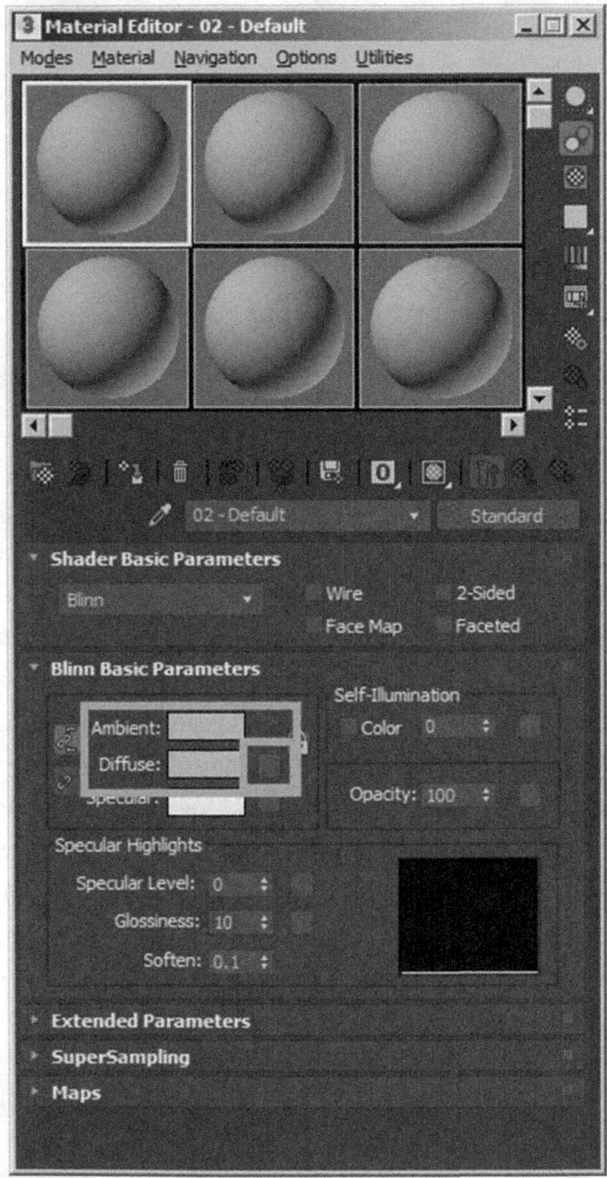

Figure 8-14. Material Editor

4. Click on the small button next to Diffuse, as shown in Figure 8-14.

5. Click on the Bitmap option from the box that pops up and click OK. Refer to Figure 8-15.

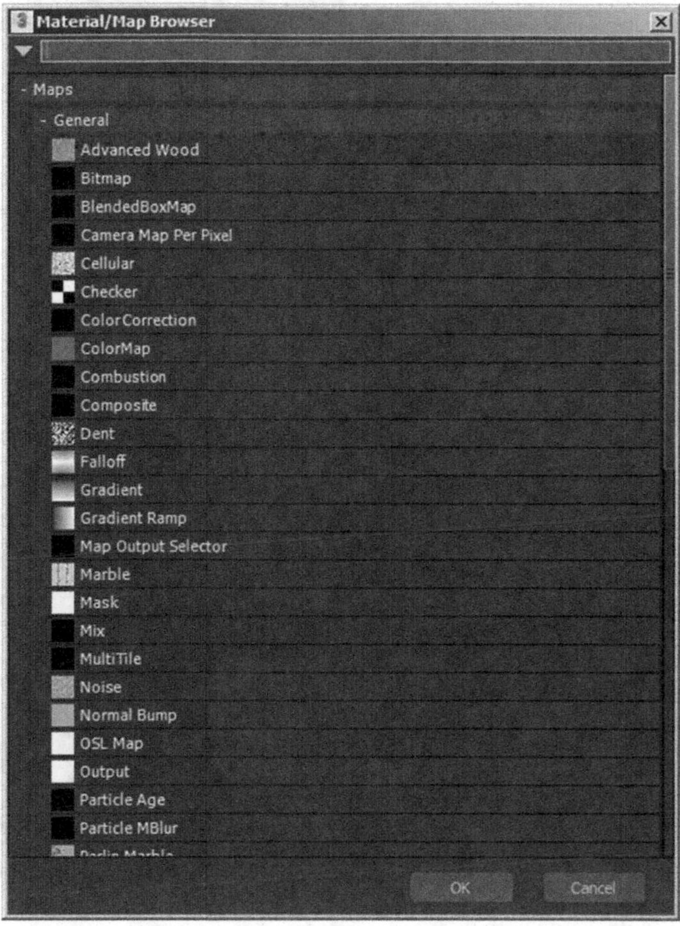

Figure 8-15. *Map Browser*

6. In the Open dialog box, browse to the location you have saved your image sequence and choose the first image. Ensure that the image sequence checkbox is checked, as shown in Figure 8-16.

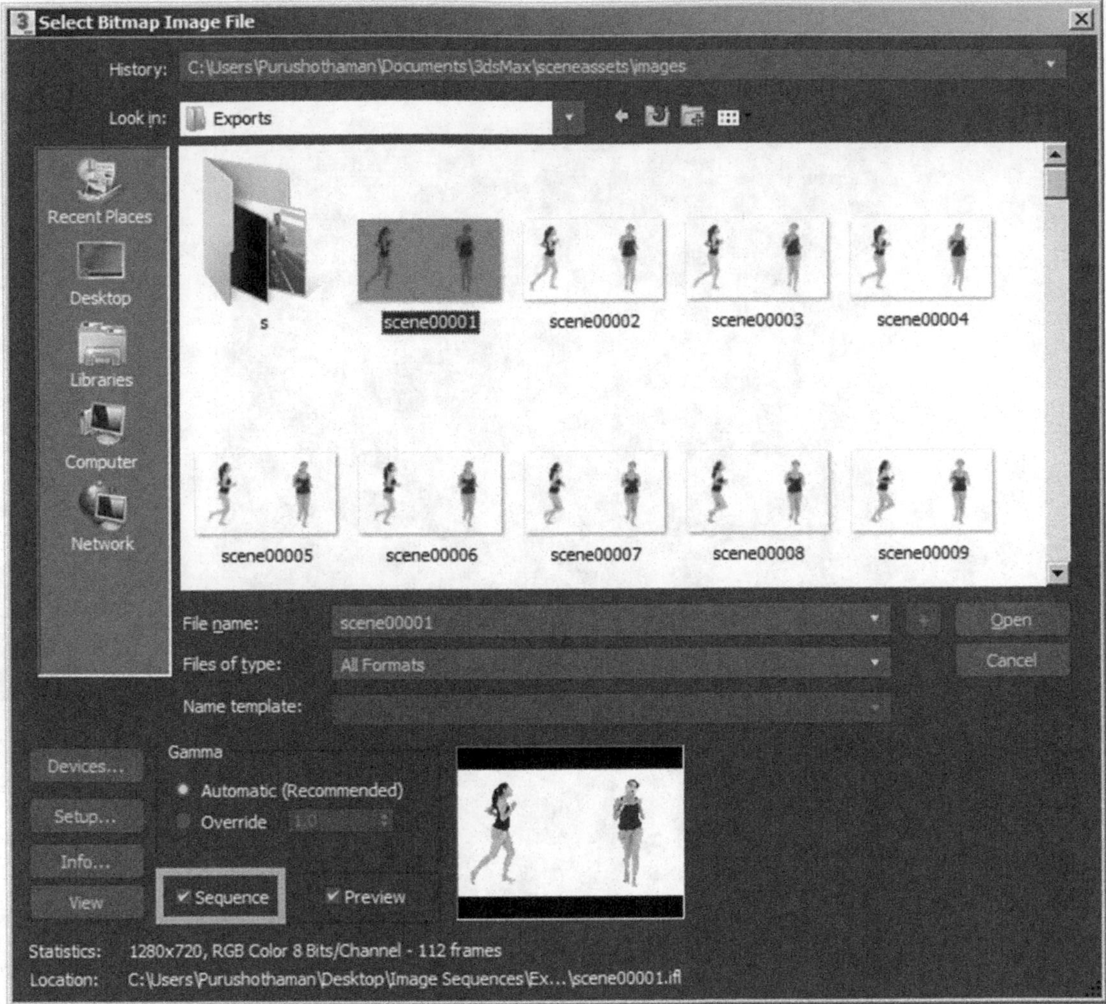

***Figure 8-16.** Select Bitmap Image dialog*

7. Once you have done this, click the Open button.

8. You will be presented with one additional dialog box; click OK to accept the settings. Note the end frame number from the file list control, as you need that number to set the duration of the timeline (see Figure 8-17).

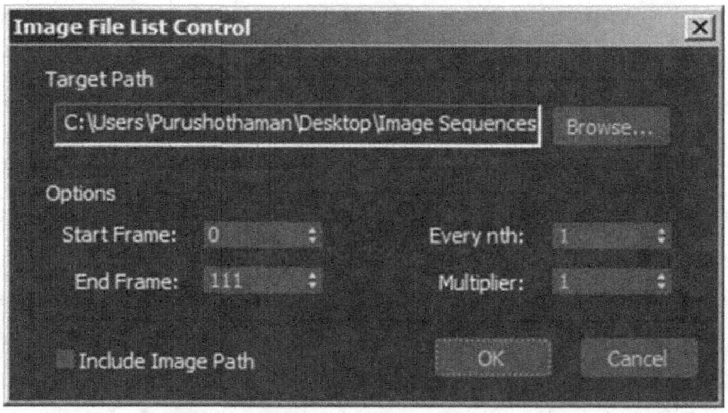

Figure 8-17. *File list control*

9. Select the material and drag and drop it on the box you created. Toggle the Show Shaded Material in Viewport option. See Figure 8-18.

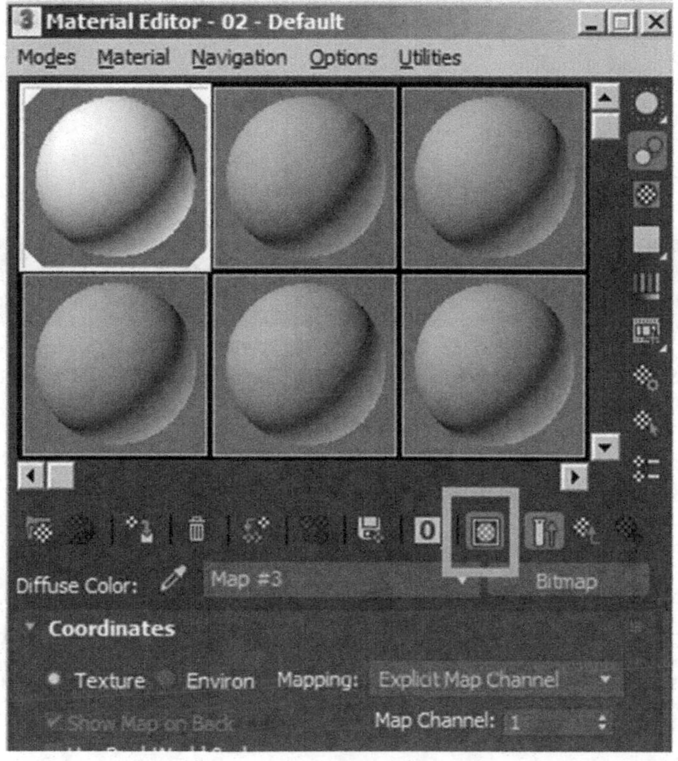

Figure 8-18. *Material Editor, show shaded material in viewport*

10. You should now be able to see the image in the box. Open the time configuration and set the end time as specified in the end frame that we saw earlier in the Image File List control.

11. Your 3ds Max viewport should look something like Figure 8-19. We are going to use this as a reference and animate our character rigs.

***Figure 8-19.** 3ds Max UI: image sequence on box (Image sequence courtesy: `https://endlessreference.com/`)*

If you use the play control and press Play, you should see that the video is playing.

12. The next step is to bring in your rig or create one. I am going to create a CAT rig. Position your box behind the CAT rig, as shown in Figure 8-20. Reposition and scale as applicable (when scaling, use the uniform scale option).

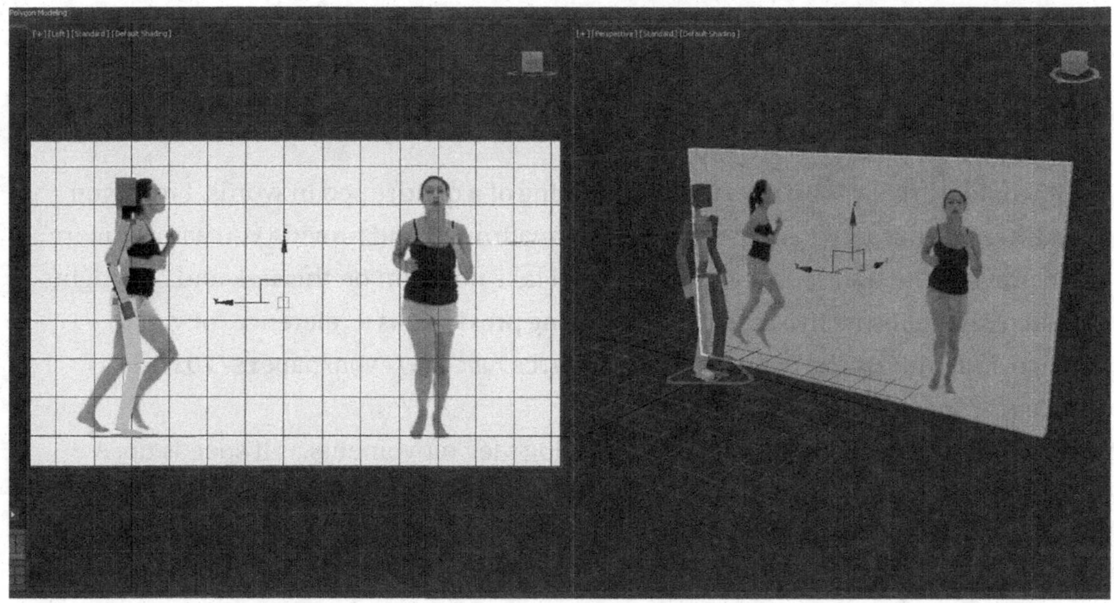

Figure 8-20. *3ds Max UI box lined up to the CAT rig (image sequence courtesy: `https://endlessreference.com/`)*

13. Right-click the box and, in the object properties, uncheck Show Frozen in Gray. Then freeze the box. This way you don't accidentally move the box.

14. Now you can start key framing the rig over time based on the backdrop shown in the box. Follow the steps in the Animation Walk Cycle section.

This is rotomation explained in a very basic way. A lot of animators use this technique to create quality animations.

Quadruped Run/Walk Cycles

A quadruped walk cycle can be of various types. For a human we can say walk, jog, and run. For a quadruped, let's take a dog as an example, the available types of walk/run cycles are as follows:

- Walk
- Amble
- Pace

- Trot
- Canter
- Run or gallop

It would be really hard to explain the footing of a quadruped in words. I refer you to an Internet source, where they simulate a quadruped and provide you with a binary file to preview the walk/run styles for a dog. (I take no claim on this link and copyrights remain with the respective author. This is being provided as a reference for you to practice and understand better: `https://www.cs.ubc.ca/~van/papers/2011-TOG-quadruped/index.html`.)

I recommend you study the pattern of a dog's leg movements as it speeds up. A rotomation technique would be a good starting point when animating quadrupeds. As you begin setting keyframes, it would be easier to grasp the patterns in the leg's locomotion.

Let's use the CAT motion editor to achieve varied walk/run and sneak results of a quadruped rig. We have already seen the CAT motion editor in the CAT rig section for a biped, so now let's look at a few options that ease the animator's life for a quadruped rig.

1. Load 3ds Max.
2. From the Create panel, choose Helpers ➤ CAT Parent. Create a Panther CAT rig from the preset. We are going to use this rig, as it can be used for a wide range of animals (cats, dogs, wolves, lions, tigers, etc.). A reference file has been created called `Panther_CATRig_Start.max`.
3. Once the CAT_Rig is created, select the base triangle of the rig and go to the motion pane of the command panel.
4. Create a CAT motion layer from the layer list, as shown in Figure 8-21.

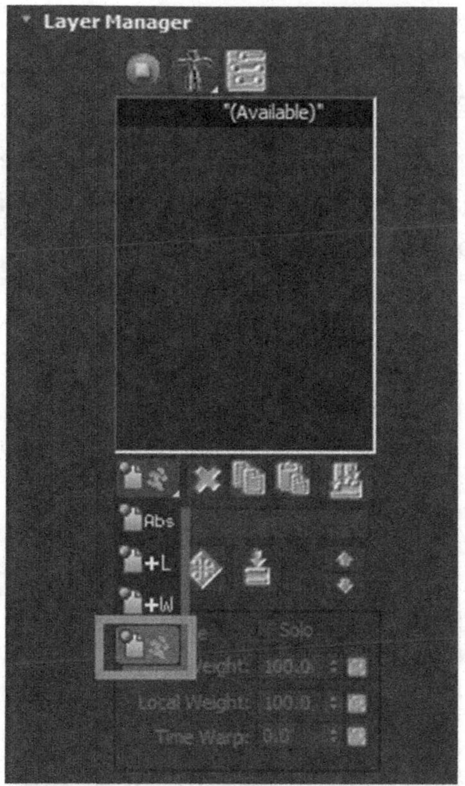

Figure 8-21. *3ds Max CAT motion layer, CAT rig*

5. Once a layer is created, click on the Setup/Animation toggle. The red Stop button is below the layer manager, as depicted in Figure 8-22. When you click it, it should become a green play icon. The panther rig will change its posture as well.

6. Press Play and you should see the rig walking in place. A checkpoint file has been created in the `scenes` folder called `Panther_CATRig_Start01.max`.

7. This is a default walk. We can tweak its speed and alter it to mimic, walk, run, and gallop using the CAT motion editor. Click on the Paw icon, as shown in Figure 8-22.

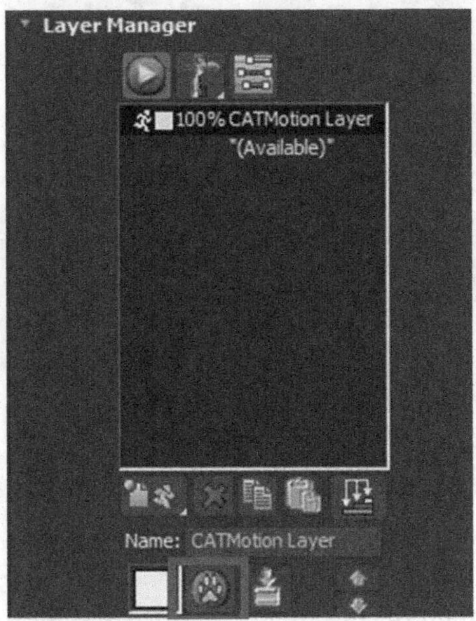

Figure 8-22. *3ds Max CAT motion editor icon*

8. Clicking on the denoted icon will load the CAT motion editor, as shown in Figure 8-23. Select the Globals section on the left pane.

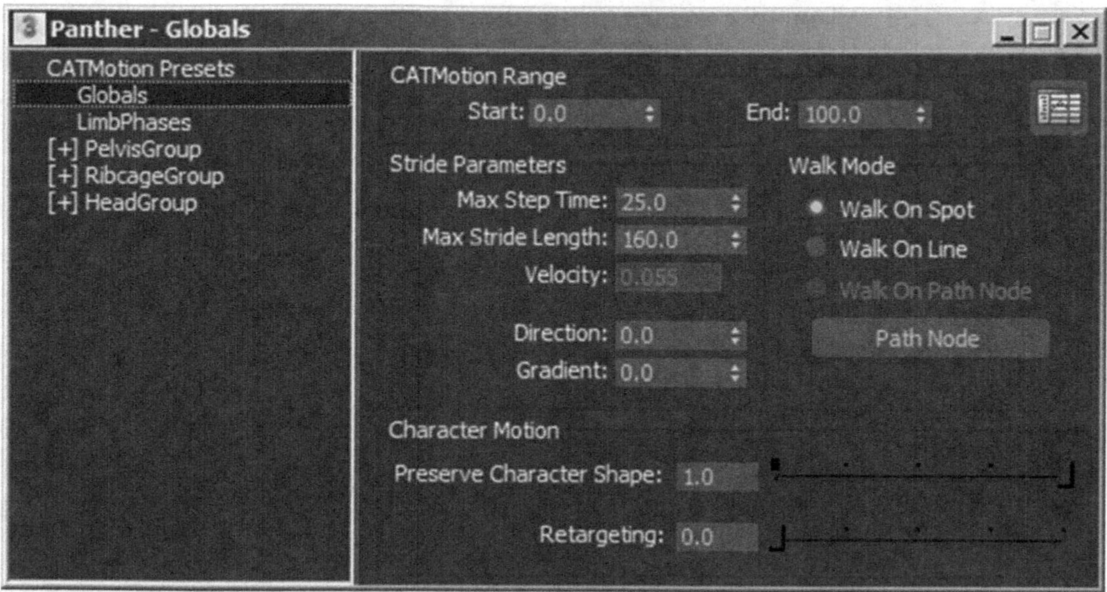

Figure 8-23. *3ds Max CAT motion editor*

9. Let's look at a few parameters in the Globals section that will help alter the walk cycle a lot. Note that you can play the animation using the play controls and tweak the values to see changes happen in real-time.

    - Max step time is currently set to 25. If you play the animation, you should notice that the character does a four-step walk. Our total frames are 100. With a value of 25, it's four steps. Now change the value to 10. The rig begins to walk faster.

    - Now let's set the max step time to 75. Play the animation and notice how slow the step is. Also notice how the animation is not looping correctly because the step time is set to 75 and our overall frame is 100. The animation restarts after a second step is initiated but is not completed, as there are only 25 more frames are left. A quick tip here would be to always have the total number of frames of your animation equally divisible by the max step. Feel free to open the Time Configuration window the play ahead and adjust the end frame to 150.

- The walk on spot is going to have the rig walk in place. Walk on line is the same as walk away, as discussed in the walk cycle of bipeds.

10. Now let's switch to the Limb Phases category in the CAT motion editor.
11. If you notice in Figure 8-24, 3ds Max names the legs in a weird way. There is no label for the front and back legs. Legs 1 and 2 are for the back, and legs 3 and 4 are the front legs.

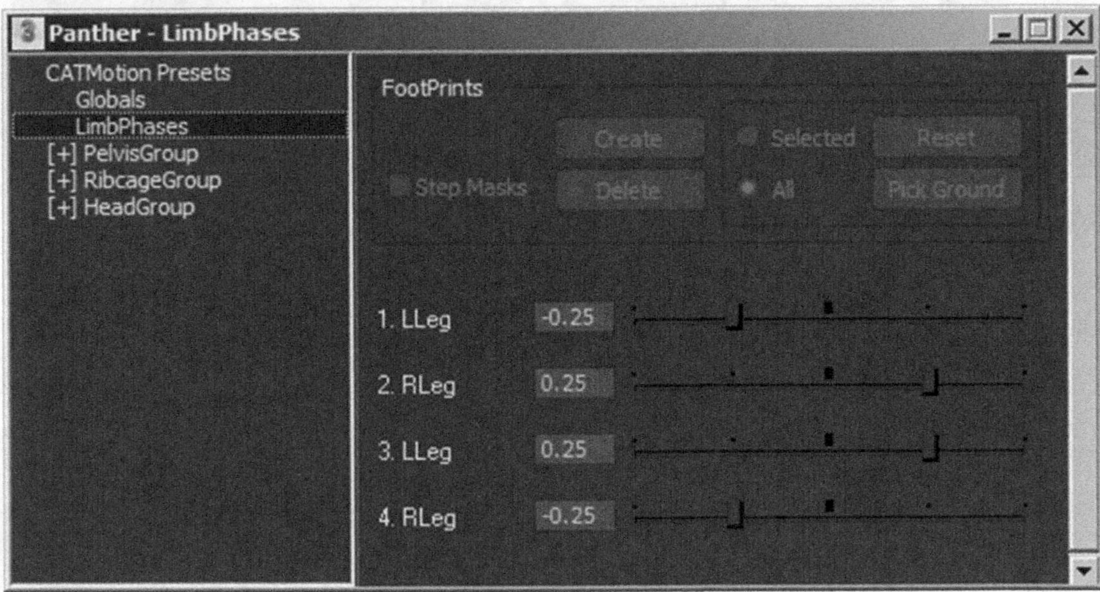

***Figure 8-24.** 3ds Max CAT motion editor, limb phases*

12. Set the leg values as follows:
    - 1LLeg to 0.25
    - 2Rleg to 0.25
    - 3LLeg to -0.25
    - 4RLeg to -0.25

Once you set these values, you should notice that the rig resembles the leg movement of a fast-running feline beast. You can now go back to the globals and decrease the Max Step Time to get a faster animation. Likewise, you can go into the other categories and tweak the values to your liking as you preview the animation.

13. At this point, I would like to show you one more option. Let's reset the leg values to their defaults:
    - 1LLeg to -0.25
    - 2Rleg to 0.25
    - 3LLeg to 0.25
    - 4RLeg to -0.25
    - Change the Max Step time to 75 so that the rig walks very slowly.
14. Now turn off Setup/Animation mode by clicking on the Green play icon in the layer manager. Your rig will go into the default pose. At this point if you play and preview, there will be no animations.
15. Select the PantherRibcage and PantherPelvis and bring them down until you see the rig get into a posture of a predator sneaking up on its prey. Move and rotate the head as needed. Refer to Figure 8-25.

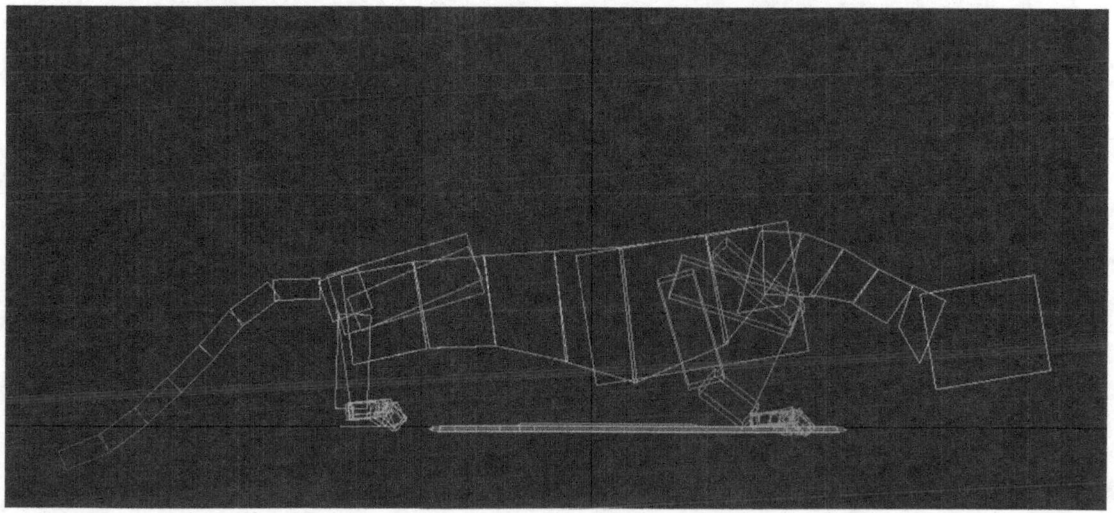

***Figure 8-25.** 3ds Max CAT motion editor, sneak posture*

16. Now select the base of the rig, the triangle, and go into motion options. Turn on setup/animation mode and preview the animation. Now you should see the predator sneaking. Notice how, by adjusting the base position, we were able to get a varied motion. Tweak it and test multiple values to get varied results. A reference file called `Panther_CATRig_Start02.max` is provided in the `scenes` folder of Chapter 8.

Note that we didn't touch the tail in this exercise. It is like a stiff stick. You can animate it by giving it twist and rolls, as well as add sway to the heads, shoulder twists, and much more. You know the tools now, so go ahead and bring the object to life.

Summary

In this chapter, we learned the key poses of walk and run cycles for a biped, as well as about a technique called rotomation that is widely used by animators. We used the CAT rigs motion tool to create procedural animation and tweaked its parameters to get walk, run, gallop, and Sneak animation by just making a few adjustments. Remember that these are still rough animations. They need a lot of refinement and tweaking before the object can be called a finished one. Look and analyze multiple references and see what the character is missing. In the next chapter, we cover facial animation using morphs and facial rigs.

CHAPTER 9

Morph Animation and Facial Rigging

In the previous chapters, we learned how to create custom character rigs using bones, bipeds, and CAT tools. In this chapter, we will look at creating facial animation for our characters. We will also learn about the techniques that are primarily used for facial animations:

- First technique is purely based on morph targets, and this technique is used for close-up shots where only the character's face is in the frame and not the rest of the body.
- The second technique is a hybrid of bones and morphs. We use the bones to give head rotations and movement, while the morph targets handle the facial expressions.

Morph Animation

Before we begin to learn morph animation, let's consider what morphing is. *Morphing* is the process of changing the appearance of one object to another. A quick example is the metal man from the *Terminator Judgment Day* movie where he changes into various people he meets. Another example of a classical 2D morph is from the movie *Saving Private Ryan,* in the end scene where Private Ryan sees the grave of Captain Miller. In this shot, you see Private Ryan morph from his young self to an older age in a seamless manner. Let's now delve deeper into creating morphs in 3ds Max.

Morph animation in 3ds Max can be easily done through the Morpher Modifier from the Modifier list. In order to perform a morph animation, you need a minimum of two objects— a source and a target object. (You can have any number of morphs. We will look at that in the face morphing exercise.)

P. Raju, *Character Rigging and Advanced Animation*, https://doi.org/10.1007/978-1-4842-5037-2_9

In order to achieve a predictable result when transforming one object into another, you need to make sure that both objects have the same number of vertices. This usually would not be a problem if you create your source object and copy it and use the copy as the target. The target can have its vertices, edges, or polygons moved, rotated, and scaled. Note that you cannot perform any modeling toolset tools, as they will change the poly count of the object.

Working of a Morpher

Let's run through a quick example of how Morpher works to begin with and then we will move into facial animation using morphers. We will morph a Cabernet wine glass type to a Burgundy one (see Figure 9-1). Of course there are a lot of other types of glasses, so let's use this to understand how morphs work.

Figure 9-1. *Red wine glass types*

Fire up 3ds Max and load `Morph_Begin.max`. (If you get an error about missing the image `Wineglasstypes.jpeg`, browse to the reference image folder of Chapter 9 and choose the image from the folder to assign it.) I modeled the Cabernet wine glass using the polygon modeling tools. If you right-click on the Cabernet glass that is modeled and go to Object Properties, you should see the vertices and faces count, as shown in Figure 9-2.

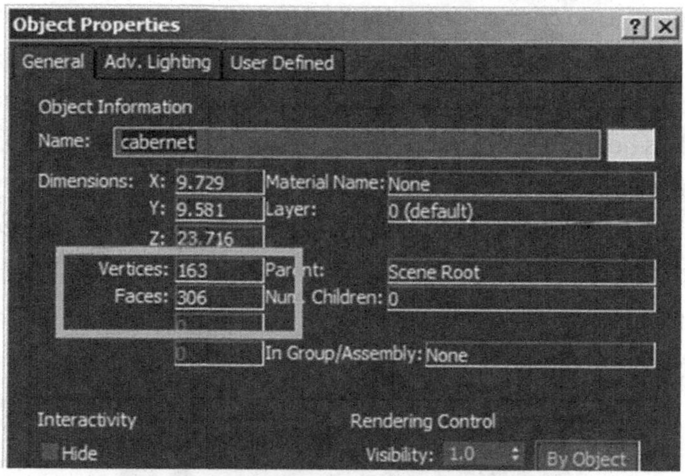

Figure 9-2. *Object properties: Vertices and Faces count*

Now we need to model the Burgundy wine glass, since we need both shapes for the morph to work. You can model the burgundy following the reference image, as set in the `Begin_Morph.max`, but you need to remember that both objects should have the same number of vertices. It's going to be hard to keep track of the number of vertices as we model (it's possible to model by keeping the vertex count in check for every step of your model, but it is not ideal to do it this way).

The easier and better approach when you want to animate using morphs is to make a copy of the source object (in our case, the Cabernet glass), hold down the Shift key, and move it (using the Move tool) to the position of the Burgundy glass in the reference image. When you let go, you will be prompted with a dialog, as shown in Figure 9-3.

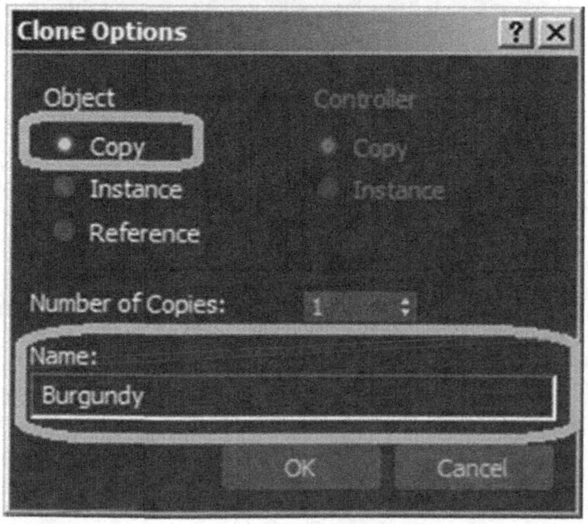

Figure 9-3. *Clone options*

We need a copy of it, so choose Copy. If you need more copies, you can change the number of copies. For now, we need only one. Rename the new copy Burgundy. When you let go, you should have two objects—one named Cabernet and the other named Burgundy. A checkpoint file has been created up until this point called `Morph_Begin01.max`.

Since we copied/cloned the first object, the second object will share the same vertex count. Now, with the second object aligned to the reference image, select it and go into subobject mode of Editable Mesh ➤ Vertex from the modifier stack. Begin tweaking the vertices to align them to fit as per the burgundy glass in the reference image. See Figure 9-4.

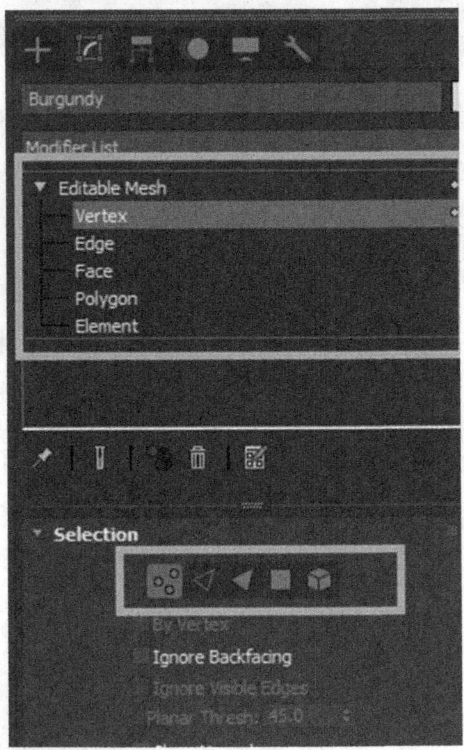

Figure 9-4. *Subobject Mode*

Remember not to use any modeling tools, as they will add/remove vertices based on the tool. See Figure 9-5.

Note You can select the Burgundy object and press Alt+X to make it see through.

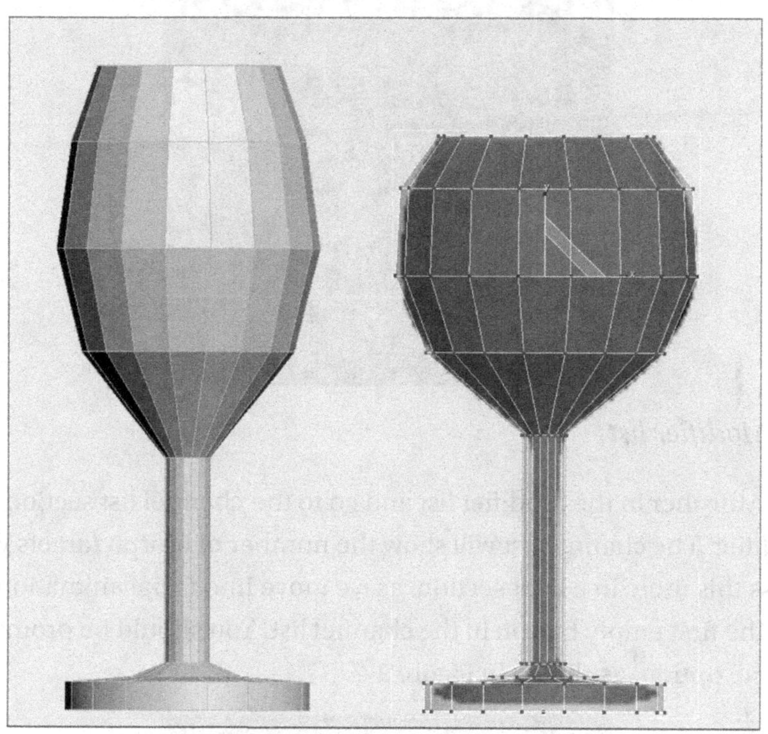

Figure 9-5. *X-ray mode alignment of burgundy object*

Once you are happy with the settings, you will have two different-looking objects with the same number of vertices and faces, which is a must-have for any object to morph. A checkpoint file has been created called `Morph_Begin02.max`.

Our intention is to morph Cabernet to Burgundy, so select the Cabernet image and choose the Modify tab in the command panel. Add a Morpher modifier by clicking on the Modifier list and choosing Morpher. See Figure 9-6.

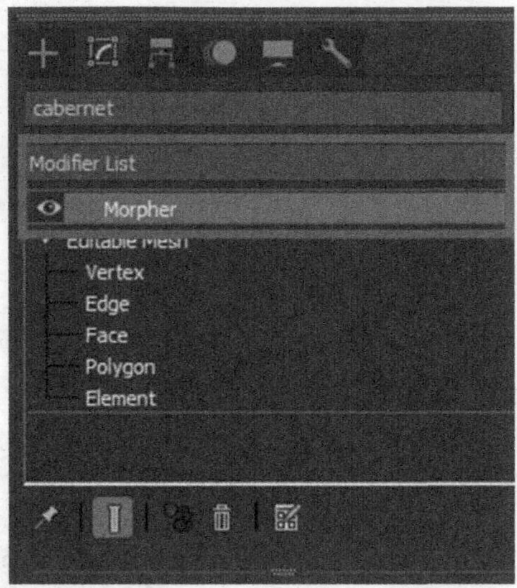

Figure 9-6. *Modifier list*

Select the Morpher in the Modifier list and go to the channel list section of the Morpher modifier. The channel list will show the number of morph targets you can add. We will discuss this more in a later section, as we move into facial animations. For now, right-click on the first empty button in the channel list. You should be prompted with the Pick From Scene option, as shown in Figure 9-7.

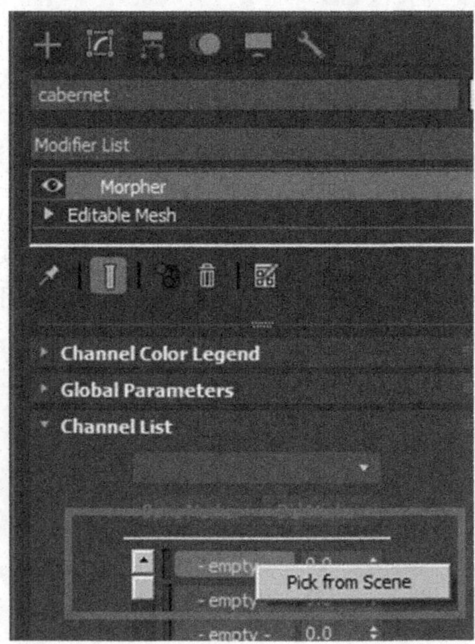

Figure 9-7. *Morpher channel, Pick From Scene option*

Click on Pick From Scene and click on the Burgundy Object in the viewport. Once you have chosen the Burgundy object, the channel list should show the first channel with the Burgundy name and a green light, which denotes that there is a morph. See Figure 9-8.

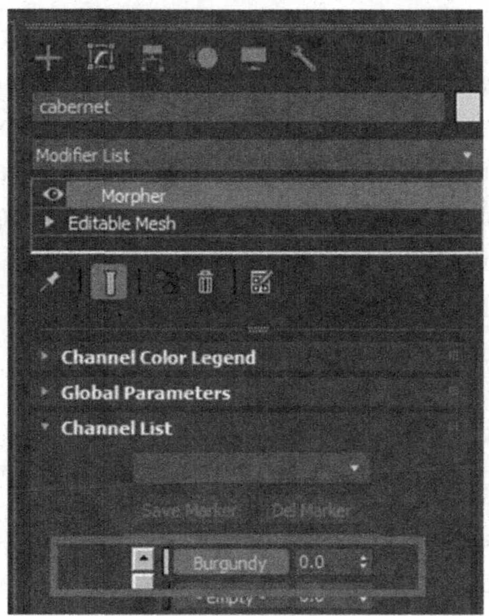

Figure 9-8. *Morpher channel, target object added*

At this point I would like you to use the spinner next to the Burgundy name in channel list and see what happens in the viewport. Your Cabernet glass should morph into a burgundy glass as you increase the value from 0 to 100. You can now turn on Auto Key and change the values as needed to animate the morph.

Note Before you render the animation, you need to hide the backdrop and the Burgundy object or move it away from the camera view so that it is not visible in your renders.

This is morph animation at a basic level. There are more than just two types of wine glasses, though. By modeling the other kinds using the same technique of clone and tweak and adding them to the subsequent channels in the channel list, you could animate to many targets concurrently—such as a Burgundy and a short glass. By adding both to their respective channels, you could even animate from a Cabernet to a short Burgundy glass (both morphs are applied at the same time!).

Facial Animation

Facial animation can be tedious and also easier based on the approach you take to achieve the animation. In earlier chapters, we completed a rig that used basic movements for a character's head. We were able to tilt and rotate the head using the controllers, but facial animation goes beyond that. We need our characters to speak and show emotions to give them more life. Let's look at facial animation using morphs.

In order to set up your character for facial animation with morphs, you need to determine the number of morphs needed. (Remember in our earlier exercise we had a Cabernet glass and wanted it to morph to a Burgundy glass.) Morphs need to be created based on the persona of the character. Let's go on a guided tour to understand the morphs used for a typical human face animation.

Typical facial animation can be split into two categories:

- Emotions of a character for expressions
- Phonemes for speech animation

Let's get deeper into each of these pointers and break them down further to see what morphs need to be created.

Emotions: Facial Expression

Humans are capable of showing diverse expressions. To recreate all those expressions is cumbersome, so in general the following animations are more than enough for characters in games or short animations, unless you intend to show more diverse expression.

- Happiness
- Sadness
- Anger
- Fear/shock
- Surprise
- Disgust

When a human character shows any of these expressions, there are a number of muscles involved in contorting the face to show what we see. At this point, I suggest you mimic these expressions in a mirror and note the changes happening in your face, especially when compared to a neutral state when no expression is shown.

You should have noted the following points. Compare these to your observations. I am just noting down key features. There is a lot more happening if you look into it in detail.

- Happiness: The mouth corners are wider and go up a bit.
- Sadness: The mouth corners are lower compared to a normal position.
- Anger: Lowered eyebrows, lips closed or slightly open to show teeth.
- Fear/shock: Eyebrows raised and mouth slightly open.
- Surprise: Eyes wide open and mouth open (more like a jaw drop).
- Disgust: Eyes nearly closed (not entirely, around 80%, although this varies based on race and culture) and cheeks raised.

Let's go ahead and create facial animation of emotions with morphs.

I detached the head of the character that we previously used for rigging and deleted the body so that we can focus on the facial features alone. I created a checkpoint file with the head alone called `Human_Head.max`.

Fire up 3ds Max and open `human_head.max`. You should see the human head detached from the body. I also renamed the object to neutral. This serves as our default facial pose.

1. Select the neutral face. Hold Shift down and move it using the Move tool along the X axis.
2. Release the mouse button, and in the Clone Options, choose copy. Set the number of copies to 6.
3. Name the copies Happiness, Sadness, Anger, Fear, Surprise, and Disgust.
4. Now comes the hardest part of the exercise. You need to go into the modifier stack of each head. (Leave the neutral state as is and tweak the polygons, edges, and vertices using the translation tools. (Remember: No modeling tools!)

5. Do not forget to use the Soft Selection in the modifier stack of the editable poly to get a smooth deformation. Enable Use Soft Selection and increase or decrease the falloff range for the desired output. Any polygon within the red-orange area is going to be heavily influenced by the translation, while the ones in the blue range are least affected by the transform. Anything not within the color range will not be affected at all. See Figure 9-9.

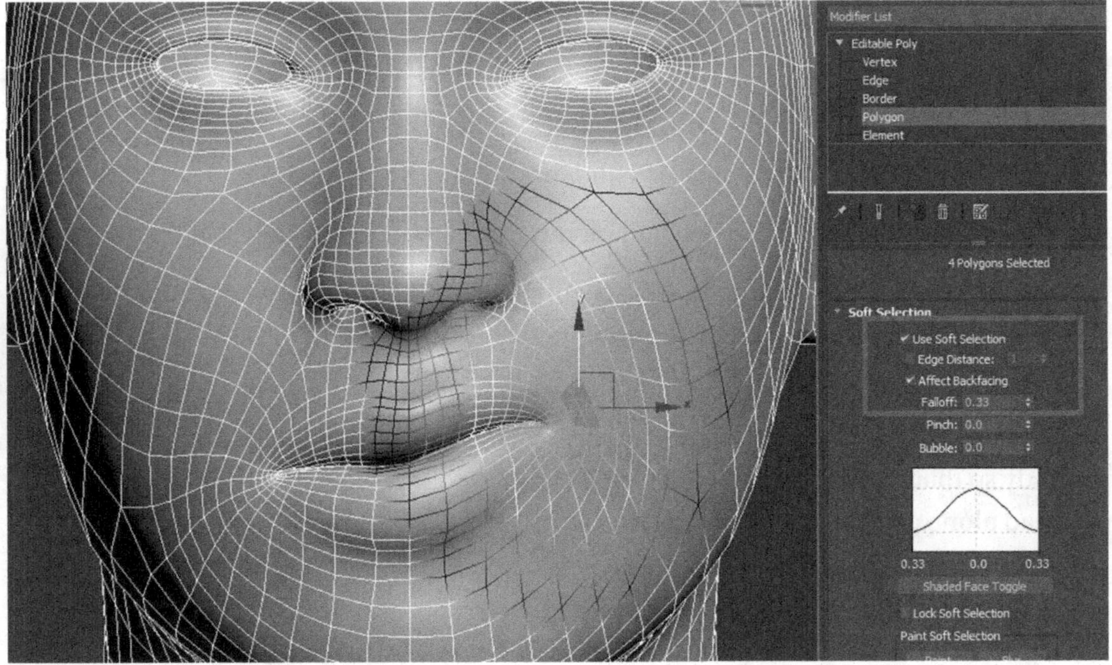

Figure 9-9. *Soft selection*

I recommend you find images or take photographs of a person who matches the persona of the character you are trying to animate and use that as a backdrop or reference. I created a checkpoint file with all the tweaked emotions. The reference file is called `Emotions.max`.

You can see these emotions in Figures 9-10 through 9-12.

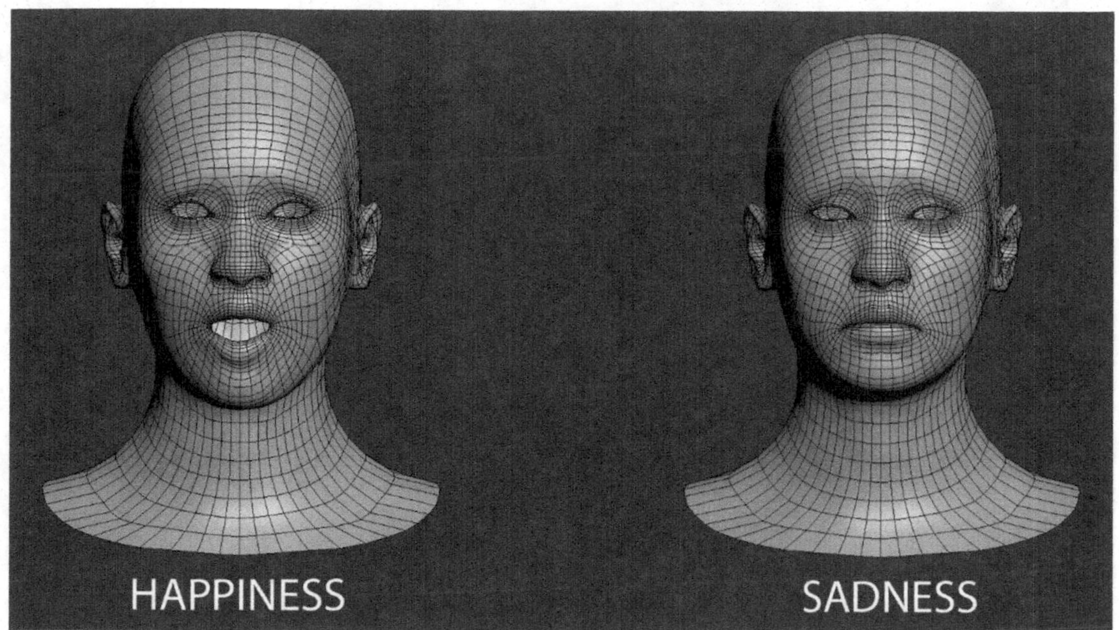

Figure 9-10. *Happy and sad emotions*

In Figure 9-10, apart from the obvious mouth open and closed state, there is a lot happening around the mouth area. Notice the shape of the chin in both states. Next up, Figure 9-11 shows anger and fear.

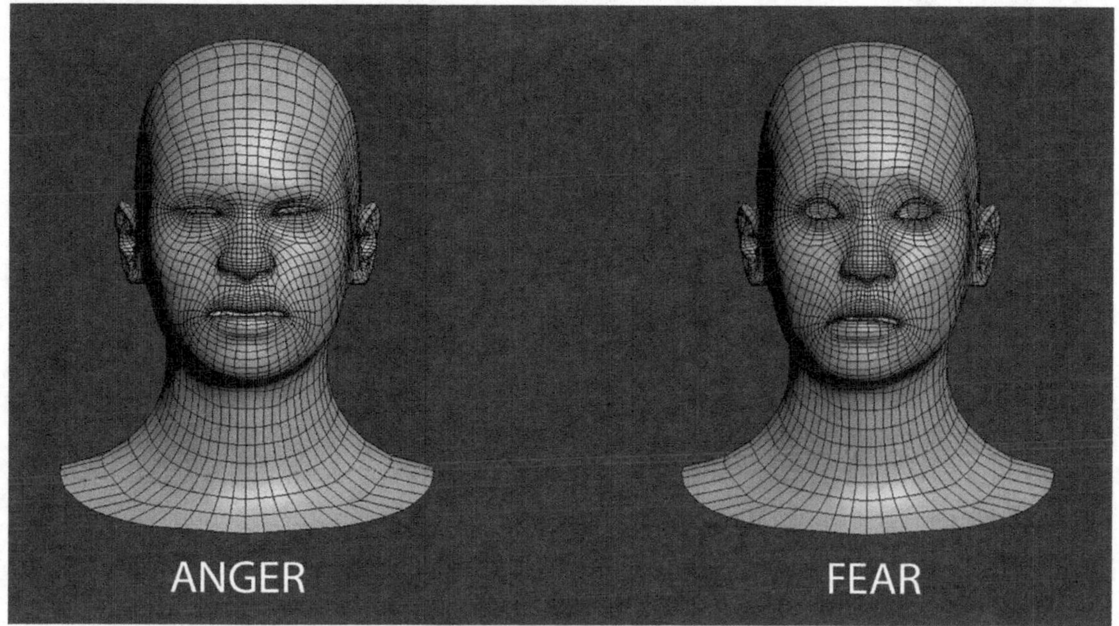

Figure 9-11. *Anger and fear*

Much of the tweaks in Figure 9-12 are around the eyes and mouth areas.

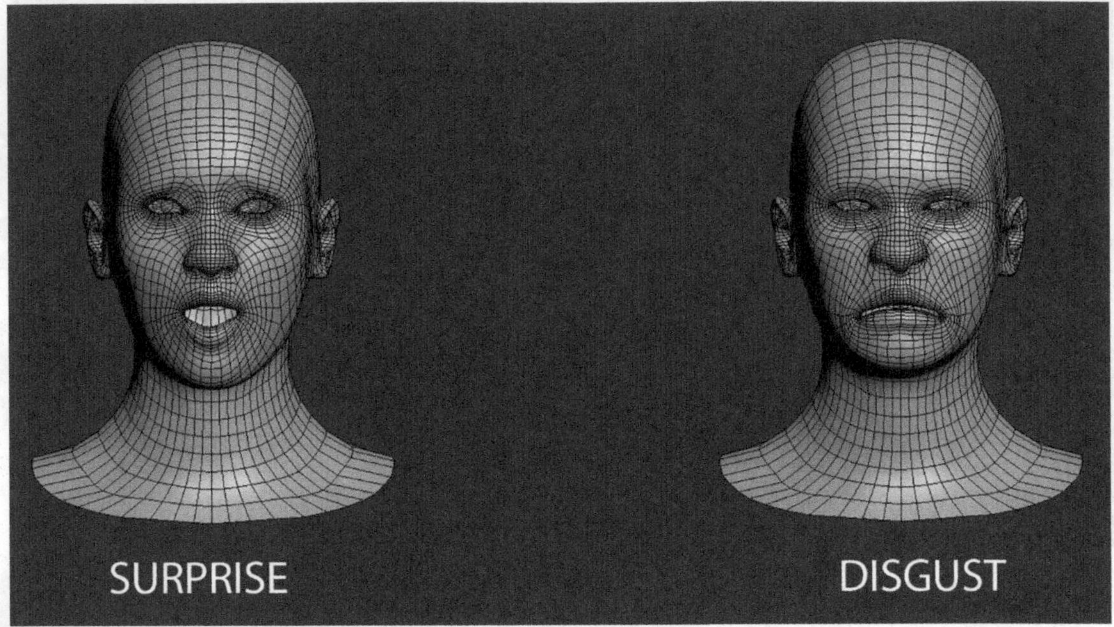

***Figure 9-12.** Surprise and disgust*

Note that fear and disgust have a lot in common, except for the eyes. This should do well for the animation.

If you are unable to find a reference image, this chapter's images are provided along with the source files in the reference images folder.

Note The quality of your animations depends on the amount of detail and time you put in getting the expressions right. Keep making tweaks and practicing and your results will be fruitful.

If you want to succeed as an animator, observe the motions around you. There is a rhythm to all motions and facial expressions.

Another key point to note is that like in rigging, where we recommend a T pose for the character, in facial animation always have the character's mouth opened in its default pose. This is because closing the mouth using subobject modes of the geometry is easier than opening it.

A checkpoint file has been created called `Emotions.max` for you to reference if need be. You can use it to follow along in getting the morph animation for the character.

Okay let's get into animating the head using morphs.

1. Load `emotions.max` or follow along if you have created your file with the poses.
2. Select the neutral head.
3. Go into the Modify tab of the command panel and add a morpher modifier.
4. In the channel list, right-click the first empty channel list and choose Pick from Scene. Select the Happiness head.
5. In the channel list, right-click the next empty slot and choose Pick from Scene. Select the Sadness head.
6. In the channel list, right-click the next empty slot and choose Pick from Scene. Select the Anger head.
7. In the channel list, right-click the next empty slot and choose Pick from Scene. Select the Fear head.
8. In the channel list, right-click the next empty slot and choose Pick from Scene. Select the Surprise head.
9. In the channel list, right-click the next empty slot and choose Pick from Scene. Select the Disgust head.

Your morphs are set! If you have additional morphs, you can load them into subsequent slots. We have set six emotions for the character, with a total of seven, including the neutral state. Your channel list should look like Figure 9-13.

At this point, you can select all the other heads except the neutral one and hide them so that they are not visible in the renderer.

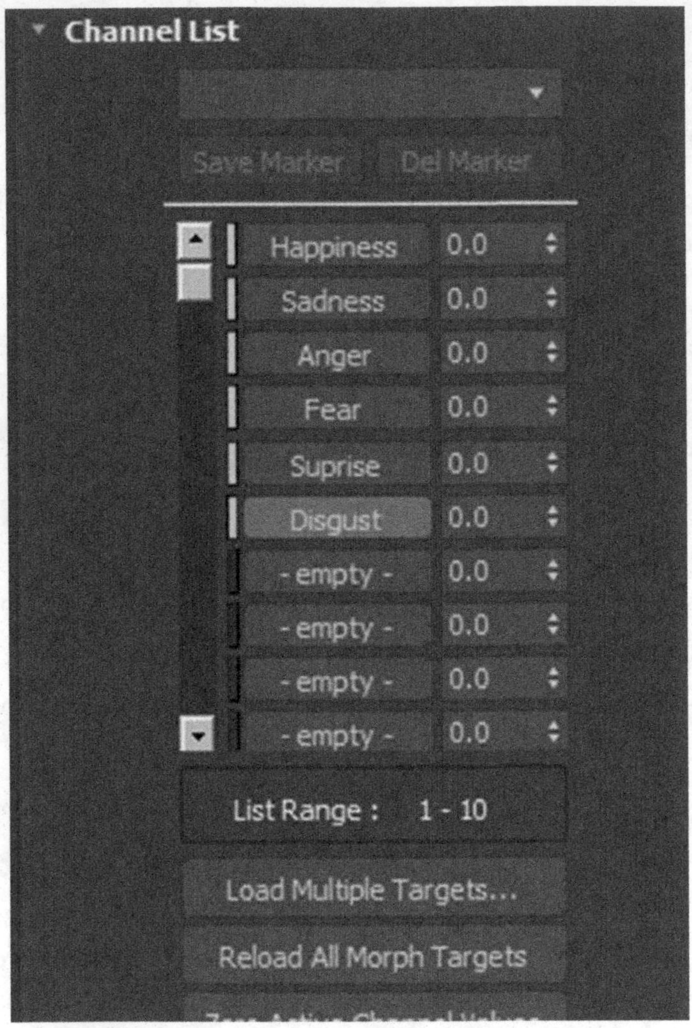

Figure 9-13. *Morph list for neutral head*

You can turn on AutoKey or use SetKey and tweak the values in the channel list. Keyframes are automatically created when Auto Key is on. To see the keyframes for modifier elements, be sure to check the modifiers in the Keyfilter mode. See Figure 9-14.

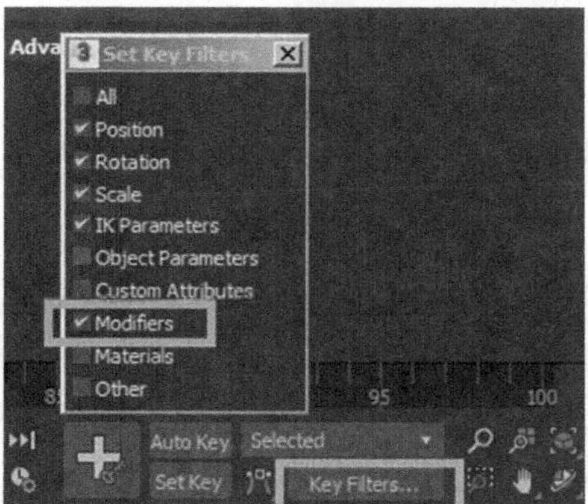

Figure 9-14. *Keyfilter dialog*

A checkpoint file is available for your reference called `Emotions_Morph.max`. Now you can tweak the values of multiple morphs to get diverse results.

Phonemes

If we want our character to talk, we need to begin setting up morphs for that as well, but how many morphs do we need to set? Maybe 26 for the letters of the alphabet? Alphabet sounds are different when they are pronounced in conjunction with other letters. Even though the English language has only 26 letters, there are actually 44 phonemes.

What exactly are phonemes? To break it down into simpler terms, it's the sound we create when we say a particular word. We don't speak by letters but by sounds. For example, the word *catch* is comprised of three sounds—c (it's more like ca), a (more like aeh), and tch—as one sound. It would be hard to explain this even further. Words as phonemes need to explained through verbal training or sound files. There are a total of 44 phonemes. Does this mean we need to create morphs for all the 44? It would be best because we would have much more control over the character with 44 morphs, but if you want to simplify this process, you can do away with some of these phonemes. In our case, we will be using nine phonemes.

I provide a file for you to see the morphs created for the phonemes; it's called `Phonemes.max`. The phonemes can be created by duplicating the head using the Move, Rotate, and Scale tools with the aid of soft selection for fine tweaks. Again remember not to increase the polygon count, as morphs rely on the polygon count to be the same.

Here are the basic phonemes that I created for this exercise:

- A and I: In this morph position, the lips are a bit wide open and you can see the teeth and the tongue resting inside the mouth. See Figure 9-15.

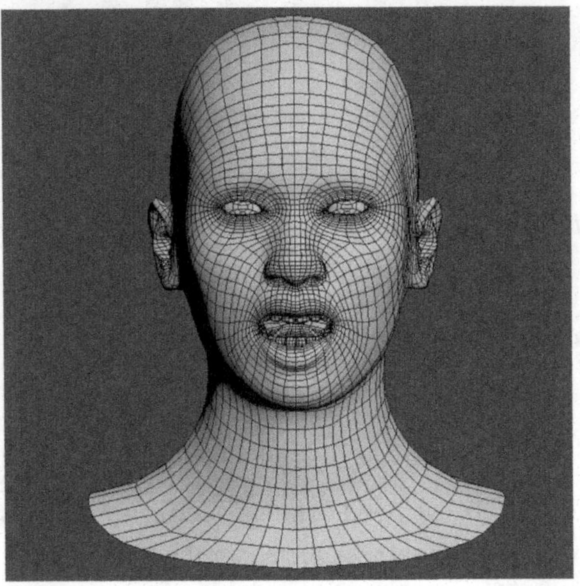

Figure 9-15. *Phoneme_A_I*

- C, D, G, K, N, R, S, T: This will be close to the neutral setup we have. The mouth needs to be open a faint bit and stretched. See Figure 9-16.

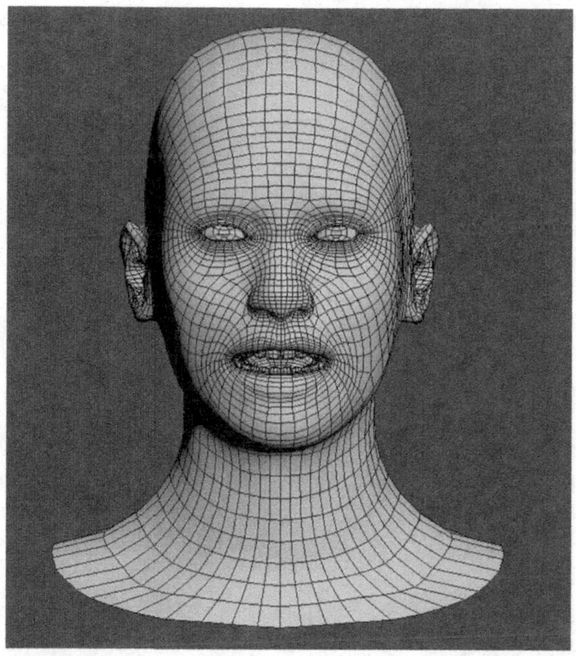

Figure 9-16. *Phoneme_C_D_G_K_N_R_S_T*

- E: This is the same as A and I but the lips are spread wider like in a happiness pose. See Figure 9-17.

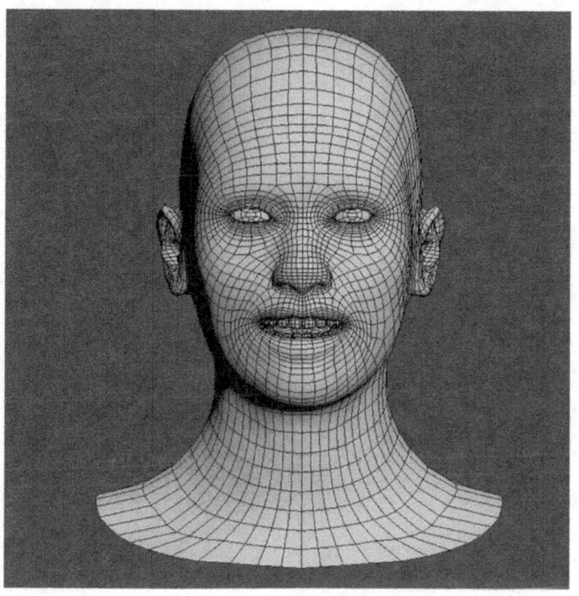

Figure 9-17. *Phoneme_E*

- F and V: In this morph, the upper jaw teeth need to be close and touching the lower lips. See Figure 9-18.

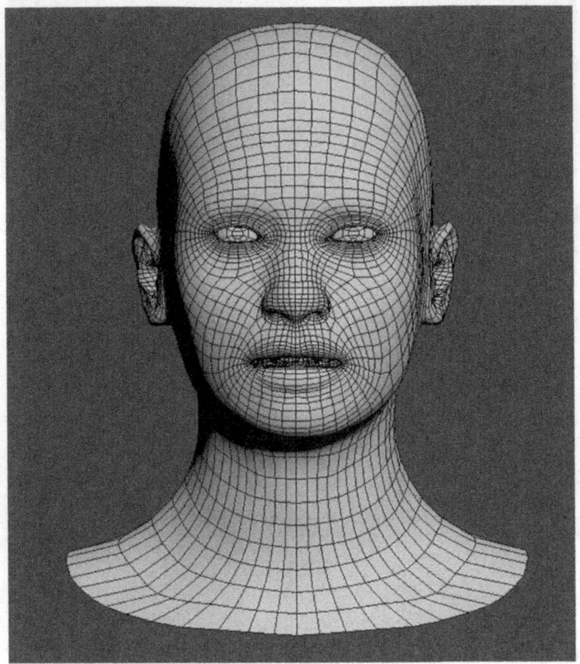

Figure 9-18. *Phoneme_F_V*

- L: The mouth is faintly open and the tongue touches the upper jaw on this morph. See Figure 9-19.

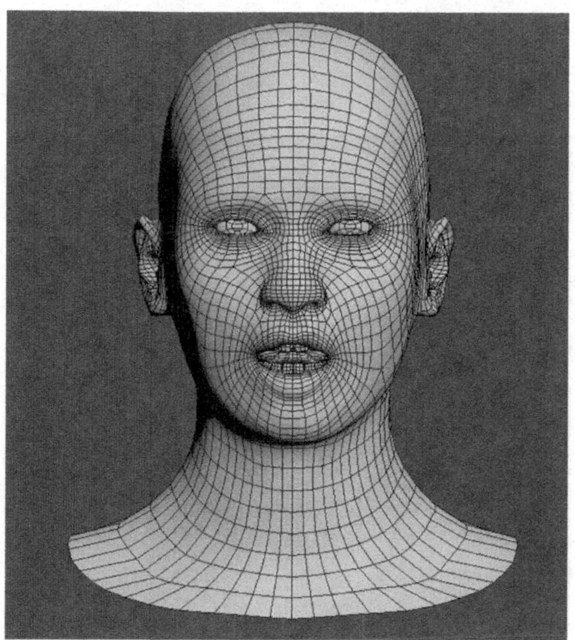

Figure 9-19. *Phoneme_L*

- M, B, and P: The lips are sealed with this morph. The duration varies with each letter, with M being the longest, followed by B and P. See Figure 9-20.

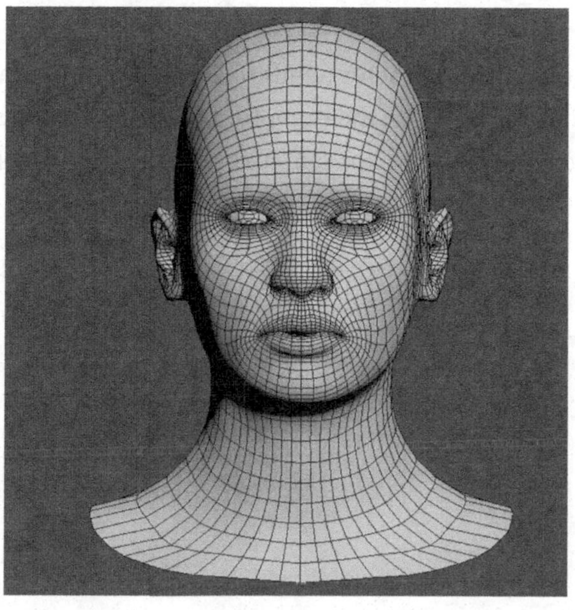

Figure 9-20. *Phoneme_M_B_P*

- O: This is the same as U but the lips don't come forward. See Figure 9-21.

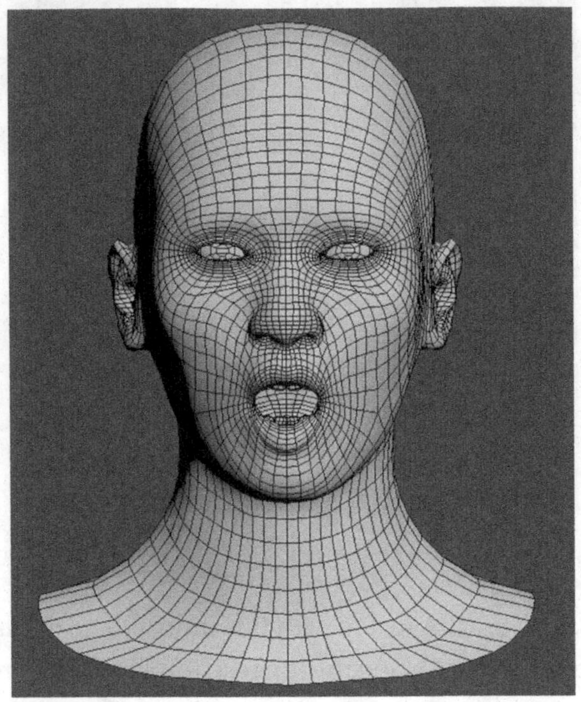

Figure 9-21. *Phoneme_O*

- U: In this morph, the character needs to have its mouth outward, like going for a lip kiss, but with the exception of the lips being spaced apart in an oval shape. The lips tend to come up front. See Figure 9-22.

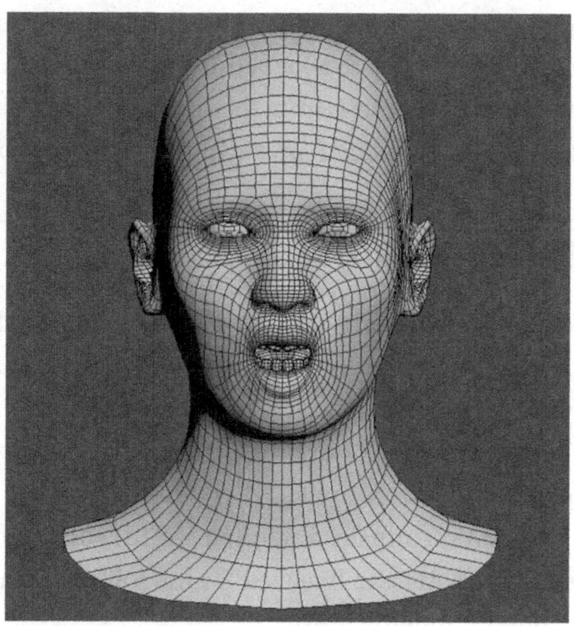

Figure 9-22. *Phoneme_U*

- W and Q: These are similar to U, but with only the bottom teeth visible, as the lower lips come down a lot more when pronouncing this. See Figure 9-23.

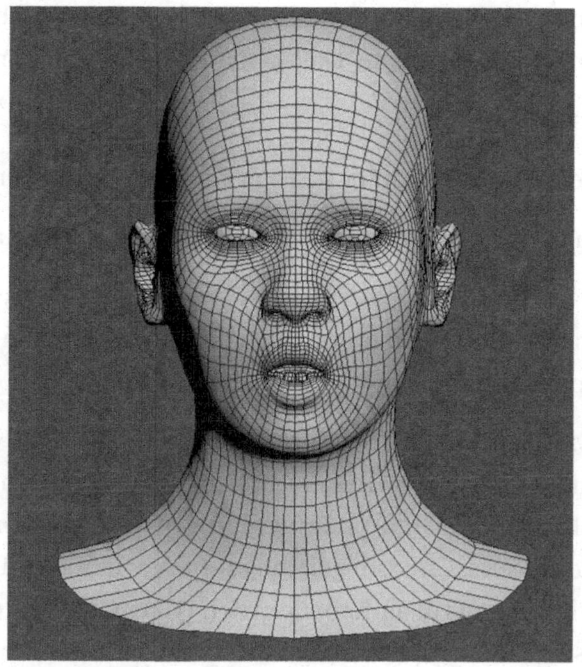

Figure 9-23. *Phoneme_W_Q*

Creating these morph positions is the biggest and cumbersome task. Once the morphs are done, the animation is easy. There are a lot of third-party tools to aid you in creating morphs easily. If you are exporting a mesh from the Autodesk Character Generator, you can export the character with morphs and a preset bone rig that has bone weight.

Audio Lip Sync: MorphTarget

Let's now use an audio file to create a lip sync. I provided an audio file called `Morph_Targets.wav` for your reference. You can follow along with this file or with any voiceover files you have to lip sync the character. Be sure you have the audio in the .wav 16-bit pcm format, or your audio might not be supported by 3ds Max. Feel free to use any converter online to convert it to .wav format.

Fire up 3ds Max if you haven't already and open `FacialAnimation_Begin.max`. Note that the file has copies of a human head tweaked for the following morphs:

The main head is named Phoneme_Rest:

- Eye blinks
    - RightEyeBlink and LeftEyeBlink
- Phonemes
    - Phoneme_A_I, Phoneme_CDGKNRST, Phoneme_FV, Phoneme_L, Phoneme_MBP, Phoneme_O, Phoneme_U, and Phoneme_WQ
- Expressions
    - Surprise, Sadness, Happiness, Fear, Disgust, and Anger

We will be using all these phonemes and expressions to achieve a good lip sync animation.

1. Select Phoneme_Rest head and go into the Modifier tab in the command panel. In the Modifier list, choose Morpher.
2. Select the Morpher and, in the Morpher Channel list, click on Load Multiple Targets. Choose all the morphs that have phonemes in them. I could choose all morphers at this point, but I am choosing phonemes only here. Choosing all the morphers at this point would put the morphs in alphabetic order. We would end up with expressions followed by phonemes and then by expressions again.

3. Now select the load multiple targets and choose the RightEyeClosed and LeftEyeClosed.
4. Finally, click on Load Multiple Targets again and choose the Expressions.

Your Morpher list should now show all the phoneme morphs and then the Blink morphs and the expressions after that. A checkpoint file has been created called `FacialAnimation_Begin01.max`.

1. Change your view to single view and frame phoneme_rest in your view (by using the Zoom Extents Selected button, which is located in the bottom-right corner of Max UI). Open the mini Curve Editor. Your UI will be similar to the one shown in Figure 9-24.

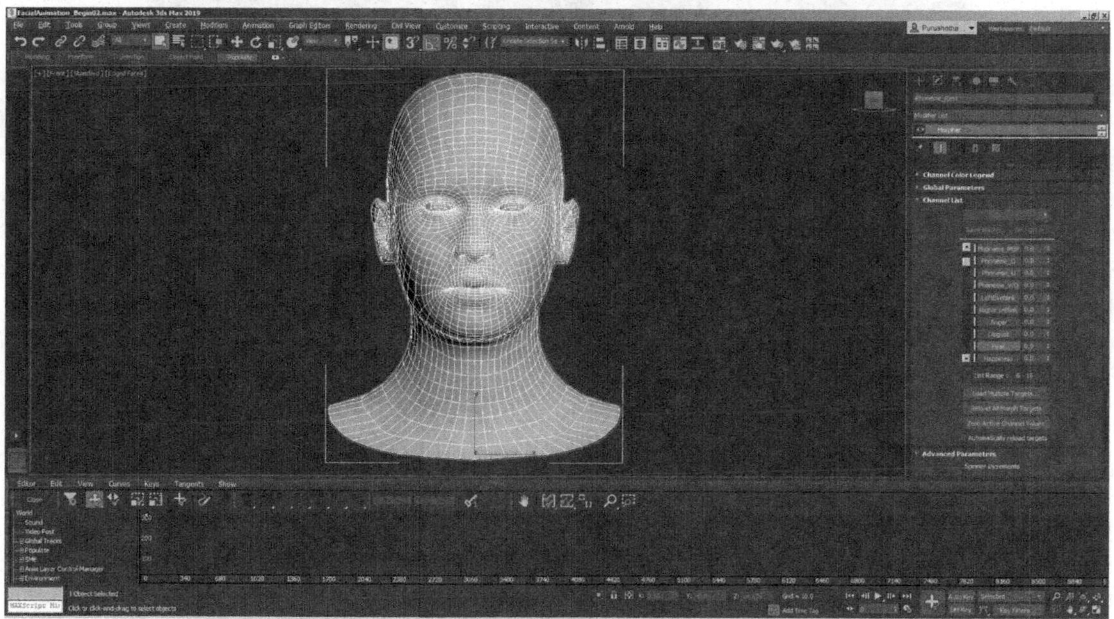

Figure 9-24. *3ds Max UI, Morpher and mini Curve editor*

2. In the mini Curve Editor, double-click on Sound in the left pane. A Pro Sound dialog option should open, as shown in Figure 9-25.

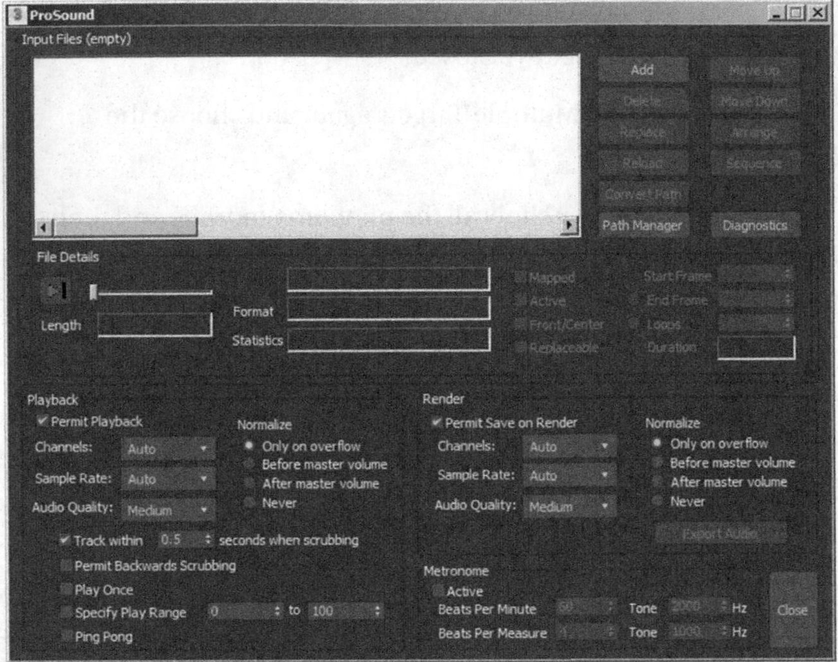

Figure 9-25. *Pro Sound dialog*

3. Click on the add and choose the `Morph_target.wav` provided in the reference audio folder of Chapter 9. If you would like to animate the head with a different voiceover, load that file and ensure it is in `.wav` format and in 16-bits.

4. Turn on Permit Backwards Scrubbing in the Pro Sound dialog. This is very useful when lining up the morphs. Without this, audio will play only when the play head is moving/moved forward.

5. The dialog box in Figure 9-26 appears once the audio is loaded. It shows various parameters. Check the endframe in the file; ensure that it's at least the same or more than the given value, otherwise the audio will not fit.

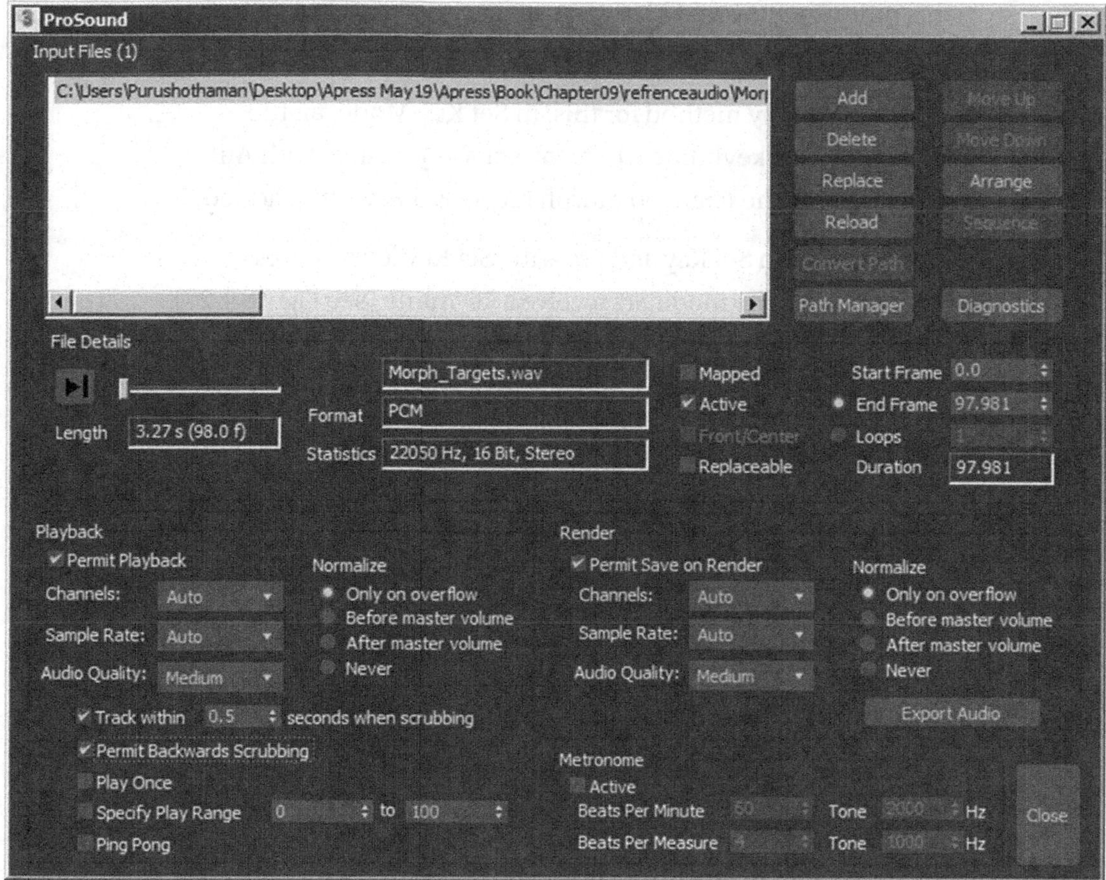

Figure 9-26. *Pro Sound dialog: Audio file loaded*

6. The animation is 100 frames long and since the end frame is 97.8, we are good. Click Close.

7. You can also close the mini Curve Editor by clicking on the Close button.

   Play the scene using the play head. Note that when the audio plays, you can scrub the time slider forward and backward to hear the audio as well. A checkpoint file has been created called `FacialAnimation_Begin02.max`.

8. Click on Key Filters, which is next to Set Key, and ensure you have the Modifiers checked in it. We are going to be animating the modifiers, without it being checked, we won't be able to see the keyframes in the timeline.

At this point if you would like, you can go ahead and hide all other geometries except Phoneme_Rest.

9. We will use Set Key method for this. In Set Key Mode, all the morphs receive a keyframe when you set a key, unlike with Auto Key, where only the changed morph receives a keyframe added.

10. At frame 0, turn on Set Key and press the Set Key icon or press K. Notice how all the modifiers receive a keyframe (see Figure 9-27).

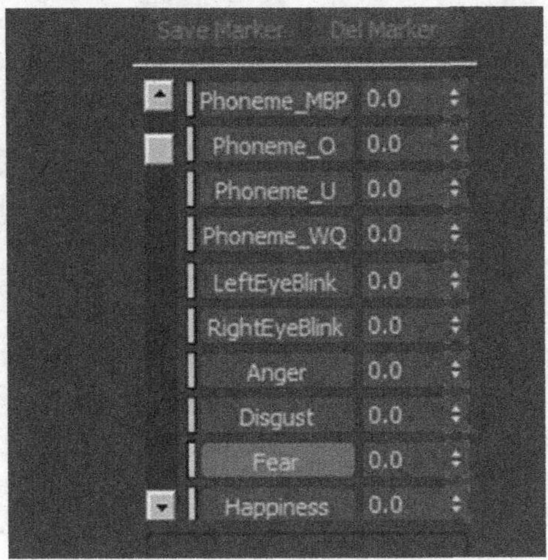

Figure 9-27. *All morphs keyframed*

11. If you scrub the timeline, you should notice that the audio part of F starts in the word *facial* at frame 6.

12. We don't want any changes to happen until frame 4, so go to frame 4 and click on Set Key or press K. I am not choosing frame 5 at this point because I want to give a preroll of one frame. This one frame preroll is not much, but it will provide a subtle result. Ideally 2-4 frames of preroll are better.

13. At frame 6, increase Phoneme_F_V to 100.

14. At frame 10, increase Phoneme_A_I to around 75 and reduce Phoneme_F_V to 0.

15. At this point, I recommend you open the mini Curve Editor and expand the Sound in the left pane of the mini Curve Editor. Expand until you see the `Morph_Targets.Wav` and waveform. In the View menu, choose Frame Extents Horizontal to frame the timeline to your scene range. We can use the visual reference of the audio waveform to position our keyframes. See Figure 9-28.

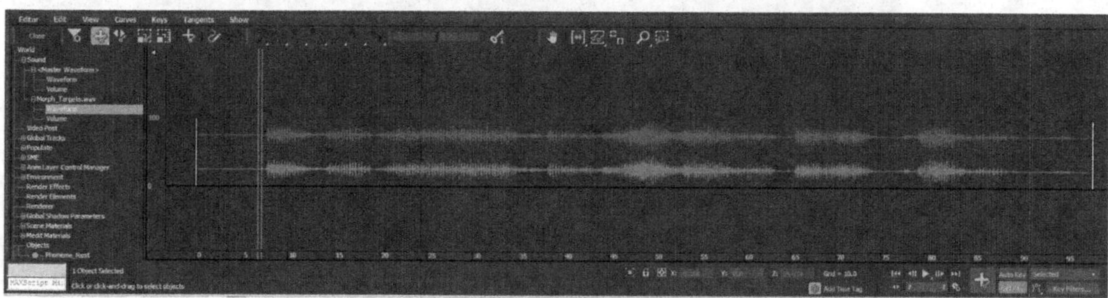

Figure 9-28. *Mini Curve Editor, waveform*

16. At frame 10, decrease Phoneme_A to 65.
17. At frame 12, increase Phoneme_C to 40.
18. At frame 15, set a keyframe for Phoneme_L to 100 and bring the other to 0.

The same process needs to be followed for the other words as per the audio. Look at phonetics and when that sound is pronounced, use the relevant morph to animate the face. There are two ways we can proceed. One is by setting keyframes for key phonemes for the entire sentence for voiceovers and then coming in and filling in between. Or, you can go in a linear process and set all keys at a particular frame before going forward to the next one. I recommend you keep the keyframes and then come back and edit/add as necessary.

1. Keep playing a particular part over and over until you are satisfied. Reposition the keyframes as needed based on the audio cues.
2. Once the keyframes are set, open the mini Curve Editor and on the left pane, choose Object ➤ Phoneme_Rest ➤ Modified Object ➤ Morpher. Select the morph. You should see the graph. Tweak the graphs to your liking using the graph tools and for fine refinement of the animation. See Figure 9-29.

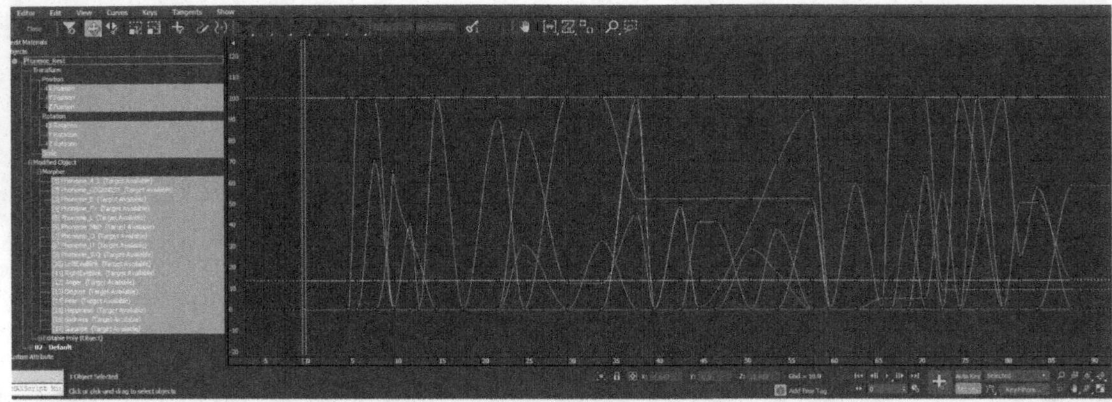

Figure 9-29. *Mini Curve Editor: keyframe graphs*

I went ahead and made a few tweaks in terms of adding more morph keyframes for phones. I also used blink and other expression morphs. A checkpoint file has been created called `FacialAnimation_Begin03.max`.

Hybrid: Facial Animation Using Morphs and Bones

Now let's take the head and make it look around as it talks. We could have created four morphs with the head, making it look up, down, left, and right. We are going to use bones to get this done.

Load `FacialAnimation_Begin04.max`.

1. In the left viewport, create two bones as depicted in Figure 9-30. You might need to lower the bone scale, considering the head mesh is very small. Rename them Neck_Bone, Head_Bone, and Head_end.

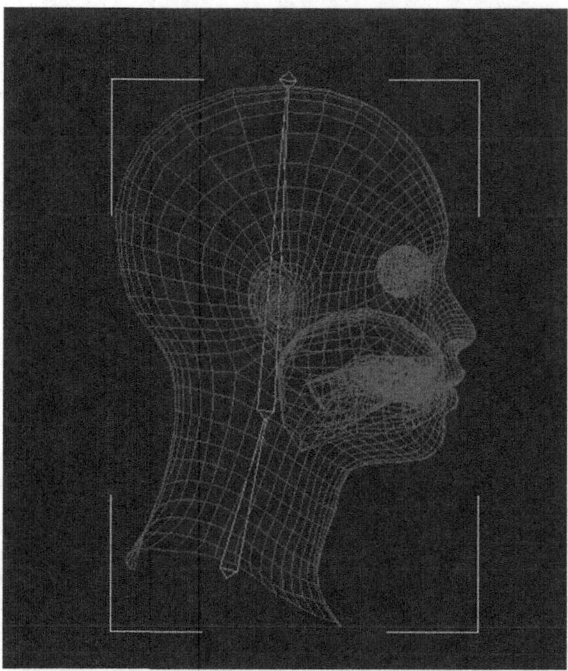

Figure 9-30. *Morph_ Head: Bone Setup*

2. Create another bone chain for the jaw, starting near the end of the neck bone. Select the newly created jaw bone and link it to the head bone. Rename the bones Jaw_Bone and Jaw_End. See Figure 9-31.

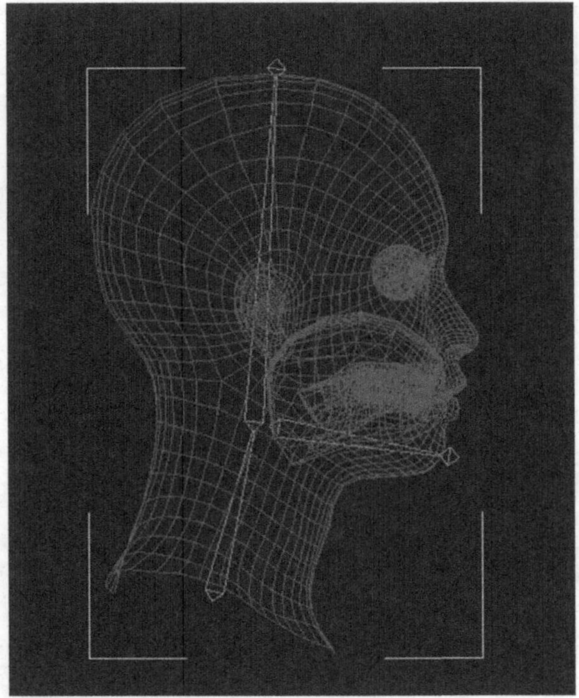

Figure 9-31. *Morph_ Head: JawBone Setup*

3. From the Create panel, create a circle shape and name it Neck_Control.

4. Create another circle in the front viewport and name it Head_Control.

5. Position both the circles, as shown in Figure 9-32, using the align tools. Use the bones as a reference to position pivot of the circles to the bones.

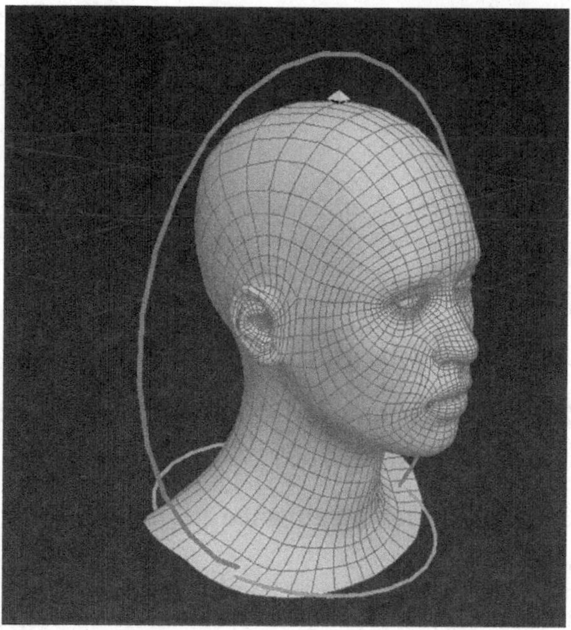

Figure 9-32. *Head and neck controls*

6. Select the Head_Control and link it to the Neck_Control.
7. Select the bone near the neck area and go to the Animation menu. Choose Constraints ➤ Orientation Constraint and then choose the Neck_Control. Your bone structure might turn in some other direction. In the Motion panel, under the Orientation Constraint pane, choose Keep Initial offset.
8. Select the bone that overlaps the head (Head_Bone) and go to the Animation menu. Choose Constraints ➤ Orientation constraint and choose the Head_Control. Your bone structure might turn in some other direction. In the Motion panel, under the Orientation Constraint pane, choose Keep Initial offset.
9. Select Phoneme_Rest Head mesh and, in the Modifier pane, choose Skin Modifier.
10. In the Skin Modifier, click on Edit Envelopes and weight them using the tools we learned about in the skinning session.
11. Now you can use the Head_Control to make the head look around as it talks using the morphers.

A checkpoint file has been created called `FacialAnimation_Complete.max`. The Neck_Control can be a child of a complete human rig so that the head moves along with the body.

Summary

To summarize what we have learned in this book:

- In Chapter 1, we learned the principles of animation.
- In Chapter 2, we learned how to create animations and refine them using animation editors in 3ds Max.
- In Chapter 3, we learned about advance animations using various constraints.
- In Chapters 4, 5, and 6, we learned to create character rigs using Bones, Bipeds, and the CAT toolkit.
- In Chapter 7, we looked at how to bind the rigs that we created in earlier chapters to a character mesh.
- In Chapter 8, we looked at animating a walk and run cycle for bipeds and quadrupeds.
- In this chapter, we learned how to use morph tools to create morph expressions and phonemes for animation.

This concludes the book. I wish you all good luck in bringing your characters to life. Observe animations and try to mimic them; you may not achieve a professional level of work right away, but with practice, it will become second nature.

Index

P. Raju, *Character Rigging and Advanced Animation*, https://doi.org/10.1007/978-1-4842-5037-2

D

E

F

G

H

I, J, K, L

M, N

O

P, Q

R

S

T, U, V

W, X, Y, Z

Printed in the United States
By Bookmasters